P9-DEY-777

COMMON SENSE IN TEACHING READING

ROMA GANS

COMMON SENSE IN TEACHING READING

A PRACTICAL GUIDE

THE BOBBS-MERRILL COMPANY, INC.
A SUBSIDIARY OF HOWARD W. SAMS & CO., INC.
Publishers • INDIANAPOLIS • NEW YORK

PRINTED IN THE UNITED STATES OF AMERICA
LIBRARY OF CONGRESS CATALOG CARD NUMBER: 63-11644
FIRST PRINTING

Foreword

The more I become aware of what makes children tick in learning to read, the more I realize how subtly and how deeply children are affected by the world of today. The more I look at today's world, the deeper is my concern that our children should learn to apply their reading to the lofty ideals that make us a spiritually free nation.

To be consistent with my view, I have placed the learning-to-read efforts of children described in this book in a present-day home, school, and community setting. I have emphasized the reading aspirations we consciously develop in children as our major goal in teaching them to read.

This book is addressed to teachers and parents because it is through their cooperative efforts that children will more surely enjoy the richness in life that reading can bring them. Much of my understanding of how children grow into independent, successful readers has been developed through many visits to classrooms across this country, as well as many personal contacts with parents. Thanks to the frank manner in which teachers and parents have discussed with me their problems in day-to-day guidance of children learning to read, I have come to see the child's step-by-step route to reading from both the classroom view and the home view. I have also acquired high regard for the valiant job of helping young readers that is being done in today's schools and homes.

Teaching children to read continues to be both a special privilege and a troubling problem. It is a privilege because, through our teaching efforts, we see a child gain mastery of the powerful skill that makes him a literate human being. It is a troubling problem because so much of what happens in the child's learning efforts is buried in his innermost mental processes and thus obscured from us. Much is known about teaching him, but many situations arise in which we must rely solely on our own common sense.

Great progress has been made in developing helpful techniques and materials for teaching reading, but no packaged process will ever meet the wide variety of personalities faced by teachers in classrooms and looked after by parents at home. This is especially true if we approach children with a respect for their eagerness to learn and if we honor the integrity of their taste. Then, instead of teaching young people as if we were feeding them packaged prescriptions, we inspire them and challenge them to invest their efforts and ideas in learning to read.

This book discusses a child's learning to read in his home and school settings and the extent to which common practices in these settings are consistent with our aim to educate him as a literate citizen. Examples throughout show the stouthearted efforts being made by school administrators, teachers, reading and guidance specialists, librarians, and parents as they carry out their obligations to youngsters from preschool age through the elementary-school years. It is hoped that the reader will respect, as I do, the patience, resourcefulness, and responsibility they reveal in their work. It is also hoped that these workers with children will be given adequate support in developing reading programs that carry us to loftier vision.

ROMA GANS

April 1962

Contents

COMMON SENSE IN TEACHING READING

CHAPTER 1

The Quest for Literacy

It is fortunate for the future well-being of our nation that parents and other lay citizens as well as educators express continuing interest in children's reading. From early times, when learning to read was motivated by great eagerness to read the Bible, down to today, when learning to read has far wider motivation, competence in reading has been and remains a symbol of education.

In this current stage of our history, we see ourselves in greater need of enlightenment than ever before. In our own country, the entire educational program, from kindergarten through advanced adult education, is planned, and frequently revised, with one important objective: the development of an improved citizenry equal to the work that lies ahead.

THE RELEVANCE OF CONCERN OVER THE ADULT READER

Commonly, a book devoted to the teaching of reading begins with a discussion of problems, practices, and methods of teaching the young to become readers. In fact, most discussions and writings on the topic take as their focus the budding citizens who are struggling year by year to become independent, self-propelled, and mature readers. Such enveloping concern solely with children's reading has much merit, but it also has dangers. We have neglected for far too long the critical appraisal of adults' reading. A few studies are found, plus polls by Roper and Gallup, but little widespread concern over what adults read and how well. Therefore, the process of educating youngsters to become good readers *for life* lacks the long-range assessment from which should come the fundamental cues for revitalizing and redirecting the schools' teaching of reading.

Unless we follow up the conduct of our graduates we are shortsighted in the truest meaning of that word. The manufacturer of an automobile is interested not only in producing all the parts and assembling them into a working machine but also in how well the finished product runs and how long it holds up. We, in education, assess our still-growing pupils from year to year until they graduate, but then our assessment stops. We hope that our "product" operates well as a reader for life, but most of our confidence that this will occur is based on assumptions.

A true quest for literacy cannot be fulfilled without a careful follow-up of reading habits and reading growth from the earliest beginnings throughout adult life. What kind of adult reader does each Judy and Jimmy become? The answer to this question will provide the "feedback" that planners of good reading programs need. Confidence based on hope is not adequate. Only confidence based on facts can assure educators that their efforts have created competent lifetime readers.

Another phase of reading also needs more consideration. Forty years ago, reading was the only means other than direct personal contact for getting at recorded ideas. To be informed, one had to read. This necessity furnished powerful motivation for learning to read and for continuing to read. Today one can keep up to date with headline news and follow major world, national, and local issues via radio, television, and films. Many youngsters and adults who are informed to a degree seldom read for information. But do these individuals represent the type of *informed* citizenry our country needs today and in the future? No doubt some rank or ranked high as readers in school work. Does their lack of follow-through in reading reflect a lack in education?

The function of reading in today's living, when other means of communication are readily available, needs careful re-examination. Such efforts at analysis will also provide cues for evaluating current teaching efforts. If the ability to read is as important as our everyday concerns indicate, then continued reading throughout the active years of life must become one of our teaching goals.

THE BIG ASSUMPTION: EVERYBODY READS

Wherever we go we encounter street signs, traffic directions, advertisements, and entertaining run-as-you-read features, all implying that those who walk can read. Highway signs carry symbols that give directions and state driving regulations. The patrolman assumes that he who drives reads. Roadways are keyed to highway symbols so that anyone who reads them can drive from East Palatka, Florida, to Pompeii's Pillar, Montana, without asking for a word of assistance. Whether we walk or ride, we see abundant evidence that we are assumed to be readers.

Business invests millions of dollars annually in advertising, on the assumption that people in general are readers. The same assumption is confidently made by the doctor, the dentist, the hairdresser, the shopkeeper, the self-service-store manager, the street-repair crew, moving-picture and television producers, the gasoline-station manager, and those in charge of churches, banks, governmental, social, and religious institutions, and, of course, libraries and schools. Our nation functions on the assumption that we are a reading public. It is safe to assume that in the years ahead more, rather than less, of such reading-to-get-along will be demanded of us.

Our most important use of the complex skill called reading is to inform ourselves concerning those major problems or issues that affect our lives. We may long for an easier-to-understand world, but as realists we know that such a world will never exist. It is up to us to face the complexities with which we are beset and to make honest efforts to grow in our understanding of these complexities, especially of those that involve us in making a decision. National and international affairs, state and home issues are affected by public attitudes, powerful special influences, and majority votes. Our decisions, be they informed and wise or ignorant and injudicious, carry weight. Therefore, we are under a strong moral commitment to inform ourselves to the best of our ability. Through mass media, chiefly radio and television, we can become aware of big problems, big happenings. But to grow in depth of understanding, to weave together many aspects of our most serious questions—these require personal reading.

DEVELOPING TOMORROW'S CITIZEN THROUGH TODAY'S READING

The question all too often asked is "How can we find the time to read?" The speed with which present-day happenings occur, plus their complexity, drives most of us almost to breathlessness. How can we develop the kind of reader who will take time out for regular reading? Furthermore, how can we help him comprehend what he reads efficiently enough to make decisions as a constructive citizen?

Obviously, knowing how to read is not enough, nor is rapidity, accurate comprehension, accurate recall, or any of the other skills commonly quoted as the hallmark of a good reader. A good reader who has developed his reading to meet current demands must utilize these skills but must have additional qualities of insight and judgment.

It is clearly of first importance that today's child be guided in his day-to-day school life and home life so that he is eager to keep up to date with important affairs, on his level of understanding. "Read to me about the astronaut," asked a six-year-old after he heard a television newscast reporting the launching of the first American in space. Creating in young children a desire and an eagerness to know is not difficult. World happenings fascinate them. They seem unafraid of new events, ideas, and objects. They also seem ready to develop lines of interest, following certain topics or questions day after day. They seem *right* for the kind of readers it would be fortunate to have them become.

Although we are a land rich in newspapers, magazines, pamphlets, and books, and a land in which education—therefore, reading programs—is compulsory for all children, we are periodically shocked by the high frequency of illiterates in our states and the low frequency of book readers among our citizens. The first of these problems is receiving the attention it should. No mentally well child in our land should grow up to be an illiterate. The second problem receives periodic attention, but the corrective what-to-do-about-it has not been faced forthrightly. Link and Hopf[1] found that seventy per cent of all books were read by twenty-one per cent of the population they interrogated. In the face of such data, book reading cannot be considered a widespread practice among adults. Will today's sprouting readers be more eager readers of books?

Studies of newspaper reading also cause considerable public concern. Newspapers with the most complete coverage of foreign and national affairs are less widely read than pictorial journals supplying minimum coverage of important issues. If this preference persists, will adult reading raise the performance level of our nation in conducting our important national and international affairs?

WHAT KIND OF READER DO WE WANT EACH CHILD TO BECOME?

Adequate planning of goals in teaching reading to today's youngsters requires a clearer picture of the demands life makes upon today's adult readers. The school's programs should then be tailored to help a child acquire those attitudes toward reading and reading skills that more nearly serve his continuing needs in adulthood. Only in this way can we be sure that today's alert child reader will become tomorrow's alert adult reader. Anything less than this will not strengthen our literacy.

Common practice today in offering proof of effective teaching of reading is to cite results on standardized reading tests. Tests have an important value in interpreting the progress of individuals and groups; they indicate the degree to which youngsters are acquiring essential reading skills. But adequate assessment of our reading programs demands that we stress the basic question: what kind of readers are these youngsters becoming? Suggestions in this book and other suggestions offered by teachers, reading specialists, and curriculum workers can become the starting point for making such an assessment.

Some parents and others involved with beginning reading tend to be concerned almost completely with the child's ability to recognize words. True, recognizing words is essential in the pursuit

[1] H. C. Link and H. A. Hopf, *People and Books.* Book Manufact. Inst., 1946.

of reading. But undue and improper emphasis may crowd out certain qualities the child needs to acquire to become a successful reader. Such exaggerated emphasis will also perpetuate the illiterate, but widely held, concept that reading is pronouncing words.

Reading is a highly personal matter, yet there are enough strong, common strands in reading as done by each individual to permit us to pull them out and examine them, then to revise and amplify our own attitude toward reading and our efforts in planning reading programs for children and youth. Such questions as the following might give direction to our inquiry:

Do we want our child to grow up not reading but wishing that someone had taught him to like it; or do we want him to grow from year to year as an eager reader?

Do we want our child to grow up able to read but uninterested in reading on current affairs, as many adults are; or do we want him to manage to squeeze reading newspapers, magazines and journals, and an occasional good book into his busy life?

Do we want our child to grow up as a headline reader, one who snatches a word here and there but never gets the gist of the whole topic; or do we want him to read accounts of important events and ideas carefully and to reflect seriously upon their meaning?

Do we want our child to grow up and read widely, question nothing, and be nondiscriminating and nonassimilating; or do we want him to be a critical, selective, and reflective reader?

Do we want our child to grow up unsure of his own judgment, reading only what others tell him to read or relying exclusively on popular books; or do we want him to develop his own taste, relying upon his own judgment for his personal reading?

Do we want our child to grow up to choose the half-baked and the shoddy because of their surface appeals; or do we want him to select the better materials?

Do we want our child to grow into a bookworm, a reader who avoids facing his own responsibilities and problems by reading, yet never relates ideas from his reading to his work or his social relationships; or do we want him to utilize his reading to help himself and to relate to others?

Do we want our child to grow up with inadequately developed

reading ability, so that he can find no satisfactions in any kind of reading; or do we want him to begin so that he will continue to read with increasing success for his developing needs and continue to grow?

The old adage of the twig fits here: If we want a child to grow into an avid, thinking reader who manages throughout his life to keep up to date through his reading, who reinforces his ideas with sound concepts gained from reading, who revels in a good book, who uses ideas gained from reading when they are pertinent, who selects newspapers, magazines, and books of genuine merit, and who enriches not only his own life but the lives of those around him: if this is our aim, then we should guide the child in this direction from his earliest years.

All too often we accept such goals but rather quickly fall into procedures that deny them. The reasons are apparent. Many of our ways of working with children and our attitudes toward them are still deeply tinged with traditions. For example, we want children to be critical readers, which means, of course, that they must be critical thinkers. Yet, when their critical thinking counters what we may say or believe, we wonder: Is this good? Will this teach my child to be less respectful of his elders? Are we encouraging him to be a cynic? Goals as inclusive as those implied are easy to accept, but anyone attempting to apply them consistently in teaching and living with present-day children will be confronted with serious problems. Should we, therefore, stick to a narrower program and spare ourselves difficulties that may arise? Only the cowardly would answer yes.

Common sense tells us that the kind of reader who will find reading an invaluable tool in his future living in our complex and threatening world will need guidance in more than the mechanics of reading. The finest tributes should be offered those educators and parents who make every effort to meet each child with as visionary a program in reading for him as careful study, intelligent planning, and good judgment can create. The following chapters include a description of widely established practices of inducting children into the literate fold and an examination of many common practices in terms of their effect upon professed goals. They also include grist for the eager reader on topics and problems to be met in everyday child-teaching and child-rearing situations in conjunction with a vigorous and visionary program of reading.

SUGGESTED READINGS ON LITERACY

CHASE, STUART. *American Credos.* New York: Harper & Brothers, 1962. Pp. 134-136 and Chapter 12.

Reports of polls of adult book reading in the United States compared with that in several European countries. Nine areas in which polls reveal ignorance on the part of American adults are included in Chapter 12.

LINK, HENRY C., and HOPF, HARRY ARTHUR. *People and Books.* New York: Book Manufacturers Institute, 1946.

A study of book-reading practices of American adults that includes nature of books, how selected, and factors that induce people to read.

MCKEON, RICHARD, MERTON, ROBERT K., and GELLHORN, WALTER. *The Freedom to Read.* New York: R. R. Bowker Co. for the National Book Committee, 1957.

A sociological, philosophical, and legal study of censorship of reading that has important implications for goals in teaching reading.

CHAPTER 2

A Look at the Beginning Reader

It is generally agreed that children show strong developmental and personality differences at all ages, but in teaching reading we tend to project the concept of a standardized beginner who will respond exactly as we would wish. Many problems for the child and his adult well-wishers spring from this common misconception.

Let's look at some five-year-old kindergarteners who in another year will come under that popular classification of "beginning readers." Here is Bettina, a rugged child, eager to climb stair rails, jungle gyms, and trees, skilled with hammer and nails, the leader in any play group but not at all interested in looking at books, listening to a story, or even telling about her important doings. In the same group is Angela, less interested and able in vigorous activity, who notices all the signs posted about the kindergarten room, as well as the names on delivery trucks. She loves to play with plastic letters and is an avid book browser at the library table. Harry, who is extremely fond of Bettina, is also strong, always ready to try new skills, and highly sociable. He loves to leaf through books, listens to stories carefully, and is an excellent, accurate narrator. Another of Harry's favorite kindergarten pals is Bugs. Bugs, an amiable youngster, responds happily to all suggestions, imitates whatever other youngsters are doing but is rather unobservant of details and comments more frequently with gestures than with words. He pays serious attention at story time, looks at books occasionally, but, as the teacher says, "There is no telling what registers." It would obviously be absurd to assume that, when these four enter the first grade, they will approach beginning reading with equal eagerness, interest, and success.

CORNERSTONES FOR SUCCESS IN BEGINNING READING

Before a child learns to recognize a word or to read the first page in a book, he has achieved some fundamental, though less observable, learnings that, if understood, prove invaluable for teaching beginners. They are the qualities a child may acquire in early years to help him in such a difficult job as learning to read. Among others, these four seem most essential: (1) an eagerness to be independent rather than spoon-fed and coddled; (2) an unquenchable zest to explore the new in the big, widening world about him; (3) the courage to try himself out at new skills and to take success and some defeats; (4) the enjoyment of being with others and learning from them.

1. *A normal, healthy youngster grows in gaining independence and the ability to look after himself.* He pushes off the hand that holds the cup and handles it himself—sometimes quite skillfully in his earliest efforts. He protests at being undressed and manages to remove his own socks, all with a satisfaction in feeling his power over the environment and his own coordination. He prefers to walk unaided. Without yet being able to put it in words, he is telling us, "Let me do things for myself. I can look after myself."

This kind of growth represents a most important beginning. The young child is learning to stand on his own two feet. Such eagerness to "do it myself" will help him to say, later on, "Don't read to me—I want to read by myself," or "Don't tell me, let me find out for myself."

A child encouraged to "wiggle his world" grows up eager to try new experiences and unafraid to venture out on his own. A child who is refused opportunities for independent activity because he might make a mistake, be messy, or disrupt household routine may acquire that shy, uneasy quality that prevents him from tackling hard jobs. "Show me how," "Tell me," and "Help me" are common requests of all children, but their too frequent use reveals a child's lack of confidence in himself.

Much of the self-confidence needed for healthy growth is acquired by children in their family life through the aid and encouragement of parents, brothers, and sisters. "Look, he can pour his milk straight" was a five-year-old's excited report as young brother Ben served himself a glass of milk from a pitcher that required two hands to manage. It is easy to see that the confidence that leads to independence is a two-way affair. Those closest to the child must be eager to see him grow up as an independent human being who is ready to try out new skills. Such two-way relationships develop in the growing youngster an attitude of enjoyment toward doing things independently. He also acquires an attitude toward himself—namely, that he can do things, that he has built-in power.

Most of those adults and older children whom we call *achievers* acquired this love of independent operation in their early years. A willingness to persevere, independent of a helping hand, is essential in learning to read. Without it, some may bog down or need ceaseless assistance and encouragement. If such help is needed, let's hope that a patient teacher and family give it—but how much easier to get started on the road to reading with the boost that comes from a family climate that encourages the attitude "I want to do this under my own steam."

2. *A second and closely related attitude is that of enjoying the new, the unexplored.* A shy child may need to be encouraged to venture forth. To some weary adults, such shyness may seem a veritable heaven-sent blessing. But for vigorous growth, a youngster must remain eager for new experiences.

It is common to see a three- or four-year-old who, in the span of minutes, inspects the whole house or apartment of a family friend. He asks, "Why do you put pencils in that vase?" "Whose pocketbook is this?" "Do you have any dogs?" In contrast, another child may sit, scarcely noticing what is about him or what is happening. The docile-eyed child may not be as "dumb" as he seems, but he could gain the impetus to seek more learning if he were free to let go, to inquire, to explore.

Parents encourage a child to react inquiringly when they arrange indoor and outdoor space so that he is free to play with a minimum of supervision. A home so arranged can then become an interesting and safe world for him. If, when he accompanies parents to new spots, friends' homes, and shops, his parents tell him what he is free to do and free to explore, they encourage him to do so. If his parents set minimum limits, they help him to learn not only "This I may do," but also "This I may not do."

Many a kindergarten teacher makes note of the differences children reveal as they take up their school routine, a way of life that acquires such importance in their thinking and in that of their parents. Some plunge directly into the school pattern, including the contacts with other youngsters. Others sit or cling to a parent, not daring to make the most of this new, fascinating world. From the first day, an alert teacher arranges materials, supplies, in fact, the whole program, in such a manner as to encourage each child to build on his already initiated independence. Those children who enter feeling a trifle shy and inhibited are encouraged to loosen up. At the end of the year, kindergarteners thus encouraged can enter the first grade filled with anticipation for more new ventures in school.

It is easy to see what an advantage this eagerness to sample new materials and experiences provides for the youngster as he approaches the complicated business of learning to read. Many of the early reading experiences will be new to him. He may have had some contacts with books and letter blocks; he may even have tried his hand at writing. In school, however, he meets new methods, materials, and occasions. The ever-ready explorer neither withdraws nor yearns for the "same old stuff" but participates eagerly. This second attitude—enjoying the new and unexplored—accompanying the child's desire to be independent is invaluable as an energy-producer for the sustained effort required in the early days of *becoming a reader*.

3. *From his eagerness to be able to do things for himself and from his never-ending appetite for exploring new opportunities, he develops a third attitude, that he is a going concern, an individual with the ability to tackle new ventures and succeed.*

Of course, the development of such an attitude assumes that in the child's early experiments he has been helped and encouraged. Tasks were not set for him; rather, he established his goals and set the pace for himself. He may have started many activities on a trial basis only to discover "This I can't do *yet*." The *yet* is important. Without it, a child may develop just the opposite of the desired attitude, namely—"This I *can't do*. I am no good." Therefore, it is important to take our cues from what children seem eager to do, encouraging them but not hamstringing or goading them, and letting them note our recognition of their efforts and accomplishments.

The child needs to maintain self-confidence in order to develop his real and fullest potentiality. The courage to think boldly and with imagination, so essential to powerful constructive living, demands that the child be unafraid, confident, courageous. Jerome S. Bruner, who has been doing outstanding research on children's thinking, makes this statement:

> Yet it seems likely that effective intuitive thinking is fostered by the development of self-confidence and courage in students. A person who thinks intuitively may often achieve correct solutions, but he may also be proved wrong when he checks or when others check on him. Such thinking, therefore, requires a willingness to make honest mistakes in the effort to solve problems. One who is insecure, who lacks confidence in himself, may be unwilling to run such risks.[1]

A child who inwardly feels "I'm all right" can afford to try things and fail occasionally without losing confidence. If an experience has been quite a heavy disappointment, adult encouragement is appropriate. Often when he is undertaking something a child seems to sense that in spite of slow or even no progress at the beginning, he will succeed if he stays at it. Many a child will achieve if he remains unafraid and free to keep trying. Forcing him or urging him at first stimulate him to act, but when freed from the adult's coaxing or urging he may stop his efforts and quickly forget what he learned.

4. *A fourth quality in a child's behavior that enhances his future as a learner is his enjoyment and imitation of others.* If he is a youngster who keeps his eye on what others do, imitates them at times, and accepts their aid at times, he increases his own learning. Such behavior implies that he is interested in people—children as well as adults—and notices what they do and how they do it. Consequently, living with others has a quality of contagion. By mixing in with the life of others near him, a child "catches on" to much. He learns by imitating them.

[1] Jerome S. Bruner, *The Process of Education.* Harvard University Press, 1960, p. 65.

Unfortunately, some observers of children regard all imitation as undesirable. True, a child needs to evolve his own kind of imagination, initiative, and creative abilities. But if he grows to feel the satisfaction of being independent, if he cherishes his opportunities to explore, and if he feels safe in venturing out on his own, then he will not become a "copycat" or submissive follower, but will use all chances to learn from life about him. Of course, some of these bits of learning that he snaps up quickly may be undesirable, but the total effect of his alertness to others will be to multiply the ease, the pleasure, and the richness of his learning. He will grow from year to year as an eager, open-eyed child. And, when, later on, he approaches the serious task of becoming an independent reader, he will be able to give and take help from those with whom he lives, at home and in school, in an easy, natural manner.

These four qualities or attitudes may seem at first glance to be only remotely associated with the way a child makes progress in learning to read. Actually, however, they are foundation stones of such learning. (Catherine Landreth, in her readable, detailed account of how children grow from infancy through the primary-grade years, gives ample evidence of their importance.[2]) From studies of children's growth and development we have come to understand the importance of these elements of personality for success not only in the first years at school, but in all of life. Each of us can recall times when we were eager to get at the job, were unafraid to begin, trusted ourselves to be equal to the task, and when necessary, were able to seek help and utilize it. The first dress sewed may come to mind, or perhaps we remember learning to read weather maps or exploring advanced mathematics. We may also recall some of our unsuccessful projects and rather accurately diagnose the reason for their failure.

HATS OFF TO PARENTS

The feelings we bring to our daily work begin in the early years of childhood in the home. Many a parent, with no child-rearing manual, has done a magnificent job of rearing youngsters who are quite

[2] Catherine Landreth, *The Psychology of Early Childhood.* Knopf, 1960.

self-sufficient in many respects before they enter kindergarten. Many parents—using the same good judgment or common sense—have not achieved similar results. Children do not always respond well to adult efforts at guiding, even when our efforts seem to fit such suggestions as those here given. Some children, starting out on the wrong foot, change their direction once they get to school—fortunately. But, in general, a warm, friendly family life has come to be regarded as the richest resource for a good, wholesome future for a child.

Much is said and written today to indicate to parents what superb guidance they can offer children, even under circumstances that are far from ideal and all too common in a society crowded with pressures of time and work. More recognition should be given to those parents whose good judgment and guidance aid a child in acquiring the personal qualities that will assure him success in reading.

THE HOME'S GREAT GIFT TO THE CHILD—HIS SPEECH

The most important skill a child acquires in his early years is his ability to speak. Learning to talk, which is an exciting phase of growth to observe in youngsters, is in many ways of greater importance to him than learning to read. In our eagerness to get the child to master the printed word, we seem, all too often, to minimize his growing power of speech once he has come to use a few words and phrases. And it is thought-provoking to note that children acquire the ability to talk, often to a very high degree, before they set foot in a nursery school or kindergarten and without a single so-called lesson—or workbook—or report card.

The age for learning to talk varies widely. Some children begin to pronounce words at seven months; others make no effort to do so until three to six months later. Some are great chatterers; others are less vocal. Marked differences are found in youngsters within any one family.

First Steps in Speaking Early speech is often characterized by an obviously listening attitude, a wide-eyed, bated-breath kind of attention as mother says "ma-ma" to the six-month-old infant.

Tongue-lip movements are explored in testing out sounds. The child observes carefully—and this is most important—how the adult is reacting to these efforts. And finally out come the sounds: "ma-ma."

We adult observers cannot be sure what the child means by *mama.* It may mean all women, or all women with spectacles, or it may have no relation to mother or any other woman. It may be merely the imitation of the sound in response to a satisfying, attention-getting collection of moments with mother. The exact meaning of *my mama* or *this mama* grows later. The word so acquired is used by the infant seemingly to evoke from the hearer reactions that he likes. Those in his presence pay attention to him, they display pleasure at what he has done, they tell him, "That's right, say it again!"

Next, the young child moves to another fundamental phase of growth. He has, up to this time, indicated his wants by reaching, whining, crying, or by some other nonverbal means. Now he begins to use key words to convey his requests. "Dink" may mean "I want to drink"; "Cookie," "I want a cookie"; and "More," "I want more," or "Do it again"—as in the case of a jiggly ride on the end of a big brother's foot. In a short time this one-word approach becomes amplified to two- or three-word statements, which often are not expressed as formal sentences. Typical are "Want more," "Me ride"—meaning "I want more" and "I want a ride."

Variety of Language in Young Children The language a child acquires and his first words in that language vary widely with geographic location and family life.

The words first used by the young child are, of course, determined by his own intimate family life. A child in Japan or in Norway would acquire words and ideas behind the words that are common to his life. Milk may be a common word to most infants in the United States, but not to many a Chinese child. Even to some American children, milk is an uncommon word.

Recently, I overheard the conversation of two boys, about four, in a sandbox at a play spot on Riverside Drive, New York. The talk ran something like this:

"You can too transfer for nothing from these buses. All you do is ask the conductor for a transfer."

"He's not the conductor. He's the driver."

"Well, anyway, he gives you a transfer—you know—pink or green paper."

"But not for any buses, just for some buses. I know because my father is a starter. He won't let you on some buses."

That same week, in a small, rural village, I overheard this conversation in the village store between a boy of about five and a girl of about four:

The boy: "My father works with your mother at the Kirk Plant. Your mother only picks feathers."

The girl: "My mother does not pick feathers. She paraffins."

The boy: "That's the same thing as picking feathers. That's what my father told me."

A simple vocabulary study of these two short conversations illustrates clearly that statement we often make so blandly—"Children are affected by their environment." The bus-transfer-starter pair might have difficulty in understanding the feather-paraffin-Kirk two, and vice versa. Each pair had grown in language usage, yet each pair reflected the experiences peculiar to their background. The language of extremely young children shows closer relationship to their background than does that of older children who, by virtue of longer experience, have shared in common more of life.

The Priority of Language Growth The child's language growth will influence the quality of his success in reading. Making sense out of words and simple stories demands, of course, that he understand what these words mean once he pronounces them. In Minnesota little Einar, who spoke only Finnish, was taught to read an English first reader. How absurd—and how tragic for Einar.

Many children with language backgrounds other than English are enrolled in today's schools. Schools along the Atlantic Coast, from Florida to Maine, are teaching Puerto Rican children. Most of these children enter school knowing no English; their parents, too, know none. New York City, with the largest number of Puerto Rican-born pupils, is making valiant efforts to help all such newcomers become bilingual in speech and reading. The West and Southwest have many pupils from Mexico and from the Orient. Many school systems, already heavily burdened with other responsibilities, are showing their tensile strength in coping with large numbers of these children of other language backgrounds, creating new ways of working with them, and giving unstintingly of effort and money to teach them to speak, read, and write English.

Language—A Personal Affair From birth until about the age of two the child seems to be highly self-centered. He actually feels that he is merged in life with others and is not, himself, a distinct person. His complete dependence on others for care makes his sense of separate identity unnecessary. Later, he must establish the fact that he is a walking, talking, important, living being, separate and distinct from other human beings. For several years he remains, to some extent, busy about establishing his separateness from others. This interest in self is not genuine egocentricity but rather an essential need of the child to grow in sensing himself as a person differentiated from others. The child's early language, therefore, reflects this need. When he points to a cat, saying "Kitty," this, to him, may mean "Notice me—I am seeing a cat." He is not yet ready to enter into descriptive conversation about someone or something disassociated from himself.

This self-centered quality in early language is an important point to remember. Certainly a nursery-school, kindergarten, or primary-grade teacher who remembers that children remain interested in themselves and in experiences that affect them personally will have a good clue toward helping their beginnings in reading and writing.

The emphasis in the primary grades on experience charts, teacher-written records based on trips and other happenings in the group life of the class, has been drawn chiefly from this knowledge of the child's interest in that which includes or involves him. Therefore a chart stating:

> We went to the fruit market.
> Alexander's father gave us a
> ride on his truck.

may stimulate more interest than:

> This is Nell.
> This is Buster.
> See Nell. See Buster.

GROWTH IN LANGUAGE BOOSTS GROWTH IN THINKING

In experience after experience, the child learns the meaning of words and phrases. In order to accomplish this learning he must be able to hear, to notice the connections between words and their meanings, and to remember. At first he may generalize: all yards have trees like his own, all homes have an upstairs like that in his own house, or—if he lives in a large apartment house—all apartments are reached via elevators. After more experiences, he begins to describe: *a small house with no upstairs*; or *a tall building with an elevator.* Such discrimination comes after he has met several kinds of houses and tall buildings, and it represents a large step in the child's ability to think.

Beginnings in Discrimination The ability to discriminate is a highly important one. To hear a child of three say, "I want the shovel. The big shovel!" should give the listener pause because at three the youngster has already recognized the fact that there are shovels and shovels, and that one is the *big* one. Does he want any old cookie or a special variety? Does he ask for a book and, after looking it over, reject it and go to the bookshelf to pull out the one he wants? If so, he is revealing the intellectual function which, if developed, will help him to become selective, to prefer one book over another. The growth of such thinking will also lead him, later, to avoid prejudice: "Some big boys hit me," not "All big boys hit."

For a child to become discriminating he must have many and varied experiences. If he had never eaten any other cookie but the same variety, he would bound his idea of cookies by this one brand. When he meets cookies in all manner of shapes, flavors, and textures, he grows not only in discrimination but also in preference, or taste. He acquires the vocabulary to report that he "likes thick sugar cookies," that he "does not like thin ginger cookies," and that he "likes vanilla wafers best of all." He is enriching a category of his thinking through experiences with cookies, he is enlarging his vocabulary, and he is learning to think, to compare, to differentiate, to discriminate, and to select in terms of his preference.

Such analysis of the value of the ordinary experiences with cookies may seem overdrawn. To the contrary, in myriads of experiences, many as commonplace as the cookie episodes, a child acquires what such competent specialists of children's learning as Jerome S. Bruner, Millie C. Almy, and Lee Cronbach tell us is a rich foundation for later learning. The child is growing in alertness, in acquiring a wide, meaningful vocabulary, and in stretching his powers of thinking. He will build upon these early developments not only in beginning to read, but also in other learning throughout his life.

Importance of the Talking Traveler Many moments for such learning occur in everyday living if a child is included in many of the commonplace operations that go on in a household. Children kept busy in a playpen or fenced-in yard for too much of a day, even if seemingly content, may be denied their fullest growth. Some time alone with challenging toys helps a child learn the satisfaction of playing solo. Hour upon hour of being alone, however, can have serious retarding effects. By the age of two or two and a half, young "sprouts" may have need to widen their world. This is the time when the everyday going-to-market-with-mother experiences, the short trips to see other children play on park equipment, the visit to a house being built in the neighborhood are rich opportunities for looking, for listening, for asking about, and for learning new words in new settings, as well as wider meanings of known words in new connections.

As children grow older and are physically ready to travel about more, they learn from experiences that can be enjoyed by an entire family. Trips to the airport to see planes land and take off, to the railroad and bus depots to see travelers en route and to watch baggage and mail bags carted and hoisted about are experiences that help youngsters stretch their awareness of the wide world and add to their understanding of many things adults discuss. Trips to cities where machines at work and people in action can be watched convey ideas to children and appeal to their love of life and motion.

In kindergartens and first grades, trips are an essential part of the program. They form common experiences for understanding today's community life and the wide variety of adult jobs, and they provide many meaningful contacts in the fields of nature study, physical science, and mathematics. A workman on an apartment building under construction explained to children the function of a plumb line and a ramp. At a nursery, five-year-olds were fascinated by the excavating and balling of a huge fir tree. In these experiences, workmen described not only what they were doing, but why. An avid five-year-old enthusiastically thanked the nurseryman and said, "Gee, you know a lot." To which the nurseryman replied, "And you are learning a lot, too." Right.

Caution: Selective Sight-Seeing The adult role in taking children on trips plays an important part in the success of the trip. Some people delight in taking children—and adults—on "guided tours." They enjoy sharing with others something they have experienced by pointing out what should be noticed, examined carefully, and appreciated. Some of us, however, have come to avoid such trips, preferring to be on our own, letting our interests and preferences guide what we take in. Children are very much like us in resisting the restricted tour. They enjoy trips best if they have ample time to pause and look carefully at something that has captured their attention. Sometimes they choose to concentrate on things other than the point of the trip. Anyone in charge of a trip must be prepared for this, as experienced parents and teachers can testify. A mother took her four-year-old Mary to the children's zoo. When they came to the pen where a child could enter and pet the young animals, such as lambs and ducklings, Mary noticed another four-year-old girl eating popcorn out of a bag. Suddenly, Mary's interest was off the zoo, off animals, and riveted on the other girl and her popcorn. A short exchange between the two took place, and then both munched popcorn together, talked and laughed, and in no way related themselves to the animals in the pen.

Even as youngsters grow older, well-planned trips may run into unexpected detours. A second-grade teacher prepared her seven-year-olds for a long trip to a large dairy. The class had read about dairy farms, the milking of cows by machine, and the pasteurizing and bottling of milk. The group formulated questions to ask the guide, such as "Do milking machines hurt the cows?" and "How long does it take to pasteurize milk?" Once arrived at the diary, the children met entirely unexpected experiences. Cows were being fed silage, which the attendant called "the cows' sauerkraut." Attached to the side walls of the barns were large squares of salt colored pink. These the guide called "the cows' lollipops." The youngsters were taken through the entire milk-processing plant, then led to an outer room where they were served huge dishes of ice cream. The next day, in discussing plans for what they would write about the trip, they were eager to talk about the "cows' sauerkraut" and "lollipops" and the big dish of free ice cream, but words concerning pasteurization had to be dragged from them. The teacher's estimation of the trip was briefly stated: "This trip was a flop."

True, some trips seem to be flops. We must be ready for such letdowns. Yet, although such trips may not meet adult expectations, children may get from them much of value. Often it is wise to take children from three through seven on a preliminary trip just for looking about. Then a follow-up trip for which the children make plans may take on more obvious learning value.

The reward for time and effort in guiding such traveling about runs high and is readily observable, as indicated by what happened when a farm couple took a neglected city child as a guest for a month. This six-year-old seemed to have little to talk about upon his arrival. The farmer and his wife included him in indoor and outdoor work and in a relaxed manner talked about what they were doing—harrowing, planting sets, whipping pudding, sterilizing the separator, and bleaching dish towels. The city boy made many jaunts to a nearby market and took in several evening baseball games, auctions, and church outings. On many of these trips youngsters of his own age joined him. That fall, the boy returned to school with new ardor and energy, and a sharp increase in his intelligence-test rating was noticed. "What happened to him?" asked the teacher. Undoubtedly, the wholesome influence of good rural family life was a high contributing factor to the change in this child, but also important was the fact that he had been given an opportunity to learn by sharing in and talking about interesting happenings.

Today's television programs create many chances for children to widen their trip and travel opportunities by discussing with parents some of the programs viewed. In many homes, however, the opportunity to talk about what is observed needs to be extended. The common statement, "TV is good because it keeps kids quiet," needs to be probed. Are we scuttling much of the value of television and limiting the learning this medium could stimulate by not entering into more conversation with children about programs of special interest?

YOUNG CHILDREN LEARN TO LISTEN

As the young child grows in his mastery of language, he also grows in his ability to listen. At first, his questions may mean, "Talk to me, so I know you are noticing me." Later, and with many youngsters this occurs at age two and a half or three, he begins to ask questions and actually listens to the answers. "How does the box open?" "Where did Peter go?" "Why is Gussie mad?" He also makes rapid strides in understanding more words than he uses. Many five-year-olds have a speaking vocabulary of 2,500 to 5,000 words but an understanding vocabulary of many times that number.

Early listening has an episodic rather than a continuing quality. For example, a young child may ask, "What bike is that?" The adult responds, "That's the delivery boy's." That may terminate the communication. Later, at three and a half or four, incidents of real conversation are noticeable. Episodes are reported—"Helen broke her bike and Sadie fixed it, and it's all right again." Youngsters at this stage often listen and produce evidence of genuinely connected discourse at times, with no major gaps in the connecting ideas. Some, however, as late as five and six, have not reached that stage. For them, continued growth in language—stimulated by working and playing with children, teachers, and other adults—is essential before attention is focused on their reading growth. Children of this type may need much stimulation and satisfaction in socializing to help them overcome this lack in their background.

VARIATIONS IN LANGUAGE GROWTH

Although other factors combine to boost his development, the child's language growth may indicate the general richness or meagerness in his preschool life. Low family financial status does not in and of itself rob a child of the conversational opportunities, affection, and other forms of attention he needs. Many a family mindful of a child's needs transcends the limitations springing from an inadequate income. Conversely, many parents either unmindful of a child's needs or uninformed of them may deny him their companionship even though they have a more than adequate income.

The very way in which a child is included in everyday family doings can boost his language growth. "I'm getting your breakfast"; "I'll plug in the vacuum cleaner, and you can hear it go whir-r-r-r"; "We'll put on our coats and take a shopping bag and go to market"; "Here comes the meter man"; "Help me find your sneakers"—all these are comments a parent can make without taking an extra second of time, but through which a child hears common words and phrases over and over until he can say them and know what they mean.

When he enters into the talking, often repeating the last word he has heard, a casual response, such as "Yes, that's right," or "Fine, you can say it too," satisfies him that his talking is being noticed. A too-silent or an unresponsive parent may dampen a child's eagerness to test himself out in talking and may thus slow his growth in speaking.

Catching Up in Kindergarten A wise teacher, rather than treating youngsters who score low on reading-readiness tests as verbally handicapped and giving them special attention in speaking, helps them enjoy a rich life out of which their verbal growth will more naturally and more rapidly develop. With good care most of these children ultimately catch up to norms appropriate for them.

The following account relayed to me recently by a kindergarten teacher is similar to reports many other observant teachers can make. Five-and-a-half-year-old Marietta entered kindergarten after a two-year period in the home of relatives where she had been scarcely noticed and where there were no children in the neighborhood to offer her companionship. During the first two weeks in school, the teacher gave her much attention and helped other children to include her as a silent partner in their play. At the end of two weeks a gradual warming up on Marietta's part was noticed.

She made one-word comments, "Me," "Look," "Here," to the children. These expanded into longer comments. At last, smiling and pleasant facial expressions grew into laughter. Then began real face-to-face conversations with one child or at times with a small group. Marietta had caught up at last in her ability to mingle and reach out in social contacts with her peers so that she could continue to grow toward "par" for her.

This knowledge that most children can and do catch up as speakers is exceedingly comforting for parents, teachers, and all who worry about the effect of retarding influences on children. Illness that causes a prolonged absence from school frequently arouses parental worry over the effect upon a child's success. Children may be temporarily delayed, but if placed in home and school situations where they feel wanted and liked, where they have companionship and receive individual help with their work, they do "catch up" to what is normal for them.

The Challenge to the School Children who experience this kind of temporary delay present a tremendous challenge for those who plan the child's entire school life—or curriculum. To concentrate too narrowly on a child's shortage may not help him to recapture or develop his proper stride. The emphasis should be on a good, rounded-out, day-after-day life that includes opportunity to practice the retarded skill of language or reading along with many other interesting activities.

Children who enter schools that maintain this broad and basic interest in their attitudes and early accomplishments, particularly in language, are indeed fortunate. In such a school, the teacher will note how each child takes hold of life in the kindergarten. Does he show eagerness to be a member of the group and a sustained interest in toys, books, and supplies, or does he cling to his mother and require constant tending and urging? Does he begin at once to inventory the kindergarten room and relate to other children, or does he sit with almost painful shyness, afraid to touch or be touched? Does he try out new equipment and materials freely and vigorously, or does he withdraw or hold back? Does he catch the spirit of the group and join with one or more in play, or does he seem to be walled off from others? Is he able to tell the teacher what he wants? Does he talk about happenings that interest him? Does he enter into conversations with other children? Does his conversation reveal a rich background of contacts in his preschool world?

In such a school, the teacher will plan the work of each day to include a variety of opportunities for experience. Some will be geared to fit specific needs of certain children, others to fit the group. All will be directed toward stimulating the growth of all the children.

Schools that reflect a broad personal concern for individual children are likely to have a broad interpretation of reading growth, as is presented in Chapter 1. Children in less favorable situations may become successful readers in some ways, but those who are fully aware of the high potentialities of children want them all to be given the advantages of deep understanding of their learning needs through stimulating preschool and kindergarten years. If each child could enter a school that has reading goals toward which to guide his growth from the very beginning, the resulting educational climate would make for not only a richer life for children but also a more intelligent and more literate United States.

SUGGESTED READINGS IN CHILD GROWTH AND DEVELOPMENT

ALMY, MILLIE. *Child Development.* New York: Henry Holt and Co., 1955.
For those interested in all phases of child growth with emphasis on emerging growth toward maturity, this book will be rewarding reading. Lucid style of writing.

BRUNER, JEROME S. *The Process of Education.* Cambridge: Harvard University Press, 1960.
A brief, challenging description of learning, with important references to the learning of young children.

HUNT, J. MCV. *Intelligence and Experience.* New York: The Ronald Press Co., 1961.
Chapter 9 presents a succinct summary of the emphasis in the entire book, which includes the relationship between experiences at an early age and intellectual development. Technical but readable.

LANDRETH, CATHERINE. *The Psychology of Early Childhood.* New York: Alfred A. Knopf, 1960.
Entire book helpful in understanding young children. Chapter V includes excellent analysis of relation of environment to child's learning. Technical but not difficult reading.

MURPHY, LOIS BARCLAY, and ASSOCIATES. *The Widening World of Childhood: Paths Toward Mastery.* New York: Basic Books, Inc., 1962.
A study of the growth of thirty-two normal children related in clear readable style. Will increase insight and depth in understanding children's everyday behavior.

PECK, LEIGH. *Child Psychology.* Boston: D. C. Heath and Company, 1953. Part II, Chapter 6.
Description of how language is learned, with helpful suggestion for parents and teachers.

STRICKLAND, RUTH. *The Language Arts.* Boston: D. C. Heath and Company, 1957. Chapters 4 and 5.
Detailed description of the growth of language in the home, nursery school, and kindergarten. Many practical suggestions.

CHAPTER 3

Beginning to Be a Reader at Home

Despite all we know about learning to read, much of this intellectual work of young children remains a mystery. We know what the youngsters tell us, what they reveal by pointing and trying to sound out, but what they *think,* what mental connections they are making, we can only conjecture. It is commonly assumed that a child becomes a beginning reader in school under the careful direction of a teacher, but, actually, fundamental ideas about and attitudes toward reading develop during the preschool years in the course of a good home life. Anyone who follows a child's growth during his third and fourth years has gained some helpful knowledge about the child's first awareness of reading.

CATCHING ON TO READING AND WRITING

Some youngsters become quite absorbed in the family's reading and writing. A child may ask, as mother reads a post card, "Who sent you that?" and "What does it say?" These questions may mean that the child has already caught on to the big idea that through writing we say something. This concept represents a fundamental realization. Whenever we read, a writer has said something to us, through letters that make up words and through words and sentences that express ideas. The child who persists in asking "what-does-it-say?" is not going to fall into the rut of word recognition but indifference to the meaning of what is read. At the outset of his learning to read the child needs to understand the general concept that through reading we "get" someone else's ideas.

Bruner, in his description of learning, places considerable emphasis on the idea that learning is acquired through arriving at a general attitude and idea first and then acquiring the specifics.[1] The child who is growing up in a home where he is included in a full, interesting life, as was mentioned in Chapter 2, acquires the general idea of reading and writing. He sees them as an integral part of life, but it is difficult to know how much he is absorbing and what ideas he may be acquiring. It is possible, however, to notice his attitude toward reading, his interest in it, and some of the specifics that become immediately meaningful to him.

THE FUN OF LIVING AND LEARNING

Alert youngsters who have had letters, messages, and stories read to them reveal some of their thinking in their immediate flow of questions and comments. "Why was Bozo in the cage?" "Can't he get out by himself?" "I could get out of that cage by myself." Such comments reveal that the young listener is following the ideas of a story and entering into these ideas. He is comprehending.

At an early age, children develop attachment to certain stories and ask that favorites be read again and again. They begin to indicate taste through preferences. They chuckle over funny parts. Certain words and phrases amuse them. They also ask for more information—"What does this say?" as a brand name is flashed on the television screen, or "What kind of dog is that?"

Books in the Family A child who has many opportunities to sit beside an adult who will read to him and with whom he can talk things over in a leisurely manner is indeed privileged. Would that this were part of the lives of all children. And would that this kind of experience were a daily affair, perhaps at bed-times. Many a bright child gradually grows into a reader through these relaxed moments when conversation and reading are geared to him personally. Furthermore, in the course of such warm relationships he is acquiring a love of books, a fondness for reading, and a firsthand knowledge of the wide variety of new ideas one can capture through reading. Bright youngsters will gather ideas at a rapid rate; slower ones will show interest and gather new meanings at their own pace.

[1] Jerome S. Bruner, *The Process of Education*. Harvard University Press, 1960.

Through contacts with books, youngsters in a lively home where books are much in evidence also learn some important facts which children who grow up in a less literary milieu must learn at school. For example, an observant grandmother recorded the following things young Kit could do before she was four years old:

1. Turn the book right side up when looking at it and start at the beginning.
2. Turn to the title page of the story in a book containing a collection of stories and say, "Read this one to me."
3. Connect ideas in pictures with the content and vice versa.
4. Notice tiny details in pictures.
5. Recognize any book asked for in her collection of more than thirty books.
6. Find any specific phonograph record in her record collection by identifying it through some clue.

A natural observation about Kit is that she's a bright child. True, but how many more children would show such evidence of brightness if they were to receive similar attention? Families with several children can plan reading moments, now to fit this one's personal wish, now to satisfy others. Older brothers and sisters, even seven- and eight-year-olds, can play extremely helpful roles in reading to younger family members, and in so doing they add to their own growth in reading. As chubby Janet in the crowded second grade of a Connecticut school proudly told her teacher, "I read to my two kid brothers every night, and I get better and better."

The importance of good family life to reading cannot be overemphasized. A Puerto Rican newcomer to New York City went to night school to learn to speak and read English. On his way to his class he passed a public library and managed to stop off one afternoon "just to look around." He saw the children's reading room and the engrossed sixth- and seventh-graders in it. He saw shelf after shelf of books on display. Despite his limited English and her limited Spanish he managed to convey to the librarian his question, "Can my kids come here too?"

The librarian, a rare soul whose mission in life was to enrich people's lives through books, said, "Yes. Do tell them to come. But you can take a book home for them now." The thrilled father took home to his surprised son his first library book—*And Now*

Miguel, by Joseph Krumgold, a highly appropriate book for a Spanish-speaking boy from rural Puerto Rico.

The librarian and the father had frequent meetings. They grew in communication; she in Spanish, he in English. He reported that he relayed everything he learned in his class to his wife and their five children, aged five to eleven. The older children were learning more rapidly than he and his wife could. The two oldest ones were reading library books by studying the pictures in them and then applying what they thus acquired to their reading work at school. The father, with an expression of great pride, said, "In our apartment we all go to school all the time, every day." The attitudes acquired by this family give a clear picture of the tremendous contribution parents can make to children's progress in reading.

Importance of a Talkative Adult Companion Many important facts about reading are acquired in before-school years by thousands of youngsters. Some, at surprisingly early ages, become interested in the individual letters. Young John, about three, looking at the telephone directory, musing and running his fingers over the cover, finally said with an air of discovery, "Hey, look, there are three *E*'s in this word." His mother recalled that once before he had asked her, "What's this letter?" "That's an *E*." From that time on he was able to recognize and remember the capital *E*.

Children in their early years become fascinated by the many signs about them, especially if we adults call attention to those that we must read in order to follow directions and obey traffic regulations. "We must wait until the sign says 'Go,'" helps a child to grow in the understanding of the use of signs and also calls his attention to this particular sign. One young father spelled signs—"S-t-o-p, Stop"; "G-o, Go"; "T-u-r-n, Turn"; "S-l-o-w, Slow"—to his two youngsters while driving. Both children became early spellers, writers, and readers.

Offer Help—Avoid Pressure In the past few decades parents—and teachers, too—have become "afraid lest I do the wrong thing." No doubt many youngsters were deprived of the fun and value of early learning through adult-child experiences. What harm can come from telling or spelling out the words on signs to a young child? The child may remember, or he may not. As long as parents accept the child's behavior without pressuring him to remember or attempting to make him sprout "genius" tendencies from that time on, no harm is done. If he remains interested for a time, remembers, then later forgets and loses early learnings, he is proving the soundness of a study made by McGraw about advanced learning of very young children; she found that they can acquire advanced skills but that they do not necessarily carry these skills along with them. Instead, they may revert back to normal for children of their age.[2]

YES, THEY DO LEARN THE ABC'S AND PHONICS

Youngsters, once they notice letters, are bound to discover the alphabet. They hear other children chant the *ABC*'s in song. One active four-year-old girl, while listening to a recording of Dohnanyi's "Variations on a Nursery Theme," said "Why, that's the *ABC*'s."

Children need to feel that they are growing. They need chances to display their power. What is more fun than to sing out the *ABC*'s, or, with excitement in the voice, rattle them off to a proud grandfather!

Alphabet blocks have long served a healthy purpose in the lives of young children. Children play with them, arrange them in interesting designs, and, later, want to arrange them in proper sequence. Playing with letter blocks and plastic letters may carry over into early word recognition. It often quite naturally stimulates a desire to write. "I can make a *T*. Watch me," said little Timmy, who also knew how to spell his name. Later, in the first grade, he forgot about such early learning. Perhaps his fascination with a room filled with friendly, busy six-year-olds crowded out all else. (This often happens to children who are unaccustomed to being with large groups.) In January, however, Timmy "zoomed" ahead, according to the teacher's report to his parents.

Early Ear Training Early recognition of letters and words is often accompanied by great interest in sounds. "That says *Danger*," said

[2] M. B. McGraw, *Growth, A Study of Johnny and Jimmy*. Appleton Century, 1935.

a nine-year-old to her four-year-old brother. "Dan-ger, dan-ger, dan-ger," repeated the youngster.

Preschoolers also enjoy making rhymes. "I can sing, I can ding, I can ring," Susan said laughingly to a trio playing with her around a sand table in the nursery school. The teacher reported that Susan's jingle started the group off on a veritable spree of rhyming, making jingles, and playing with words. For example, while washing off a table, Gerard chanted "Swish-swoosh-swish-swoosh," washing in time with his chant.

Again, these early experiences may be forgotten. But, as careful observers have noted, a child who notices differences between letters and can detect which is *B* and which *P*, although he may later fail to recognize *B* and *P*, is likely to retain the ability to notice detail carefully—a great asset in learning to read. Similarly, the youngster who, through early fun with rhymes, reveals a good ear for sounds may not acquire specifics in phonics but does acquire a more accurate sense of hearing. Eyes and ears gain valuable exercise from rich early experiences with symbols and sounds. Certainly such experiences provide an advantage for a child when he enters school.

When learnings of this sort are retained, and they often are, they boost the child's efforts during the beginning reading stage. A caution needs repeating here. Normal give-and-take with before-schoolers involving letters, words, and sounds can become harmful to a child if interested adults become overly ambitious for him, expect him to continue to show high verbal tendencies, hope he will skip grades in school, and even show displeasure and marked disappointment when he lags in such interests. Unfortunately, some children respond to such adult treatment by striving to please their elders. At first they may seem to be helpfully affected, but in later years they may reveal tension or resentment toward those who have goaded them on, and even toward reading. It is important for parents and teachers not to exert such pressure. Stone and Church call to our attention the seriousness of undue pressure: "Some children try hard to measure up to their parents' expectations, but the very effort that goes into trying produces anxiety that interferes with learning."[3]

[3] L. Joseph Stone and Joseph Church, *Childhood and Adolescence—A Psychology of a Growing Person*. Random House, 1957, p. 362.

The language arts are naturally interwoven by children. They flit from one activity to another—now looking at letters, now writing them, now sounding them out, then noticing them in books or signs. Ideas are expressed in words that are written in symbols to which we have attached sounds. An intellectually nimble child grasps this inherent connection early. This big step in learning is part of the essential mystery of becoming a reader. The "catching-on" also reveals the intuitive thinking powers young children reveal if they are eager and unafraid.

Noticing Early Learnings To us, who read without thinking about the skills involved, certain fundamental steps may be overlooked. We may fail to register appreciation when a young child bringing in the family's morning mail says, "Here's a letter for me," and upon looking, we find that it is indeed for him. If we were to take the time to unravel what this one incident reveals we would note:

1. That the child is aware of personal messages via mail.
2. That he knows an envelope bears writing that indicates for whom a message is intended.
3. That, by some kind of careful inspection, the child can recognize his own name.
4. That his name communicates to him, "This is mine."

Incidents of this kind require recognition and approval. This is as big a step as the applauded first step in walking. When a child looking at labels on the seasoning jar says, "This says 'salt,' " it is rewarding for him to be told: "You are right. It does. What do you think is in that jar?" He may even be able to describe to you how he could tell. One must be ready to be surprised by the answer. The cue for recognition may have nothing to do with letters. It may be "the jar nearest the biggest one" or "the one with a black top"; on the other hand, he may say, "It says S here." If the child refers to the letter S to identify the jar, he is telling us that he understands the function of symbols. The letters that spell *salt* have no resemblance to the article. The child makes a mental connection between these symbols and what they stand for.

Only recently I had a visit from red-headed Carol, who held a paper in her hand on which her seven-year-old brother had written two words, *Carol* and *doll.* Carol excitedly showed me the paper, saying, "Look, here it says Carol. That's me. And look, here it says doll. That's for my doll." She had discovered that these strange pencil marks stood for her and her cherished plaything. To a casual observer, such a discovery means little. In the child's real struggle to learn to read, it is a big event.

BIG GAINS FROM SMALL MOMENTS WITH PARENTS

Through countless small moments of being read to, looking at signs, watching television programs, browsing through books and magazines, playing with alphabet blocks or letters, and attempting to write letters and even single words, many bright youngsters learn to read. Some may acquire the ability to recognize favorite words and parts of stories by following along carefully while books are being read to them. What a wonderful way to learn to read! Such youngsters are often described as "self-taught." This is, in a way, an appropriate description because the children themselves do the exploring and inner intellectual work without being set to the task.

Every Child's Right—Books, Books, and Books No experience can match the value and satisfaction a child derives from sitting close to an older person, parent, friend, or relative, and looking into a book that is being read to him. As this child becomes better versed in looking on and listening, he may begin to link key words with their sounds. He may notice far more than he indicates. Most of all, however, he is discovering the genuine fun that books contain for him.

In this age of mass book production for the very young, more books that present information appropriate for children are becoming available. Not so many years ago, a young child's questions were not recognized as indicators of the eager learner but were assumed to be purely attention-getting devices. Stories were his only book fare. Fortunately for today's child, we now understand the normality of his readiness and eagerness to know. "Read to me about the kangaroo," "Tell me again what kind of machine this is," and "What kind of pudding does this label say?" are requests for facts and implicitly tell the adult, "Read to me or tell me. I want to know." Sometimes children do plague us with questions merely to establish contact with us and to get attention. We are safe if we honor their questions as sincere requests, giving them short but honest answers. And it is to be hoped that our patience has the elasticity it often needs when youngsters deluge us with questions.

To characterize such early progress as effortless is to err seriously. Children work with genuine intentness and real vigor, even if for only small periods of time and almost as they run. The vast amount of detail they learn at such an early age can be accounted for only by their ability to dig in and persist at it. Many adults could take a lesson from them in this hard business of learning new skills and acquiring new ideas.

That Superb Teacher—The Parent The role of the family in these satisfying experiences with beginning reading and writing cannot be overemphasized. In a good home, when a child's interest is aroused over a certain point, he can quickly get answers to his questions, whereas in school he may have to wait his turn. The delay may be only a few minutes, but a young child's interests often cool quickly. Then, too, at home he is talking to a person who usually understands what he is talking about. During the preschool years children are often still unable to convey ideas clearly to one who has not become as intimately acquainted with them as has a parent.

LANGUAGE GROWTH AND LEARNING POWER

All too often the language growth of young children is taken lightly or overlooked once the infancy period is past. The child's growing collection of words and phrases that he can understand and use properly is a resource upon which he will build and from which he can draw all the rest of his life. His very success in reading depends upon his facility in understanding the ideas that words convey.

Growth of Language Through Discovery Language makes other major additions to a child's learning that later will be reflected in the kind of reader he becomes. A child who discovers things going on in his immediate world and who has comfortable associations with parents and children asks and talks about what he sees. At four, many a suburban or city child can differentiate between a Diesel truck and a gasoline-fueled motor, between an electric engine and a coal-fueled engine, and between a helicopter and an airplane. Such a child has observed and can converse about road construction, house building, and garden planting. He has enjoyed lifts in elevators and on escalators. He has acquired a tremendous repertoire of radio and television advertising jingles and trade names. He understands much of the work that goes on in his immediate family life. He knows many people, has been to many places, and may already be an experienced shopper.

Rural children may acquire much of the same kind of learning on trips to towns or cities. They may also learn much about the work that goes on around them, especially if they live on a family-operated farm where they can enter into day-by-day conversations about the work. A child needs the chance to share in conversation and to test out his growing vocabulary in order to gain real language-learning value from experiences. A "talking world" about him helps him bloom.

A natural result of this active way of living in preschool years is a wide and growing array of interests. Many of these, such as his interests in modern inventions in transportation and great happenings in science, the child will carry along for years. A child so ignited with a love of learning and living will never be described as "bored" or "uninterested" in a home and school that are also pulsating with life. It is readily understandable that the "eager beavers" invariably grow into successful readers, able to understand, talk about, and think about what they read.

Nursery schools and friendly neighborhoods contribute much to this early learning. Central to it, however, is the home. A child who has many venturesome trips with his family, who engages in simple chores with older brothers and sisters, who shares in table talk, and who is encouraged to explore and inquire, leaps ahead in his language skill and accumulated knowledge; and, as discussed in Chapter 2, he develops wholesome attitudes toward himself that give him the courage to tackle and achieve difficult learning tasks, including learning to read.

COMMON SENSE—A GOOD GUIDE FOR PARENTS

When parents assume a helpful role by responding to children's questions, numerous problems may arise. As was stated earlier, sometimes parents fear that they may be doing the wrong thing. For example, when a child points to a letter and says "What's that letter?" common sense should tell us to answer him in a matter-of-fact way, "That's a *W*." "But," said a young mother whose older child, Beck, was in the second grade, "Beck's teacher says she is trying to break him of pointing." In the early years of research into reading, pointing was regarded as a slowing-up influence on reading. During that period pointing was discouraged at the very outset of instruction in reading.

The Importance of Pointing Pointing and following along the line while reading may be absolutely essential to some youngsters. The child who says "What's this letter?" has no other way of indicating than by pointing. Those who use their fingers to indicate what they are reading in first and second grades are not only helping themselves to keep their eyes on the right place but are also using the contact with the page to keep them alert.

Some youngsters need to touch, feel, and handle more than others. To deny them this may slow up and even stop learning. Such children may be like some of us older folk who, in order to enjoy the beauty of a fine piece of glassware, must pick it up and feel it. A sedate matron at a shop counter filled with antique china commented audibly, " 'Don't touch.' Well, that spoils it for me," and so saying walked from the shop. Although letters are not embossed and cannot be felt, the very process of running the fingers over the words satisfies the desire to "get the feel" of reading. This desire should not be thwarted. Later, as the child increases in reading ability and grows hot in the pursuit of what's coming next, he will stop pointing. If he, by chance, does not, his teacher should then help him desist.

It is well to recall that the no-pointing influence appeared about 1920, before the spate of research into the behavior of young children occurred. At that time great concern was expressed for proper use of the eyes in sweeping over the lines in rhythmic fashion and reading by clusters of words rather than by short, abrupt jerks.

Pointing was linked with slow reading and was considered a retarding influence on young readers. Some of this thinking still persists in spite of the increased respect for children's need to touch, wiggle, and manipulate as a part of their way of learning. Careful observers of young children see the wisdom of allowing touching and pointing tendencies, even in beginning reading.

The essential need of sensory accompaniment to learning is now being explored in several research projects. A report of a symposium on sensory deprivation states: "A number of investigations have shown that deprivation early in the life of an organism creates permanent adaptational difficulties in adult life."[4]

Many careful studies have been made on the function of the eyes in reading. Some practices based on these studies border on quackery. The eyes are facile organs that adjust easily to the work they are called upon to do. In China they help young readers to read characters that seem to us to have almost no distinctive characteristics. Chinese youngsters read these from top to bottom, one theory being that the early Chinese used bamboo rods on which to carve their writing. When these young readers reach the bottom of a column, they go to the top of the column to the left. If a child were born in the Near East, he would read character after character from right to left.

Do you recall the pictures of eye movements to be found some years back in all technical books on teaching reading? From some of them one might deduce that the human eyes were born to lope from left to right, then swoop back to the left and continue. A reader's eye movements depend on the language he is reading, not on a natural tendency of the eye. The movement of the eyes is acquired behavior, and, thanks to the facility of eyes, they adjust to reading the print of the Orient, the Near East, and our Western culture.

Grace M. Fernald at the University of California found that running their fingers over the forms of letters helped some children to become readers.[5] Arnold L. Gesell, in his well-known studies, found

[4] Philip Soloman, ed., *Sensory Deprivation—A Symposium Held at Harvard Medical School.* Harvard University Press, 1961, ch. 8.

[5] Grace M. Fernald, *Remedial Techniques in Basic School Subjects.* New York: McGraw-Hill Book Company, Inc., 1943.

that some preschool children leaned more heavily on some senses than on others in learning. Those of us who have done much work with young children have noticed marked difference between "the need to look closely to learn," or "the need to feel to learn," or "the need to hear it to learn" that children reveal. Those who need to explore through touching may be furthered in learning to read by being able to do so; those not permitted to do so may be kept from achieving.

Helping the Very Young Scribe Many other questions trouble parents of young children in helping them learn skills related to reading and writing. When a four-year-old says, "Show me how to write my name," what writing tool should the parent use? What style of writing should be used—longhand with both capital and lower-case letters, or printing all in capitals? It seems sensible to use a crayon or a soft pencil, although if a child insists upon a pencil or pen that he hands to mother for the occasion, no harm will be done. Capital letters are simpler for the novice scribe to write than "longhand" or cursive letters. Also, the child often sees signs and television advertising all in capitals and may already recognize some letters. Manuscript writing, which closely resembles letter forms used in books and signs, is commonly used in the beginning years at school. Some schools make available to parents copies of the alphabet in manuscript style—a helpful practice that should be more widely followed.

The parent can let the child watch exactly how writing is done. A slow, careful manner of demonstrating will help him see whether to begin at the top or bottom when making certain letters. If the child's interest in writing is momentary, this demonstration will satisfy his short-time need. If he continues to write his name, he will be ready for suggestions on how to make each letter. The main point to remember concerning most of the requests by preschool children is that one should offer them as much help as they seem ready for. The precise method used is relatively unimportant; the essential element is the cheerful responsiveness of the parent.

NOT "HANDS OFF," BUT HANDS BE HELPFUL

In recent years, in various parts of the country, pamphlets prepared by curriculum workers and primary teachers have included suggestions to parents on how to prepare a child for kindergarten. Some have drawn a sharp line between what parents should and should not do. Some have advised parents to keep hands off reading and writing, because such matters are in the province of the school; they have made the point that this type of work demands professional competence.

No one will deny that tense, uneasy parents may cause a youngster to become upset in his first efforts at reading and writing and thus rob him of the very joy and eagerness with which he should enter into such learning. However, the vast majority of parents possess considerable common sense. To tell them to keep hands off reading and writing is to create many situations in which they will feel frustrated and their children will feel denied. Imagine young Katie saying "Show me how to make a K" and the mother replying "Wait until you get to school. Your teacher will show you how to make a K." Katie would not regard this as a reasonable answer from a parent who, as a rule, was helpful. Katie would be right—such a response is unreasonable.

The value to a child of being guided, under good home situations, to be exploratory, eager, and confident in some knowledge of reading and writing is evident even in the satisfactions the child displays. No matter what follows in kindergarten and first grade, such a youngster has had a fine romp in a literary way before he crosses the school's threshold. He may "park" such learning in the excitement of beginning kindergarten, but undoubtedly he will pick up and proceed later in the year. A few of the nimble ones may even master preprimers and primers in the kindergarten years. Wise teachers in good schools, however, do not push reading, even at the bright youngster. Learning to live in a busy but relaxed way in vigorous group play is the best kindergarten program for most children of this age. Responding to their questions and comments about signs, letters, and books in a matter-of-fact way, as wise parents do, gives them all the help in reading they need at this time.

What about the child who does not reach out for reading before he enters kindergarten? There are many children of this sort. Some are the physically well-cared-for children of well-to-do negligent adults who choose a baby sitter with less care than they choose the mechanic who handles their car or the man who repairs their television set. Others are the children of hard-pressed parents who may have to hold two jobs to cover the family budget and who are absorbed in financial worries. Still others are youngsters whose parents are busy, wholesome people, but who in their lives have not been ignited by the spark of reading. A good school program can bring to children in these categories a delayed delight in books. Finally, there are those children who may approach the world of things and physical action with satisfaction but not the realm of ideas, symbols, and the fun of figuring things out. They may be slower in most learning or they may be "late bloomers." What happens to all these strong personalities in the beginning reading program is described in Chapters 4 and 5.

SUGGESTED READINGS ON LEARNING PROCESSES

ALMY, MILLIE C. "Wishful Thinking About Children's Thinking." *Teachers College Record,* 62, No. 5, February 1961.

A presentation of evidence that indicates that children think differently from the logical manner of adults. Therefore to expect them to learn as adults do is unsound.

BRUNER, JEROME S. *The Process of Education.* Cambridge: Harvard University Press, 1960.

This short book is punctuated throughout with pungent ideas about the way in which children learn, the importance of wide and frequent experiences in a given area, and the difficulties of "structuring" learning. A timely study.

HUNT, J. MCV. *Intelligence and Experience.* New York: The Ronald Press Co., 1961.

The importance to the growth of intelligence of varied and satisfying experiences in early years is clearly presented throughout this volume and documented with research. The concept of fixed intelligence is refuted. An essential book for all educators. Although written in textbook style, a valuable book for parents.

MCGRAW, M. B. *Growth: A Study of Johnny and Jimmy.* New York: Appleton Century, 1935.

A detailed experiment with twins. A helpful reference for professional workers in situations where excessive pressures seem to be placed on the learning of young children.

SOLOMAN, PHILIP, ed. *Sensory Deprivation—A Symposium at Harvard Medical School* (foreword by Stanley Cobb). Cambridge: Harvard University Press, 1961. Chapter 8.
Entire report has value for educators probing bases for children's learning. The study by Donald O. Hebb reported in Chapter 8 indicates timeliness of challenging practices that quell children's tendencies to use sensory accompaniments as they explore and learn.

CHAPTER 4

How Kindergarten Helps the Beginning Reader

The kindergarten was first organized as an induction into learning through play. Although some kindergarten theorists included work projects planned to develop certain skills, the child's freedom to explore, to inquire, to discover, to add to his fund of knowledge, and to grow in the ability to socialize, away from home, with others of his age became the predominant theoretical influence in the United States. Learning to read has been only recently emphasized as a reason for making kindergarten an integral part of the elementary school.

The anxious attitude of many young parents about reading is a widely accepted reason for starting to teach reading in a formal way in the kindergarten. The age in which we live has been labeled an anxious age, and no one can deny that there are well-founded reasons for anxiety. The shortage of college space has made some parents begin to worry about their child's admission to college even before he enters kindergarten. Success in school demands competence in reading, and some people hold the erroneous idea that the earlier a child is taught to read, the more surely will he be academically successful. Some bright preschoolers learn to read at home and continue as successful readers throughout their school lives. No one could keep them from succeeding. Others, not as bright or similarly motivated, can become bored and even resentful toward help in beginning reading because they are not yet intellectually or culturally interested in deciphering words. Such children are, perhaps, not even interested in listening to someone read to them. These youngsters must be encouraged to develop interest in reading in the course of living.

As early as 1931, when Morphett and Washburne did their research in the Winnetka schools,[1] studies were made concerning the age at which instruction in reading should begin. Although the outcomes of the studies vary, all indicate the waste and undesirability of starting a youngster off on his pursuit of literacy at too early an age. Because it is essential for a young child to have a relaxed, tension-free attitude toward reading, a look at the kindergarten programs as they are now related to beginning reading is relevant here.

THE COMMON FEATURES OF TODAY'S KINDERGARTENS

Most children start their school career by entering a public kindergarten. Kindergartens across this land vary widely in their programs, but they have many characteristics in common. First, they are usually equipped with a variety of materials that can be utilized for playing alone or in groups, for building, for painting, for browsing, for vigorous physical activity, and for moments of rest. Shelves and storage places are low enough for the child to reach. Cubbyholes or individual lockers are located so that each child can establish the habit of managing his own wraps and other personal belongings. More than any other part of a school building, the kindergarten is equipped and arranged to make the young inhabitant feel that this is his domain.

The second important common characteristic of kindergartens is that they are filled with eager youngsters who vary widely as to home and neighborhood background, language development, vigor in meeting new experiences, and readiness to share several hours per day with a number of other children under the supervision of one adult, the teacher.

The element of varied backgrounds is important for us to remember. In the previous chapter, the potentials of privileged home lives that result in valuable learnings were described. Children from such backgrounds may find that sharing one teacher with so many

[1] Mabel V. Morphett and Carleton Washburne, "When Should Children Begin to Read," *Elementary School Journal,* 31 (March 1931), pp. 496-503.

others is difficult to accept. They may grow impatient while they wait for the teacher to satisfy other pressing demands before meeting theirs. They may feel jealous at times, and they may also become truly exhausted from the amount of noise and motion about them. Many eager children may grow so excited by kindergarten life that they come home "done in" and ready for a nap. Nevertheless, they are pleased with school, even if it is exhausting.

Along with the outgoing, energetic ones may be the overly shy, the fearful, who spend the first few days in tears, worried lest they are lost from home and mother for good. Others may wander about, half hearing, half seeing, almost too confused to know what is happening; the teacher has to accompany each suggestion to these children with physical assistance in order to help them become a part of the group's life.

Any observer who spends one day with a good kindergarten teacher, watching her do her level best to manage twenty-five five-year-olds and to see that each has a happy, constructive day, must marvel at such teaching art—and physical stamina. Contemplating the thousands of present-day kindergarten teachers with more than thirty young pupils in the morning and a second edition of equal size in the afternoon, one appropriately asks, "How do they do it—and survive?"

School leaders and parent groups who realize clearly the importance for children of kindergarten life with a good teacher try to limit kindergarten size to twenty-five or under. For the first few weeks at least, in such communities, a second adult, a parent or student assistant, or a member of a high school Future Teachers of America Club is on hand to assist the teacher with the group. Those who think schools in this period of our history are extravagant in their demands for personnel and facilities need only visit a large kindergarten to see under what difficult circumstances the youngest pupils of our rich land begin their education.

READING READINESS—DIFFERENT POINTS OF VIEW

Beyond the common factors of classroom equipment and a wide range of youngsters, kindergartens vary widely, chiefly in the purpose and content of their programs. One of the chief differentiating factors may be their attitude toward beginning reading and the interpretation of that variously defined term "reading readiness."

Readiness to learn is observable in children even in infancy. A child starts to reach out for articles he wants, to pull himself up on rings in his crib, to handle his feeding spoon, and to repeat babbling sounds. In education, we have put the emphasis on what we consider he is ready to be taught. Almy states, regarding readiness:

> Readiness is an educational concept concerned with the timeliness of what we wish to teach the child in the light of his ability to make use of it. It would seem, therefore, to put emphasis on understanding of the child's total development. One asks not only "Can the child learn this?" but also "What effect will this learning have upon him?" Unfortunately, however, the concept of readiness, particularly in relation to reading, has often been taken in a much narrower sense. . . . The answer too frequently is a program in which the child is to be given opportunities to practice the various elements involved in the reading process, without sufficient regard for the many other important experiences which he might be having, which in the long run would also contribute to his abilities for reading.[2]

Kindergarten programs are influenced by two widely held points of view regarding readiness. These two views, which are actually in contradiction, can be best described by presenting two programs: Program I, which emphasizes a systematic approach to reading readiness and daily use of workbooks and other preplanned materials; and Program II, which uses the environmental challenges to reading that occur in the daily life of the kindergarten but puts emphasis on a varied active day, a wide range of experiences, including many trips, and work with a variety of materials for dramatic play, art, and construction. Program I attempts to acquaint a child with prereading materials that require a definite, prescribed response. Work with these materials also teaches the child to conform to the uniform behavior of the rest of the children who are working on the same material. In Program II, no effort is made to teach a child prereading skills through precise direction or to stress uniformity of behavior in intellectual pursuits.

[2] Millie Almy, *Child Development.* Holt, 1955, pp. 272-273.

PROGRAM I. READING READINESS—PREPLANNED

The total program in Program I, like that in any good kindergarten, is planned with respect for the child's growing interests in the world about him. Trips are taken to interesting neighborhood spots, and free and animated discussions following the trips are encouraged. Big-muscle activities, such as building with blocks and vigorous outdoor play, are provided for. Children's interests in drawing, dramatic play, music, painting, and other activities commonly called creative activities, are also encouraged. Books are available for browsing, and a story hour is usually a daily affair.

Program I may emphasize early in the year the group's response to following directions, and in some schools much use is made of mimeographed outlines for coloring, with instructions dictated for coloring and cutting. Such work, it is explained, encourages a child to listen and to grow accustomed to paying attention in a manner that will be helpful to him in the more closely directed reading-readiness work later on. Signs and appropriate labels on lockers and boxes of supplies are commonly used, and youngsters are commended for noticing them and discovering "what they say."

Reading-Readiness Test Use After the winter holiday season, many schools following Program I give "reading-readiness tests." By this time, it is assumed that the youngsters who entered school in the fall are at home in the kindergarten atmosphere and will be at ease in taking what for many will be their first test. Other schools with a similar point of view defer such tests until the end of the year or until the beginning of the first grade.

The reading-readiness tests may be standardized or they may be a part of a basal reading series. Although they vary, in general a child is required to provide certain responses which will indicate his ability to interpret pictures and to recognize similarities and differences in letters and in words. He will also reveal his readiness to follow instructions, such as those essential to the test. Children who show alertness to signs, who reveal a facile vocabulary, and who do well on the reading-readiness test are organized into reading-readiness groups. These groups meet around tables and "learn to stay quiet" for periods of about twenty minutes while they follow the detailed reading-readiness workbook material selected by the school from one of several publishers. They follow instructions given by the teacher in using the workbook and other materials. They cross out letters and figures, underline, and color, according to the plan of the exercise.

Other activities, such as looking at books, noticing the teacher's notes on the blackboard, and reading signs during trips, are considered to contribute to reading readiness, but the real teaching emphasized is the page-by-page work in prescribed reading-readiness materials. Some teachers describe this part of the day as the formal part, resembling the formal instruction in the primary grades in many schools, and they consider it essential for children to meet this educational experience before entering the primary grades.

Children considered unready to take part in the reading-readiness period continue to pursue freer work planned for them by the teacher. In large kindergartens, a teacher may plan quiet work at this time to keep the reading-readiness group from being interrupted. In some schools all children are included in the prereading work, even though some of the immature are unable to grasp what they are doing. Where Program I is used, children's success in kindergarten is evaluated in part on their achievement during the reading-readiness period and is used in recommending that a child be promoted to first grade. The degree of importance of such evaluation may vary from slight to major; in some cases it is the deciding factor in assessing a child's achievement for the year.

By the end of the school year, approximately three-fourths of the children in kindergartens using a preplanned reading program are able to pass a test fitted to the materials. Individuals vary in competence, but many have gained, among other skills, the beginnings in recognizing words by key letters, the beginning of phonics, and the ability to recognize letters and words that look much alike. Some may be able to read preprimers successfully.

Teachers' Attitudes Toward Program I Although many teachers following this program say that it does not prevent the total kindergarten program from maintaining its broad social outlook and that it does not cause the many other abilities of the children to be overlooked, some careful observers differ. In some classrooms, the major concern hinges upon the reading-readiness period; the remainder of the half day (most kindergartens are on a half-day program) becomes of minor importance.

Many teachers, some of them experienced, like the commercially prepared kindergarten reading-readiness program. In communities where uneasiness is expressed about the adequacy of the school's reading program, they are able to describe and show readily what goes on; these teachers also believe that at the end of the year they can gather test data that are concrete and assuring to inquiring parents. Furthermore, under the pressure of looking after so many details for so many children, the teacher who may be too exhausted by late afternoon to plan creatively for prereading and beginning reading experiences has materials and plans available for use. The less apt teachers often state that the materials are a blessing.

Other teachers, however, both experienced and inexperienced, find serious faults with preplanned programs. One teacher called them an "appliquéd patch" that was difficult to relate to the children's other experiences. Frequently teachers raise the question of appropriateness of the work to the wide range of abilities of the children. Other teachers regret the effect on children of this age of placing stress upon conformity. Still others reject the implication inherent in the program that *this is how one begins to teach reading*.

Some Responses of Children to Their Reading-Readiness Work

What happens to those youngsters who enter kindergartens from homes that have helped them sprout many of the skills to be developed with reading-readiness materials?

Some continue to gather more reading competence at home while getting satisfaction from being with a group at school whose work is sanctioned and in which they can demonstrate power. A few may be less attentive than if they were truly challenged. In a Minnesota town Roger, who could read simple books when he entered kindergarten, told the teacher when she asked him to be more energetic in his reading-readiness period, "This isn't really reading." For many others, the graduated materials with specific instructions seem challenging, and they work at them with serious effort.

A child is helped in learning if he sees the connection with its ultimate use of the exercise he is asked to do. For example, Judith studied a page with rows of figures, each row containing a misfit. When the teacher asked, "Do you know what you are going to do?" Judith answered, "First, I want to know why." The teacher patiently explained that the exercise was a check to see how carefully Judith noticed the differences in little pictures. If she did this well, she would notice the differences in letters and numbers. This was the help Judith needed, and she set to work.

Not many youngsters are as able as Judith, however, or as vocal about their quandaries. The majority fall in quickly and do as they are told. For the teacher with more than twenty-five to observe, this willingness to conform may be considered a great help. W. H. Auden, the poet, who learned to read by being tutored individually, asked a panel on a television program, "How can a teacher teach more than one child at a time to become a reader?" The miracle is that the teacher does accomplish this, and, furthermore, that the individual children do learn to read by group instruction, from kindergarten throughout their entire school life.

Limiting Effects of Preplanned Reading-Readiness Work What about the less agile, those who do not seem "ready" for the daily reading-readiness work? For such youngsters, the kindergarten program may be a genuine denial of essential learning. Many of these young people need active exploring through trips so that through these experiences their vocabularies can grow, their interests widen, and their eagerness to learn become more acute. A teacher required to meet a quiet reading-readiness period each day must tailor her schedule accordingly. The work of the entire group must, therefore, be planned to provide time in the classroom under quiet conditions. Obviously, the freedom to take trips of value to five-year-olds and the encouragement of vigorous, sometimes noisy, group activities must be curtailed. Bright, as well as less agile, children suffer from this curtailment, even when a sensitive teacher tries to avoid it.

Those kindergartens that stress preplanned, organized daily lessons in reading readiness vary in many details. In their major daily emphasis, however, the general description here given maintains. Central to the point of view is the belief that a child of five or a little older is ready for and can profit from daily lessons based on prepared materials through which he acquires certain skills. Among these skills are recognizing letters, word elements, and words.

Obviously, with this belief goes the assumption that this early foundation will influence reading progress in the later school years. Some parents as well as teachers also emphasize that the child learns to pay attention, to work precisely, and to follow directions. He learns "to act like a first grader" in controlling his responses. A further evaluation of Program I follows later in the chapter.

PROGRAM II. READING READINESS IN EVERYDAY EXPERIENCES

In Program II, reading readiness is recognized, and children learn skills in beginning reading. Some become able to read simple books and other materials unaided. The program is aimed chiefly at giving children a wide range of individual and group experiences through which they learn to enjoy life away from home, to work and play with peers, to extend their creative powers in art, music, and dramatic play, to explore new community resources, and, in general, to add to their growing fund of information about more and more facets of their world. Their language growth, which is central to all future learning, is a key concern in Program II; consequently, much free and informal conversation is encouraged, and time is allowed for it.

In this program beginning reading, or reading readiness, is an integral part of such experiences. For example, when children want to identify their own paintings, their names are written on them—at first by the teacher, later, when they show the desire to do so, by the youngsters themselves. Some children are ready and eager to put simple messages on pictures or greeting cards for their parents; some copy their names from the identification cards on their lockers. Attention to letters and writing comes about in many other ways. Some, less eager, may pay little or no attention to such work or to any signs or labels about the room.

Use of Books and Other Reading Materials Growth in reading is also stimulated through the use of books. The library table or corner is an important spot. Here children browse, talk over books with their close friends, and acquire a love for books and knowledge of them. To many children this kindergarten experience is an extension of early home experiences. To others it is their first contact with the rich world of literature for children. From browsing on their own, many gather ideas of what some books are about. They derive an aesthetic satisfaction from some books that they find appealing, and many enjoy running their hands over the glossy pages. The appetites of the mature are whetted for more reading.

During story time, when the teacher reads to the group, the majority find additional satisfaction in, and stimulation for, reading. A wise teacher helps the children to share in story reading by having them take turns in selecting the book to be read, encouraging discussion of the story, and even, at times, encouraging the children to interrupt the reading with their own comments. Story time is a great social event.

Today, with excellent books providing factual information geared to the interests of young children, the story hour may become an exciting experience with geography, or natural science, or biography. At five, a young child is ready to explore new fields of learning. Ideas that he can deal with from books are, therefore, his due. From contacts with such books, he begins to understand that "We learn from books" and "We read and find out."

Some kindergarteners may talk quite glibly about ideas in the book. Here a wise teacher appreciates that they may sound as if they fully understand but that they do so in a five-year-old's way. They grow in understanding in a rather circuitous way, not necessarily adding one point after another, but gradually evolving more adequacy in thinking. Frequently the children pore over the book from which the teacher has read. Some gain the ability to recognize names and key words from the text. Some can be heard reading aloud parts they recognize.

In addition to these experiences with reading and writing, children in Program II are exposed to innumerable other contacts with ideas in print. The kindergarten room contains calendars for keeping track of dates, notes written on the blackboard, signs, and labels. Children usually notice these aids to kindergarten life, but if not, the teacher calls them to their attention and encourages youngsters to notice and use them. Finding the correct day of the week, telling what the new sign says, and observing the teacher as she writes the directions for help in remembering an important event—all these are real beginnings in useful reading for the more mature five-year-olds. Similarly, on trips, signs and printed matter are noticed.

This program is close to the day-to-day living of the young child. He notices, he reacts, he inspects, he experiments, he learns, and he acquires a growing knowledge of reading. Central to the success of the program, however, is the teacher's ability to judge the way in which children react to various types of experiences. For the nimble, who show independence in recognizing their names, eagerness in learning to write, and ability to read key words in simple notes, continued opportunity to grow in reading is essential. Simple books, including preprimers, are properly introduced at this point.

Helping Ready Readers with Books What about the intellectually agile youngsters who not only can do a little reading in simple books but also are eager to read more? Obviously, to ignore their ability and their eagerness is callous neglect. A teacher in a crowded kindergarten in a northern city found herself with three such youngsters. Bobby, who became the spokesman for the three, entered the room each morning saying, "Give us kids our reading lesson today." Each day, while others were at a variety of games and construction, the teacher met with the three (and others who joined them occasionally) to read short stories to them, to hear them read parts, and to help them recognize words. Two of these youngsters needed much encouragement to join with classmates in more vigorous work and play. Left to follow their own interests, they would have kept to individual quiet work with crayons, paints, and books, avoiding socialization with other youngsters. By the end of the year, the three early readers and four others had grown in reading independence so that each could read simple stories, primers, and some parts of first readers without help. They also had acquired a firm grasp of word-recognition techniques and could write their names and short sentences.

The teacher of these children emphasized two points in describing her work that year: (1) She guided the beginning readers through a varied, rich program so their early reading development did not prevent their rounded growth. (2) She received their interest in reading with the same attention that she gave to the growth of other pupils in singing, skipping, or relating an incident. Early readers need continued guidance, but they also need protection from exploitation through being unduly lauded or publicly displayed.

Guarding the Child's Creative Powers The workbook type of exercise with instructions for coloring and pasting mimeographed materials is not used by those who accept the underlying bases of Program II. They express the concern that such work stifles the creative child and puts a premium on unquestioned acceptance of authority. Children less closely directed may "think around the edges" of what they are doing and acquire experience in reacting personally to what goes on around them. For the less mature, materials and activities appropriate to them, but changing to fit their growth, are similarly essential.

Is Reading Readiness Neglected in Program II? One challenge to Program II comes from those who question whether proper recognition and help are given youngsters who are ready to begin reading. The teacher who is alert to both eagerness and boredom and changes the daily work to encourage the eagerness and prevent the boredom is meeting the goals inherent in the plans for Program II. Large kindergarten groups and crowded daily schedules may cause some youngsters to miss strategic personal boosts. The same could be true in Program I, however, and at all age levels and in schools with all manner of program viewpoints.

What happens to a child who is bored and obviously ready to go beyond his current learning level? Evidently children can, to some extent, assimilate delay, boredom, and a too-easy program if they are not made to feel embarrassed and inadequate as individuals, and if their boredom does not lead them to reject school as a "dumb place." However, sensible teachers keep a weather eye open to notice the degree of stimulation and satisfaction which children meet in their daily work.

EVALUATING GROWTH IN KINDERGARTEN

Careful over-all evaluation of the two programs remains to be done. Studies of certain aspects reveal that children begin to read in both programs and that success in reading in the primary grades, as measured by standardized tests, occurs with children from both types of program as well as with some who have had no kindergarten experience before entering first grade.

In evaluating prereading and reading experiences, it is dangerous to view them as separate from the total kindergarten program. The danger lies in assuming that throughout the United States kindergartens now base their right to exist chiefly on their contribution to a child's beginning in reading. Such an assumption would be an error of great magnitude. The main function of the kindergarten from its inception has been to help the child feel at ease while he engages in a wide variety of activities in a group, away from his home. These activities are planned to stimulate his growth in vigorous physical action, in getting along with his peers, in a wide array of new experiences through which he increases his language powers, and in many contacts with books and other printed materials.

Current studies of the way in which children approach learning situations reveal the error of assuming that children are learning what we think they are learning merely because they comply with our directions and give back the responses we solicit. Almy refers to some such assumptions as "wishful thinking about children's thinking."[3] Bruner, in commenting on young children's thinking, observes that they examine, "hunch," and arrive at some learnings "intuitively."[4] The logical, carefully planned, sequential reading-readiness work is not consistent with findings of specialists such as these.

Other practices of the structured reading-readiness program need to be questioned. Certainly the belief that a group of ten or more children at the early age of five learns valuable attitudes from

[3] Millie Almy, "Wishful Thinking about Children's Thinking," *Teachers College Record,* 62, February 1961, pp. 396-406.

[4] Jerome S. Bruner, *The Process of Education.* Harvard University Press, 1960, pp. 13-14 and Chapter 3.

uniform prescribed "lessons" is open to serious question. Since not only educators but also other competent judges of American society are decrying the high degree of conformity and the corollary lack of originality found in today's citizenry, teaching a child to conform in a realm as intellectual as reading, and at the impressionable age of five, is not good educational practice.

Finally, there is the matter of determining the stage at which a child is ready to read; in other words, his degree of "reading readiness." No responsible educator believes that reading readiness appears in a child at a given date—that before this magic date he is not ready for beginning reading experiences and that after it he is. Unfortunately, some parents and teachers speak as though such a definite point were ascertainable. "He is now ready for reading"—or "He is not yet ready for reading" implies this definiteness. When such statements are based upon test results, the mistake is further compounded.

Successful readers have been developed even from those who had late starts. In some European countries, children enter school a year or more later than do children in the United States. They become readers. In adult education classes in the United States, oldsters are taught the prized skill of reading. Whole nations have successfully carried out literacy programs for adults. In Russia, for example, children who were becoming readers in school went home to teach their parents to read. In a literate country such as ours, however, the danger lies in what delaying beginning reading does to the child's attitude toward himself. Deferred help on reading can be harmful to the child if he feels embarrassed over not beginning or if he acquires a sense of inadequacy because of the delay.

Reliability of Reading-Readiness Tests Specialists in measurement and students of child development raise serious questions about making important decisions based on the findings of reading-readiness tests. First, these tests are group tests, and although they may be carefully given to small groups of five or six youngsters at a time, studies of young children in such group situations reveal how unreliable the results of such testing may be. Thorndike and Hagen, who are widely recognized authorities in the field of measurement, state: "Especially with younger children, maintaining continuity of attention and effort on a group test may be a problem, and variations in this respect are certainly a significant factor in test score."[5] The scores may show a tendency of an entire group, but they should not be relied upon as the most important factor on which an individual child's reading ability or "readiness" is judged or on which his fitness to pursue certain kinds of work is determined.

Schools, as a rule, are mindful of the difficulty of accurately measuring a young child's ability in a group-test situation; they usually combine the scores of reading-readiness tests with other essential data in making an evaluation of the child's ability. In many ways it is fortunate that children do not lend themselves to such precise diagnosis as is sought by some types of testing. There would be real danger in a static interpretation of a child's ability, not only in learning to read, but also in other learning. Studies of children who were moved from limiting environments to richer fields reveal exciting results of intellectual as well as other personality changes. A program too tightly geared to the pace for which a child seems ready may deny him the chance to stretch his abilities and reveal new interests and greater power.

Individual Records of Growth Guides for parents and teachers in evaluating kindergarteners are included in books on teaching young children and in materials published by individual school systems and districts. Each child is studied in terms of key points of growth; these include his general health, his ability to give and take in work-and-play relations with others in his group, his ability to look after his own needs, his language growth, and the knowledge, ideas, imagination, understandings, and ways of thinking that he communicates through his speech, gestures, and play.

Teachers find it helpful to use check lists; records, even if maintained in a highly informal manner, are essential. A good understanding of each five-year-old, even in a group consisting of only twenty, demands concrete evidence about each Ted and Tess. Vague general terms, such as "doing fine," "growing," or "disinter-

[5] Robert L. Thorndike and Elizabeth Hagen, *Measurement and Evaluation in Psychology and Education.* 2nd ed. Wiley, 1961, p. 241.

ested," are of little value; they do not aid the teacher in understanding the child's growth and her responsibility in guiding him, in describing his growth for school records, or in communicating with parents. Observations tersely recorded, such as, "Remembers from one day to the next," or "Enjoys books during his quiet time," are explicit and telling.

In general, attaching "labels" of any kind to children, especially in the early years, is frowned upon by educators, and wisely so. For example, a child denied rich language contacts in preschool life may enter kindergarten as one of the less verbal members of his class. After the middle of the year, he might flower forth. If typed as an unalert or nonverbal child, he might be considered unready for vital growing experiences for which he actually is ready.

Many teachers and students of young children put their emphasis on the continued observation of children's reactions; they thus avoid definite typing or labeling or predicting of the child's future conduct in a matter as specific as learning to read. A child who is provided with an opportunity for which he is intellectually ready and who is also aided and encouraged by a warm, sensitive adult will learn. His future success in the first grade is enhanced if in kindergarten he continues to enjoy his associations with children and books. He will best prepare for first grade by continuing to look forward to school and by eagerly and successfully meeting new challenging experiences.

In summary, a proper evaluation of each child's growth in kindergarten would reveal the increase in his independence from home, his growth in congenial work and play with his "pals," and his widening spread of interests. It would also indicate his increase in a number of skills, such as motor skills, singing, and manipulation of a paint brush, as well as beginning writing and reading. Furthermore, an adequate evaluation would note the child's eagerness to learn, his courage in trying new tasks, and the way in which he reveals his growth in thinking. With satisfactory steps in such directions, he has added to the preschool vitality with which he entered kindergarten. He has also increased the assurance that he will continue to thrive in school, throughout first grade and all the later grades.

SUGGESTED READINGS ON THE KINDERGARTEN AGE

ALMY, MILLIE. *Child Development.* New York: Henry Holt and Co., 1955. Chapter 8.

This chapter, "Testing Their Powers—Psychodynamic Aspects of Development From 3 to 6 Years," offers much help for those interested in evaluating young children's broadly conceived learning.

ASSOCIATION FOR CHILDHOOD EDUCATION, Washington, D.C. *Reading in the Kindergarten???* Bulletin.

A series of articles by authorities who question the inclusion of reading in kindergarten programs. Data from research are included to support their point of view. An essential bulletin for parents, teachers, and administrators.

BRENNER, ANTON. "Nature and Meaning of Readiness for School," *Merrill Palmer Quarterly,* III, Spring 1957, pp. 114-135.

A fresh, much needed view on the concept of readiness.

GANS, ROMA, STENDLER, CELIA, and ALMY, MILLIE. *Teaching Young Children.* Yonkers-on-the-Hudson: World Book Company, 1952. Part II, Chapters 4 and 6.

Several theories of programs are presented in Chapter 4, indicating their consistence with current understanding of how young children learn. Evaluation in relation to a soundly based program is described in Chapter 6.

LANDRETH, CATHERINE. *The Psychology of Early Childhood.* New York: Alfred A. Knopf, 1960. Chapter 11.

Clear, concise presentation on the reliability of the testing of very young children.

MOORE, ELEANORA HAEGELE. *Fives at School.* New York: G. P. Putnam's Sons, 1959.

A detailed description of kindergarten children and their learning in home and school, with timely recognition given to "downtown children" and "suburban children." A helpful book for all interested in five-year-olds. Sprightly style.

THORNDIKE, ROBERT L., and HAGEN, ELIZABETH. *Measurement and Evaluation in Psychology and Education.* 2nd edition. New York: John Wiley and Sons, 1961.

For those interested in and responsible for selection, use, and interpretation of test data, this book is invaluable.

CHAPTER 5

First Grade—a Crucial Year

Children entering the first grade at about six years of age are expected to become readers during the school year, with or without previous kindergarten experiences. And, according to a variety of standards and ways of measuring first graders, approximately seventy-five per cent of them actually do. One who discovers how complex and intellectually taxing a process it is to learn to read must respect the power children reveal by their ability to learn—and the power teachers reveal in teaching them by the roomful.

In this chapter some of the difficulties children and teachers face in relation to beginning reading will be examined. Of no minor matter are the pressures that spring from two sources—those who hold to the assumption that all mentally normal children should learn to read successfully in first grade, and those who assume that if their preferred methods were followed by teachers, all children would so learn.

Innumerable methods are in use for teaching beginning reading to all varieties of youngsters. The claims of some are akin to the medicine-show claims for snake oil, a guaranteed cure for all aches and rheumatic diseases. Alert teachers are aware of the unique qualities youngsters reveal in their approaches to new situations and the complex intellectual demands involved in learning to read. Would that more theorists taught in a day-after-day, week-after-week first-grade situation for at least a year before offering suggestions to teachers.

FACING SOME FACTS ABOUT BEGINNERS

The success in reading achieved by so many beginners is amazing, especially by those children who have had no opportunity to work and play away from home in a room filled with other children or who are low in language development because of a bleak preschool life. For some, the ride to and from school in a crowded bus and a classroom filled with strange children and an adult stranger—the teacher—may be too much to assimilate even without initiating work on reading. The shy child who acts as if he were afraid of children may meet as great difficulty in facing first grade as does the friendly plodder. Even when a few weeks are given to a modified program that is intended to serve as a gradual change from kindergarten to first-grade work, some youngsters in each group may not take hold.

Many factors affect the child's start in reading. The first factor of importance is the nature of the child himself. If he is the eager beaver described in Chapter 2, unafraid to listen, look, or tackle new tasks, he may start off under any condition and yet progress according to common expectations. If, on the other hand, he is shy, uneasy with the other pupils and the teacher, fearful to venture forth, he may be slower in starting. Some may begin gingerly but speedily overcome their cautious approach. Some may seem extremely immature, more like kindergarteners. Others may appear to be firmly moored on a plateau; they require much time, patience, and individual encouragement to take hold. This may be true of such children no matter what methods or materials are used, the claims of enthusiasts for various unique or specific methods and materials notwithstanding.

The child's ability to attend school regularly is of major importance in the first grade. A child who is absent, even if for only one day, finds re-entry a large, absorbing problem. Linnette, a quiet six-year-old in an Oklahoma first grade, after a two-day absence asked her teacher, "Are these all the same kids?" Routines, materials, fellow pupils—all may take on a look of strangeness after even a brief absence from them. A longer absence may make the child afraid to return to school. Studies of first-grade reading failures list irregular attendance as one of the highest factors contributing to failure. Incidence of illness, even under the best home supervision, cannot be prevented. However, the teacher's efforts to re-establish the child's ease at school and parental encouragement at home aid greatly in minimizing the effect of absence.

A CLOSE-UP OF THE READING PROCESS

A composite of several difficult skills makes up the process of reading. Look at the word *pony*. As an experienced reader, you scarcely note the letters or their sequence. You may simply look at the word and think immediately of a pony. You may now be totally unaware of the steps you took to bring yourself to this seemingly automatic response. First, you probably grew up in America, where we have a twenty-six-letter alphabet with a given form for capitals and lower-case letters. Basic letter forms may vary according to the type used, but the general configuration of each letter remains similar. In our language, these letters are arranged in words from left to right, and the words themselves are arranged in succession, from left to right and from line to line. Had you learned to read in the Near East, you would have had different letters to learn and their succession would have been from right to left. In China, you would have had different characters, placed in columns in right-to-left succession, each column reading from top to bottom.

Establishing the Left-to-Right Habit The left-to-right order in our printing and writing is something a child must learn. Following this order is not a natural tendency, as is taking one step after another. Many beginners learn this order from casual contacts with reading at home. Many are taught this characteristic of our form of recording in kindergarten. Many learn it only in the first grade. But, wherever he learns, it is essential that the child get the left-to-right sequence firmly established in his thinking so that he does not later become confused in reading and in writing.

When a beginner looks at the word *pony*, he must perform some big mental leaps. He must first look at the word, then he must take the next step—pronouncing it. He must translate this collection of little figures arranged in a precise order from left to right into their correct sounds. The sounds blended into the word then evoke the meaning and, finally, the mental image of *pony*.

The Importance of Repetition From previous contacts with pictures, the beginner has easily grown to understand "this-is-a-picture-of-a-pony." Two-year-olds often point to pictures and correctly name the objects portrayed: "baby"; "dog"; "Mommy." They have learned to see the picture and call out its correct name. Seeing the word and thinking the image is a task more complicated than seeing the picture and saying the word; it includes additional difficult steps. This process must be performed often enough so that it becomes virtually automatic. A child who is beginning to read needs to meet the word *pony* often enough so he sees the word, pronounces it, and promptly thinks *pony*. For some bright youngsters, the process is rapid; for the slower, more time and more repetition, or drill, are needed.

Patience and a listening attitude on the part of the teacher are invaluable to the struggling beginner. Even we adults, when wrestling with a difficult situation, appreciate the presence of a patient person rather than one who tries to speed up our effort and thereby completely stalls us. Teachers who can wait for a child to come out with an answer and who make no effort to hurry the youngster are indeed a blessing to beginners.

The Importance of Oral Reading A young child may have an absolute need to hear himself read in order to know that he is reading. This was clear with Gerhard, a transfer from a nearby village school. He had had one-half year of schooling, which included much satisfying individual oral reading. When the teacher suggested to him that he try to read "with your lips closed," he said, "How can I tell then if I'm reading?"

We know that beginners love to hear themselves read and love to display their new skill, no matter how plodding and hesitant the demonstration. But they may also need the physical feeling that accompanies their oral reading to appreciate fully that they are reading. Their nerve connections no doubt tend to function more readily on a see-think-then-say response than a see-think-but-hush basis. We adults never read without some nonobservable muscular reaction, but we, like children once they gain experience, have mastered the inhibition of our sound effects. Some quick learners acquire this mastery almost as quickly as they can learn to read a line. It therefore seems sensible to encourage *much* oral reading by child to classmates or to the teacher, older brothers and sisters, and to his parents. Such reading is not only good practice, but doubtlessly helps exercise the neural routes of reading.

For slow learners particularly, the process of learning to read is difficult enough without adding the burden of inhibiting the tendency to read aloud. Will such use of oral reading in teaching retard speed? The concern for speed without a corresponding recognition of other factors can lead to poor results. Those who read adequately will acquire the necessary speed. If some "pep-up" in speed is needed, that is successfully managed in later grades, high school, college—and today even in industry.

A wise teacher carefully plans individual oral reading so that it occurs frequently, especially for those just beginning to sprout the ability to read a line or two. Quite commonly, children are organized into oral-reading clubs of two or three members who take their books, sit together, and read quietly in turn. A busy teacher with a crowded classroom who, nevertheless, provides the opportunity to test out reading power through oral reading is to be commended.

CHILDREN'S LANGUAGE AND LOGIC

A genuine difficulty for the teacher—and for any observer of a child's beginning reading, for that matter—is the fact that what goes on in the child's thinking may be completely hidden. He may look, pause, knit his young face with effort, and say "pony." What went on in that pause we may guess at, but we cannot describe it with sureness. Or he may go through similar reactions and come out with the word "boy." A teacher may conjecture that the *p--y* of *pony* gave him a clue to the word *b-y*. But again, an adult observer cannot be positive.

Adding to the mystery of what goes on inside the child's thinking is the fact that a youngster at this early age often lacks the language with which to describe his intellectual process. This lack of adequate means of expression was revealed clearly in work with some nimble beginners in a New York City school. A teacher sitting with a group of six beginners who were reading aloud asked Henry, after he paused, then correctly pronounced "wanted," "How could you tell it was *wanted*?" The best answer Henry could give was, "I just thought." As they grow older, however, children may become more aware of what aids they use in meeting specific tasks.

We adults are able to be logical, taking intellectual steps in proper order. We can look at a new word, notice its elements, and deduce both its sound and its meaning. But children see connections and relationships that may not be apparent to us. According to recent studies they "hunch," or "imagine," and may, at times, come up with the right answer, for their own unique reasons. Certainly it will be a help to conscientious and professionally minded teachers in the field of reading to have more light thrown on what actually does go on in the thinking of beginning readers when they enter upon this complex task.

ENTER PHONICS

Phonics is that step necessary in translating letters and collections of letters into their sounds. Associating the sound with its symbol is a form of generalization. For example, a child who has become familiar with many words starting with *p-o* generalizes and starts sounding out the word *pony*. Many a child independently catches on to the initial *s* sound. After learning to recognize such words as *see, so, say,* and others beginning with *s,* he makes his own deductions. His agility in making this generalization may be due to hearing acuity, experience with rhymes, jingles, and words in general, and quickness in making the mental connections necessary in learning.

Even before entering kindergarten, some extremely alert youngsters acquire many phonic elements from looking on as they follow an adult who reads to them from books and from noticing television advertisements and a variety of signs. However, the majority of children need specific help in acquiring the ability to use the variety of sounds of individual letters and groups of letters in the pronunciation or sounding out of words.

There is a wide divergence of opinion about teaching phonics. In no single phase of reading is there as much all-or-nothing emphasis: either it must be taught in the adherent's specific way or a child will fail to learn to read. Key points in several theories regarding the teaching of phonics are therefore included here.

THEORY I. PHONICS IN RELATION TO CLUES FROM CHILDREN

Many experienced teachers and specialists in the field of reading accept no one time or method as best for teaching all beginners. Instead, in light of what seems best for the child or children involved, they utilize situations as they arise. A wise teacher takes her leads from the manner in which children respond to incidents. These give her clues to their alertness to reading, as well as to other important learnings that they have already acquired or for which they seem ready.

Individual Differences in First Approaches For example, the first-grade teacher in Colorado who placed each child's name on his locker the first day of school assumed that Barry and Benny might get their names confused. She was just beginning to know this group, but she already had observed that these two boys were open-eyed, alert youngsters. She called both to the lockers, which were close together, and asked, "Do you know how to spell your name, Barry?" He did not. "Can you tell it when you see it?" "Yes," he replied and quickly pointed to the name on his locker. The teacher asked the same questions of Benny. Benny could spell and even write his name, he reported. "Well, let's look at your names and spell them aloud together." Both boys responded, Benny more readily. Then she asked "How can you tell which is yours?" After a real pause Benny took the lead and said, "Look, mine is B-e-n-n-y and Barry's is B-a-r-r-y. Mine sounds *Benny* and his sounds *Barry*." This brief moment told her some important facts about both boys; one of these was Benny's ability to recognize the distinction between similar words and to use some phonics.

With Janice and Jenny, the teacher worked differently. Neither seemed aware of names or letters, neither reacted with a listening attitude to the teacher as she tried to help each notice the name and location of her own locker. "See, Janice, your locker is the one nearest the door. Your name is on it. Jenny, your locker is right under the clock. This will help you to find it. Your name is on it, too."

After trying out learning possibilities and noticing the reactions of children, the teacher then plans work appropriate for each youngster. Pupils who react with alertness are given help that leads them on; those who do not respond with alertness are given opportunities of another kind. A competent teacher in the first grade plans many similar trial-and-observation situations in the beginning period of reading. Some children who are able to recognize words at sight or who can unlock the sound of some words through their beginnings in phonics may start reading simple books; others, less verbal, less experienced, and less observant, will begin such work later.

Providing Opportunities in Phonics Taking cues from children's comments and other observable signs of readiness demands that the teacher must be given the freedom in her teaching to develop such leads. A busy day presents many opportunities from which to select. The discussion at the beginning of the session may include a word relating to a news event, such as *carnival* or *accident*, which the teacher writes for all to see. Story hour, which includes not only reading but discussion, also furnishes many chances for stimulating interest; the teacher can record the names of principal characters in the stories, as well as words that sound interesting to the children or words whose meaning has special appeal.

The teacher's writing, preferably done on a large sheet of paper with crayon or a free-flowing pen, and where the children can readily observe, is an extremely helpful practice. The teacher and children may comment about the letter being written: "Notice how tall the *l* is"; and "There are two letters alike in this word. Who can find them?"; and "This sounds something like Betty's name." Such discussion evokes increased interest and alertness in the young observers. Their responses also reveal to the teacher which elements some already recognize. The specific learnings derived from one such chat about words may not be discernible, but through many similar associations with writing children notice and make connections. For the slow, such activity builds increased awareness and alertness; for the quick, this type of work may be all the help they need in becoming able to recognize words through the use of phonics.

Most six-year-olds have a strong interest in their own names. The phonic elements common to several children's names may be the basis for a talk in the first week of school. One first grade had six *J* names: Janet, Jean, Jill, Jimmy, Joan, and John—a bonanza for the alert teacher. In that same group was Wilmetta who could boast the longest name in the class. Barbara commented that she had a good name to write because it started with *Bar* and then added another *bar*.

To an imaginative teacher, names are filled with phonic teaching potentiality because a child not only has a genuine personal interest in recognizing the appearance of his name in writing but is also likely to want to learn to write it. When he writes, he will reinforce the sound of the letters and their sequence as he spells.

Progress in Learning Phonics By being helped to notice the association between letters or groups of letters and their corresponding sounds, a child acquires a fundamental awareness of phonics. From first experiences, he progresses according to his own awareness, acquiring the sounding of initial consonants, vowel sounds, and suffixes, such as *s, es, er, ed,* and *ing.* His learning in this important matter is not left to chance but follows a sequence related to his state of readiness. First-grade teachers use a variety of sources for guiding their efforts to be sure that the full value of phonics in recognizing words is acquired and applied by each child according to his intellectual power. Dolores Durkin's *Phonics and the Teaching of Reading*[1] is a particularly helpful reference now available to teachers as a guide for insuring that important elements of phonics are included or not overlooked.

Other ways of recognizing words are also utilized in the early reading stages, in conjunction with attention to phonic elements. In fact, it is impossible to ignore such practices as recognizing words by configuration or by cue because the process occurs spontaneously in the life of children. The suggestion that children should be taught to recognize words by phonics *first and only* is an academic matter, because so many eye-open youngsters look at whole words as they travel about at home, in neighborhoods, on highways, and in shops and quickly grasp their identification. They learn to recognize trade names, signs, and words in stories that are read to them as they look on. They also recognize many words from watching television. The learnings can all be described as "natural"; they are scarcely noticeable to adult companions.

Furthermore, many words that spark such learning represent persons, objects, or ideas that appeal to children. Anyone who is close to young children can understand that the whole word *lolli-*

[1] Bureau of Publications, Teachers College, Columbia University, 1962.

pop makes a quicker appeal to the child and can be recognized and remembered more easily than any of the separate letters or combinations of letters in the word.

Common-Sense Use of Multiple Word-Recognition Techniques Those who teach and observe young children as they learn to read realize that multiple approaches to word recognition are more appropriate to the varied characteristics of children than a single, all-phonic approach. Children learn to notice the length of a word, the tallness of the letters, and other distinctive characteristics of word configuration. From early contacts with nonphonic words, they learn many of them at sight—*one, sure, son, cough,* and the like. A close contact with a first grade reveals what a wide and rich amount of knowledge about words youngsters of this age can acquire with the guidance of a wise teacher who points out and helps them notice word characteristics.

Variations in Learning to Read Marked differences among children in ability and response are observable, but, as the school year progresses and as the teacher works with children on simple books —now in small groups, now individually—the majority grow in phonics ability and in other important word-recognition skills. Some words and phonic elements will be more difficult to master than others. Some youngsters may need far more repetition of new learnings than others. In all first grades, variations are present, even in a school with homogeneous grouping. In a wholesome classroom situation, all will learn and move ahead if they are fairly regular in attendance and maintain reasonably good health.

Important in this crucial year of development is the relaxed and approving attitude of parents toward the child. A child who feels that his teacher and his parents believe he is doing well will be encouraged to release his full power and do his best.

Above all, in this personal-experience-centered reading program, respect for individual differences is a matter of routine. Obviously, promotion-failure issues are out of place. In a program geared to each child's ability, a slow child is encouraged to grow at his rate and is not held back or branded a failure if his reading work is marginal. Of importance to the future well-being of a child is emphasizing any small reading success and establishing a feeling of self-worth in the child. This need is now widely recognized. The relationship of academic failure to a child's loss of interest in school, to persistent reading difficulties, and to a consequent early drop-out from school is also well established.

A teacher who guides a first grade is, therefore, not only helping a child begin his career as a reader but is also in a position to encourage him to believe in himself, to like school, and to enjoy learning. Those who use the child's growth status and his unique learning abilities in inducting him into using phonics as well as other ways of recognizing words are emphasizing the inclusive and far-reaching effect of Theory I as a teaching method.

THEORY II. THE PREPLANNED APPROACH TO PHONICS

Strongly opposed to the foregoing plan of inducting children into word recognition only partly through the use of phonics are those who advocate a uniform, systematic approach to teaching phonics as an introductory part of the entire reading program. There are several systems, varying only slightly, which stress a carefully planned approach. Some require that the child first learn to pronounce the letters of the alphabet in sequence. One system recommends that a child say *"a—ä, b—bä, c—cä, d—dä,"* and so on through the alphabet. Next, in this system, a child is introduced to simple words that he sounds out, letter by letter. Bed is sounded *"bä-e-dä,"* then blended into *"bed."*

Some Challenges of All Phonic Systems This method and others that include the alphabet approach are challenged on two counts. Those informed about the thinking of young children question the soundness of attributing to children the step-by-step, logical approach to learning. If children did acquire skills and knowledge in this tidy sequential arrangement, the early, formal days of schooling should never have been abandoned.

The second challenge comes from specialists in speech. Such consonants as *b, c, d, f,* and g are not always found as *bä, cä, dä,* and the like. The letter b might be blended with others to form *bo, be, bi, bu, br,* or *bl.* Furthermore, first pronouncing *bed* as bä-e-dä, and then as *bed,* is not only confusing to the child but is erroneous teaching.

Adherents of the phonic approach to teaching reading tend to slight or ignore another important aspect of the English language: namely, that a goodly percentage of the words do not sound as they are spelled. Among those not phonically consistent are those common words previously cited—*one, sure, son,* and *cough.* These are among the words that a child guided under the first theory learns to recognize at sight. Through meeting some words in many daily situations, he recognizes them at a glance, without spelling them or trying to sound them out. Frequently words like *little, by,* and *happy* are among an early sight vocabulary acquired by beginners because these words have distinctive configurations. However, adherents of the phonic emphasis in teaching beginners object strongly to the recognize-by-sight inclusion before the learner acquires considerable experience in the phonic approach.

The Linguists' Approach to Phonics and Beginning Reading Exceedingly careful research in the English language by Leonard Bloomfield led him to plan a linguistic approach to teaching reading. He recommends

> that new words should be presented according to their form; that is, regular forms should be presented first, irregular forms only later. By getting all the associated facts together, the child's power to recognize words in his reading is greatly facilitated. After learning the first list or two, a child should be able to learn a whole list of words almost as rapidly as he learns one word now by means of the word method.[2]

His beginning lists would include word "families," such as *pin, nip, pit, tip.* Using combinations of letters in words that are regular, according to Leonard Bloomfield, prevents what he considers the serious fault in some phonic methods:

> The authors of these methods tell us to show the child a letter, for instance, *t,* and to make him react by uttering the *t* sound. . . . This sound is to be uttered either all by itself or else with an obscure vowel sound after it. Now, English-speaking people, children or adults, are not accustomed to making that kind of noise. . . . If we insist on making the

[2] Leonard Bloomfield and Clarence L. Barnhart, *Let's Read—A Linguistic Approach.* Wayne University Press, 1961, p. 26.

child perform unaccustomed feats with his vocal organs, we are bound to confuse his response to the printed signs.[3]

The careful analysis of words into phonemes and phonic elements by linguists is a valuable aid to teachers in helping them actually to *hear* words and be alert to their phonic complexities. *A*, rather than merely having a long, short, broad, or schwa (*ä* as in infant) sound, has over forty sounds. Such phonemes as *ough* have a wide array of sounds, as for example, *ought, rough,* and *though.* A teacher who is alert to the variations and irregularities in the English language can be more helpful to the child who is attempting to work out his system of identifying words than is the instructor who takes a rigid attitude toward the language.

The Augmented Roman Alphabet Approach to Reading This quest for a right way of inducting young readers into phonics is going on not only in the United States but also in England. J. A. Downing has described the research conducted in schools in various locations in England with the "Augmented Roman" alphabet.[4] This alphabet is composed of "43 lower-case Roman" letters involving forty sounds, and is used exclusively in the primary grades. After learning to read with this alphabet, a child transfers easily to the traditional orthography. Any method, phonic or see-and-say, can be used; the emphasis is on the print, which closely resembles the sound of the word. For example, *of* is spelled *ov*; *reading* is *reeding*; and *should* is *shood.* The old Roman combined vowels *œ* and *œ* are among the forty-three alphabet characters.

According to data gathered from experiments, more children learn and, in the course of learning, make more rapid progress than with the traditional orthography type, no matter what methods are used by teachers. This experiment comes to grips with a problem inherent in the English language—namely, that similar symbols do not necessarily indicate the same sounds whenever they are used. More research along such lines is warranted. Perhaps, rather than struggling with the problem of how to guide a child into an intelligent use of phonics, we might bypass the problem by streamlining the alphabet into symbol-sound consistency.

[3] *Ibid.*, p. 28.

[4] J. A. Downing, *The Augmented Roman Alphabet.* London: Pitman Publishing, 1962.

VARYING THE APPROACH TO BEGINNING READING

Meanwhile, common sense should prevent us from gross mistakes in teaching beginners to become independent in identifying words. Too strong an emphasis on phonics may hold back those who react with alertness to certain visual phases of reading. They can become apt at seeing words whether they remember them by their configuration or "by sight"; they then become able to pronounce them from memory. Other children may sound a word out and "hear" the word. Their hearing may be more acute, or they may have had more listening experiences—or both. Still others may need more tactual experiences to help them recognize and remember words. They may want to run their fingers over the letters as they spell and sound them out. They may need to arrange letters on a flannel board to get the "feeling" of the letter. This procedure helps them to remember letters and add words to their growing reading vocabularies. Writing, for them, is a great reinforcing method of learning.

A set, uniform approach to the teaching of beginning reading, one which would work equally well with all children, would indeed be a panacea. To achieve this, one would first have to produce a "standardized" six-year-old. Such standardization achieved, teaching first grade would then be a simple matter.

Nevertheless, the wide acceptance of theories of systematic, preplanned teaching of phonics and the pressures on schools to use a given method add to the crucial decisions teachers and school leaders must face in planning the work of the first grade. It is clearly evident that children vary in their backgrounds, alertness, sensory approaches, and other learning qualities. If the attitude of children toward school is to be respected, no method should be selected which will hold the nimble back and threaten others with failure. This consideration is paramount for those who are responsible for selecting the approach to first-grade reading.

Variations in the Need for Repetition An essential need for all beginning readers is the opportunity to fix or remember items learned. But offering drill and all forms of repetition of the amount and variety required by each child day after day is a big order for the teacher. Obviously she must be concerned about this need and must try to meet it to the best of her ability. An extremely helpful practice is guiding the children to become aware of their own needs. True, their judgment must be checked, but when first-grade Betsy reported to the teacher, "We seven girls know every word in this whole book," the teacher's information about their reading growth was greatly aided. Slower learners may not show much ability in assessing their own state of knowledge at the age of six, yet it is wise for the teacher to try out this concept and, in so doing, spark their competence. Those ready for the idea can then proceed and add this essential step—self-evaluation—to their maturing powers.

Loss of time, as well as feelings of frustration, can result when children in beginning reading have enjoyable periods with books and good, helpful lessons in word recognition but insufficient opportunity to practice new learnings sufficiently to anchor them in memory. An observer of young children will note how they automatically drill themselves. As a new word is learned, they use it over and over; as a new skill, like riding a two-wheeler, is acquired, they practice and practice to perfect their skill. So too, do youngsters need drill to retain or perfect their memory of new words, phonic elements, or other specifics in the reading process.

Obviously, the precise amount of help needed by each child in even a small class cannot always be determined by a teacher, no matter how able. Therefore, the ability to recognize and report their own learning and to become aware of their own next needs is a great asset in boosting children's learning. Young Benjamin, who had had a fine background in a spirited first grade, reported that he was "working on three words that always stick me, *some, was,* and *it.*" He asked his teacher to write them on a bookmark, which he then kept in the book he was reading. His teacher helped each child to remember words by writing them on a marker that the child kept handy.

Slower children need more suggestions from teachers as to what to do, yet a teacher must notice as closely as possible how appropriate for them such suggestions turn out to be. Individual conversations with these youngsters often bring out their reactions.

Teachers working with crowded schedules feel the importance of these personal contacts and regret that adequate time is lacking for more of them. Observations of such obstacles to closer teacher-child contacts make us realize that we may fail to bring slow operators into full bloom because of the limiting circumstances under which so many must be taught.

GAMES AS ESSENTIAL LEARNING AIDS

A further observation of the way in which children manage their own learning reveals the importance of games. "Let's make a game of it" actually means, "Let's put some challenge in this learning." This same comment also means, "Let's have some winning end points." Fine games in word-recognition techniques that include phonics are available commercially. Skillful teachers also make many games of this sort and encourage youngsters to make their own.

In a large first-grade class, children cut up cards on which words had been carefully written in manuscript by the teacher and placed the pieces in an envelope labeled "Scrabble Game." Making words quickly and accurately was a popular game played individually or in pairs. In this same room several boys, as they identified new model cars, asked the teacher to write on a separate card the name of each car as identified. They vied with one another to see who collected the largest pack of cards, and they learned to identify quickly the name of each car.

Many games played at home have high reading-practice value. The able son of a college professor, through a number of unhappy experiences, grew to dislike reading and to reject help in learning, but taught himself to read with the popular game Monopoly. Games that possess the qualities of good games—not those that are fakes or sugar-coated exercises—serve an essential educational purpose. A game shelf for housing games in frequent use is an integral part of some classroom libraries. In this day of expanding the items housed in school libraries, the possibility of including games seems a sensible one.

STARTING TO HEAT SEVERAL IRONS AT A TIME

The multiple learnings expected in first-grade programs cause an interested person to ponder. Six-year-olds about to undergo the major event of losing first teeth, who are eagerly mastering new physical skills and who may still sing only near key, start to make a successful dent in learning to read, write, spell, compute, and explore various fields of music, art, and science, all within the short span of a few months. Although a sensible teacher tries to pace the program so that interest in reading does not become interrupted or diluted with interest in arithmetic, writing, or any of the other learnings, he does not always find it possible to do so. Not only is the regular program varied, but children with their avid interests in the life about them bring ideas into the classroom program. Such inclusions may stimulate others in the group. A program is enriched, stimulated, and made more satisfying by such additions, yet youngsters' efforts may become diffused. Certainly teachers need to adhere to essential purposes and plans. Without plans, the program may blow about, now on this topic, now on this skill, with efforts too scattered to permit real learning.

ENTER WRITING AND SPELLING

Writing and spelling are so closely interwoven with reading that, if properly viewed, they may add to rather than detract from children's reading achievement. This is especially true today, since beginning writing no longer resembles the flowery letters of earlier days. Some of us can remember learning to write our *ABC*'s with "sweeping light lines." Now, the simplest form of all handwritten letters, called *manuscript*, is widely used. Manuscript is not only easier than script for a child to acquire, but it also more closely resembles the print in his books; therefore, it is an aid to him in recognizing letters and words. This last point has been considered so important that books for beginning readers are now usually printed in a type closely resembling manuscript writing.

Many late four-year-olds and early fives are eager to try their hands at writing and, therefore, may come to first grade with some previous writing experience. They can write their names and copy simple greetings or messages that the teacher has written on the board. Soft-lead primary pencils and crayons are provided in classrooms where such efforts are encouraged.

Individual help is given to the child in acquiring the correct way to write each letter. Good, clear letter forms are displayed to him as a guide. Some teachers use script pens with black ink, and large sheets of white paper, for all the writing that they do in the presence of the children. This writing is far clearer than that written on the so-called "blackboard"; moreover, the symbol of black-on-white is similar to the black print in the child's white-paged book.

Special Problems in Writing A teacher prevents confusion in demonstrating writing if she remembers that the child needs to see the writing in process as it travels from left to right. A teacher who comments as she writes, "See, I start here at the left hand and go to the right," until children have established that practice, lessens mistakes.

A left-handed child may become confused by seeing the teacher start with the right hand and move away from the center point of the body. He may then, using the left hand, move out in the wrong direction. Today's teachers are informed about left-handedness and expect to have in each class at least one southpaw whom they will encourage in using his left hand while others use their right. Many of us can still recall the pressure on the left-handed child to make him use his right hand. Problems in speech and other emotional upsets followed such errors in guidance. Attention to direction in writing for both right- and left-handed children, even if they already seem to have established left-to-right direction in reading, is helpful teaching.

Beginning to write entirely in capital letters works well, and unlined paper is preferred. Lined paper injects another complication into the skill of writing—that is, keeping letters in a proper location with reference to a line. This additional element was clearly demonstrated by Bobby at the age of six. One October day, I received a special delivery letter. Inside the envelope was a plain piece of paper. Toward the lower half of the paper appeared B O B, on the reverse side was B Y. All the letters were very clear, but the arrangement had a considerable list toward the bottom of the paper. That evening I received a telephone call—long distance—to hear an excited voice say, "Did you get my letter? I can write my name now." So, in the beginning, the correct letter forms and their sequence are the all-consuming first step. Keeping lines straight is another step and can better be taken once the formation of letters is mastered. As letter forms are comfortably managed, the use of ruled paper and the introduction of lower-case manuscript letters follow.

Enjoyment in Mastery of Writing the Alphabet Learning to write the entire alphabet in capitals and lower-case letters—and in sequence—is often accomplished by a majority of first-graders. Some educators may raise eyebrows at such activity and brand it outmoded formal education. Nonsense. Today's child, once motivated, thrives on proving to himself and others what he knows. Obviously he quickly grasps the fact that we have a twenty-six-letter alphabet and that we can write each letter two ways, as a capital letter or as a small letter. From early contacts with alphabetical lists of children's names, and a look at indexes of some books, and even from a cursory contact with a dictionary, the child becomes intrigued by the sequence of the alphabet. Perhaps the majority have chanted along with older children who sang it at play. It is a natural aim to be able to say and write the alphabet in correct sequence. Depriving children of doing so is robbing them of some of the real fun of being a learner.

The particular letters with which they begin their writing may be chosen according to a child's special eagerness. It would be unfair, would it not, for a young William and Yetta to wait to learn how to write their names until the class starting with A got that far?

For writing, more than for early reading, a knowledge of spelling is a necessity. (Think of the numerous adults who are excellent readers but who remain inadequate spellers.) To be able to write his name or any word, the child must know the letters and their sequence. Writing stimulates interest in spelling, and both, in turn, feed back greater word knowledge in reading. For this reason, "language arts periods" in schools are now common, and under the leadership of a good teacher there is much excitement and real satisfaction in using and sprouting new multiple skills during this period.

Using Phonics in Spelling Knowledge of phonics is immediately applicable to spelling. Children reveal their use of phonics in efforts to spell independently of adult aid; hence, spelling is commonly used as one of the bases for diagnosing a child's adequacy in phonics. When young Phil wrote in a note explaining his tardiness to the teacher, "I phel daun," he was commended for thinking how words sound. Then he was given the correct spellings of these words and told, "Some of our words can't be spelled as they sound. We have to learn how to spell them."

The comment made by this teacher needs to be made over and over. It is a statement of a fact too often overlooked by those who deplore errors in children's spelling.

In teaching spelling, as with reading, children are helped if teachers encourage a multiple-sensory approach—seeing, hearing, and touching. Children love to spell orally, often turning spelling into a chant: *b-i-g, b-u-g, b-a-g,* and *f-u-n-n-y, b-u-n-n-y, s-u-n-n-y.* Some children must "hear themselves" spell. To silence them is to stifle their learning efforts. Fear of retarding their later speed in reading and writing by permitting the oral spelling seems unwarranted. As skills are mastered and as they are used in motivated experiences, speed is stimulated. Of course, some who walk slowly, talk slowly, and think slowly may never reach great speeds in doing anything.

Again, in spelling, as with all types of learning, repetition and review are essential. It is not uncommon to hear an adult say, "I used to be a good speller, but I now dictate and seldom write. I've lost my former accuracy." A spelling test planned for children should be taken by successful businessmen in nonwriting positions and by active, civic-minded women who seldom write. Can you imagine what a revelation this might be? Psychology for years has reminded us that "disuse leads to forgetting." How many parents have faced the reality of this fact while trying to help a junior-high-school son or daughter with a mathematics assignment?

ALL THIS—AND THINKING, TOO!

By the time half of the first-grade year is over, one-third of the children in a normal school situation show evidence of growth in independent reading. They unlock words by sounding them out, and they read simple news items or parts of stories without any help. They use essential techniques in recognizing words: phonics, word configuration, and clues from context. Many words are so familiar to them that they recognize them at a glance.

Highly essential to this skill development is the guidance of independent thinking by children. A good program not only includes such guidance but regards it as fundamental to the child's proper education. When stories are read, they are discussed. Children give their reactions as to why things were done or why they were not done. They speak up in response to "What if" questions by the teacher. They react also in terms of their acceptance and approval or rejection. Helped by a good teacher, they are encouraged to express their feelings, independent of the comments of others. Here children show great variation in ability. Some may not yet be able to react to common questions, whereas others may bring forth surprising reactions. Such times give a teacher an excellent opportunity to study the way in which they think and how honest and independent they are in their reactions.

This first-grade year is an important time in the young child's development to establish the beginnings of taste. He is encouraged to think independently and even pause while he turns ideas over in his mind. In a stimulating first-grade class in New York State, the teacher had just finished reading Hilary Knight's *ABC* book.[5] "How about it?" she asked. "I like it" and "So do I," piped up a few, not yet taking time to react. "Oh, that's an easy book," said young Freddie, who was making rapid strides in reading and feeling his oats. "Well," said Emily, "it is a different *ABC* book from the one I've got." "What do you think about it, Ernest?" Ernest looked very thoughtful. He responded, "Yes, it sure is different, but I haven't made my mind up yet." Emily added with a note of finality, "I like this one better." The teacher commented, "Some of you are really thinking about it."

[5] Hilary Knight, *ABC*. The Golden Press, 1962.

This was an excellent classroom for developing reflective, honest readers. The teacher took time to listen to the children and gave them time to "just sit" and think. The more facile, more alert youngsters seem readier to profit from such informal discussion, but close observation might show how much rubs off on others in the group who may remain silent. One realization that comes to anyone who works with young children is that at times they do not respond immediately. A day or more after a question has been raised, they may startle us by coming out with an answer, sometimes after we have even forgotten the question. They do think, but they think differently from us, and not on demand.

EXPECTATIONS AND PRESSURES IN FIRST GRADE

Teachers often feel an atmosphere of increasing urgency toward the spring of the year. It is at this time that the variations in children's growth become more obvious, and anxious parents and older brothers and sisters ask uneasily about a child's standing. Perhaps a third of the group begins to take hold the latter half of the year, and some may blossom rapidly from that time on. A few may be far beyond beginning reading and capable of a wide range of independent reading. Others are interested at times but seem intellectually or experientially unready to master item after item, no matter how varied the program and how individually helpful the teacher tries to be.

Early studies of the relation of age to success in beginning reading indicate that a child of normal intelligence learns most successfully at the age of six and one-half. For some, even six and one-half is too early. Such youngsters in some schools may spend an added year in first grade, or take an added year to complete the three primary grades. Their intellectual growth cannot be forced, no matter what method is used. Helping such children to remain eager and anxious to learn is of key importance.

Some schools defer beginning reading to the second half of the first-grade year. Other schools have altered the entrance age for kindergarten admission in order to send youngsters into first grade four to six months older than heretofore. One naturally asks, why not vary the program to fit the ability range of the individual? In this way, teachers could start beginning reading in early fall with the eager ones, and later, even in second grade, with those who have not yet reached the appropriate stage of learning. Some schools have done this; many continue to do so. However, learning to read *as young as possible* is one of our cultural pressures. In times of general anxiety this pressure seems to ascend.

Despite evidence that children can start at seven, eight, and even older, as they do in other countries, and develop into successful readers, the general idea, "come six, come reading," persists. Successful accomplishment in the first grade is, therefore, a deeply rooted expectancy for six-year-olds. The majority meet this standard and more; they also have made good beginnings in writing, spelling, and mathematics. In addition to such important learnings, many have acquired a respectable fund of knowledge and skill in such fields as science, civics, music, and art. They happen to be youngsters who were ready to take such strides and who were in a classroom that offered them the chance to do so. Their behavior is normal *for them*.

Would that all youngsters might approach this crucial first-grade year with eagerness and no awareness of the existing pressures! School and parent groups sensitive to what is important to children's well-being do not put stress on a set standard of accomplishment for young children, lest it induce fear of failure, tension, and feelings of frustration regarding learning. The teacher who approaches each child with an attitude of helpfulness and who provides each child with frequent encouragement will stimulate the best response from each beginner. At the close of first grade every child and his parents should feel the satisfaction of a year spent in successful learning in terms of his individual qualities and background.

Learning to read is only a part, although a very important part, of the curriculum of the first grade. There are different points of view as to which type of curriculum pattern seems best adapted to the success in reading and the all-around growth of six-year-olds. In the following chapter we shall describe common curriculum patterns and the problems that arise in their use.

SUGGESTED READINGS FOR THE FIRST GRADE

BLOOMFIELD, LEONARD, and BARNHART, CLARENCE L. *Let's Read—A Linguistic Approach.* Detroit: Wayne University Press, 1961.

A linguistic point of view regarding the use of phonics in beginning reading. The Bloomfield System of teaching reading the linguistic way is included.

DOWNING, J. A. *The Augmented Roman Alphabet.* London: Pitman Publishing, 1962.

A description of the use of the Augmented Roman letters in a continuing experiment with beginning readers in several schools of England and the results to date.

DURKIN, DOLORES. *Phonics and the Teaching of Reading.* New York: Bureau of Publications, Teachers College, Columbia University, 1962.

A monograph addressed to teachers, with information on the phonic structure of words and helpful suggestions for teaching phonics.

GANS, ROMA, STENDLER, CELIA, and ALMY, MILLIE. *Teaching Young Children.* Yonkers-on-the-Hudson: World Book Company, 1952. Chapters 7 and 8.

The development of a child as a reader, writer, speaker, and listener is detailed in these two chapters, with descriptions of home and school situations that highlight sound and unsound approaches.

HEFFERNAN, HELEN, ed., Committee of the California School Supervisors Association, *Guiding the Young Child.* Boston: D. C. Heath and Company, 1959.

Entire book a rich resource for those working with young children at home and at school. Excellent guide in planning curriculum for kindergartens and primary grades.

MCKIM, MARGARET G. *Guiding Growth in Reading.* New York: The Macmillan Company, 1955. Part II, Chapter 3.

Widely accepted points regarding reading-readiness teaching and pre-reading and beginning reading practices are included. Suggestions for teachers follow closely those included in manuals of basal reading series.

CHAPTER 6

Differing Attitudes Toward First-Grade Reading

The variations in methods of teaching beginning reading in the first grade are apparent to anyone who visits schools across the country and reads published curriculum materials. Parents who must transfer offspring from one school to another are well aware of these wide differences. Because local initiative in planning school affairs is a highly prized quality in community living and because state departments of education not only respect but encourage local initiative, differences from school to school are to be expected. Although some programs are tagged as "name brands," their description in terms of a few characteristic emphases may allow readers, both educators and laymen, to see their differences.

The practice most widely used in teaching reading in the first grade is that which considers reading as a separate skill, along with writing, spelling, arithmetic, and other subject-matter areas. A special period is devoted to reading, to spelling, to arithmetic, to health, to social studies, to music, to art, and so on. Sometimes the language arts are divided into separate periods for spelling, oral English, writing, reading, word study, and the story hour. It is not uncommon to visit a present-day American first grade that, in the number of very brief periods for classes and the assignment of these periods for separate subjects, harks back to the first grade some old-timers attended. Many schools, however, perhaps a majority, have made large strides in cutting down on the number of short periods and in making efforts to relate subject matter to some extent.

EMPHASIS I. THE BASAL-SYSTEM APPROACH TO READING

The basal-system approach involves the adoption of, or reliance upon, textbooks and accompanying manuals offering suggestions to teachers for use of the books. Schools adhering to this point of view use basal materials for all children in first-grade reading; often this system is used in succeeding grades also. Basal systems usually include workbooks, practice materials, manuals for teachers, and tests for measurement of reading.

Two reasons may underlie the decision to accept a basal plan. First, such materials and suggestions to teachers are often the result of much research by reading specialists; therefore a scientific aura hovers over them. Second, with today's many crowded classrooms and many inexperienced teachers, the task of teaching beginning reading seems for many teachers too great without detailed plans and materials to follow.

Some Common Features of Basal Reading Systems The basal reading systems vary, but they have many qualities in common. As a rule, their content is built with a controlled vocabulary that is introduced gradually and repeated with studied regularity. Topics are selected with an eye to their general appeal to six-year-olds across the country, and pages are highlighted with colorful pictures. The brief introductory books, called preprimers, are planned so that the pictures carry the ideas which the simple vocabulary does not include. For example, instead of having the child read, "Here is Jasper in his wagon," the caption "Jasper" may be placed under the picture of a boy in a wagon. The manual for the teacher includes proposals for helping youngsters to recognize the words, to make note of word characteristics (including phonics), and to remember them. Suggestions are also given for discussing the meaning of the content, although the material even for children of this age is meager.

Some systems employ large charts through which children are introduced to some of the first words they will meet in the preprimers. Much of such preprimer work resembles the reading-readiness work used in kindergartens. Individual exercises in workbooks give children an opportunity to reinforce the learning they gather from charts and preprimers.

From these beginning experiences children acquire a *sight vocabulary* that is also included in the first reader and the supplementary readers. They also establish or reinforce already budding word-recognition skills; these skills comprise the careful inspection of how a word looks, from its beginning at the left to its end at the right; some knowledge of specific letter sounds and elements in phonics; some ideas about context clues; and the sharpening of the ability to remember words. They also strengthen the practice of reading from left to right and increase the child's information about the organization of books in general—such as which part of the book is the top, how to use the table of contents, how a book is paged, the fact that sections of a book often bear titles.

In some schools, work with reading workbooks and charts starts for all first-graders soon after the initial day, no matter what their state of eagerness. One need not comment on the lack of insight in such teaching. In other schools, reading work is introduced only to those who, by performance records in the kindergarten and by other evidences, show readiness. In most schools, this group usually comprises one-third of the entire class. A second group may be started off after the Christmas holidays; the remainder, a month or so later.

Three groups at varying stages of progress with the basal materials meet at separate periods or simultaneously, the teacher going from group to group. This is considered the reading period or lesson. During this time, a teacher has a chance to hear children read individually, to note their successes as well as the errors they make, to note what additional help they may need in phonics or in added drill, and to give them directions for the individual work periods that usually follow. Some youngsters who are found to be misplaced in ability level are changed from one group to another. Some may reveal difficulties which indicate that more careful diagnosis is desirable.

Measuring Reading Progress Individual checks on progress are given at certain periods, and a more inclusive test, which is a part of the basal system, is given toward the end of the year. These final tests, measuring the success of the first year of reading, are actually more appropriate than standardized primary reading tests because they are devised to test the specific vocabularies and reading techniques that the children have been taught.

The program during the year includes other reading experiences, as well as guidance in writing and spelling. The story hours in some schools are as regular as in kindergarten. Books for browsing and "library books" for individual pursuits are used by the abler youngsters. The central theme in reading, however, is the progress in the basal system. Differences in children's ability are allowed for by starting the bright on given work earlier than the slower child. The materials, in general, are uniform.

Variations from Classroom to Classroom Although they may subscribe to a systematic approach to the teaching of reading and the use of basal materials, schools vary widely in their methods of utilizing such a system. Some encourage teachers to use the basal materials as they see fit and to supplement them with other materials of their choice. Other schools prescribe strict adherence, with page-by-page reliance upon the manual, leaving little time for other materials. Most of the authors and the publishers of these materials endorse the free and imaginative use of their materials, and many school principals and supervisors encourage teachers to incorporate their own ideas and include a variety of materials in their daily work in reading.

Even in schools demanding considerable conformity from teachers, particularly teachers in the primary grades, great differences among first-grade teachers can be found. A teacher who is creative and who enjoys working with children relates the work to ongoing experiences of the children and keeps them eager, alert, and learning happily. A less imaginative teacher, who belabors youngsters with boring instructions and repetition of minutiae, makes children dislike reading and everything connected with school. One cannot overemphasize the importance of a "peppy," creative teacher—no matter what the philosophy of reading involved.

For example, in a large suburban school where the same basal reading system was used throughout the six grades, one first-grade teacher had in conspicuous places a "News of the Week" chart, notices of two big events—"Our First Visit from the Dentist" and "All-School Assembly Today"—and, in a sheltered spot, a small desk and chair below a sign reading, "For Writing Our Letters." There was an atmosphere of industry within this classroom. Children worked independently in small groups while one group of three worked with the teacher. Across the hall, in another first grade, the only sign visible was "Attendance—Jane, Carolyn, Matthew." The pupils were divided into two groups; each child in one group was working on the identical page of a workbook, while the other group listened as the teacher described what they were to do during the next period. In this classroom there was much restlessness and little evidence of eagerness or independent child activity.

The differences in these two situations were caused, not by the materials or basal system adopted, but rather by the teachers themselves. The first teacher used ideas that increased learning. She obviously worked in a way that developed independent work habits, because this independence was evident in the children's behavior. The second teacher lacked such spark. In short, no plan, no matter how brilliantly devised or inclusively organized, can prevent an alert teacher from helping children notice more in the world about them, talking about interesting words, enjoying good stories and news events, and adding to each day countless high learning moments in addition to those recommended in the basal manuals.

Further variations in basal-plan use are found in schools. For example, many teachers report "Yes, we have adopted a basal system, but we use it only when it fits with certain children." Often able readers are encouraged to use books not of the basal series while those pupils who are more dependent and slower to blossom forth use the basal books. Such practice reveals a waxing respect for individual differences and may induce the teacher to extend even further a program of reading tailored to fit the individual child.

Respect for Variations in Teachers' Ability One can readily see that to teachers with little experience in first-grade teaching and to those who lack initiative and ability to plan carefully, the basal system is not only an aid but also a safeguard for children's learning. For the able, experienced teacher and also for the alert beginning teachers, too-close reliance upon the basal system is a limiting influence. Building on children's individual interests and varying backgrounds is hindered if all must use identical materials. Therefore, where there is respect for differences in individual teachers' ability, the work in basal systems is not mandatory, but rather based upon the teachers' needs. Schools which show a genuine concern for increasing teachers' resourcefulness and general competence may, as a result, not represent any one curriculum and reading theory, but may, instead, include a variety—basal systems, as well as other materials and procedures, depending upon the wide range of teachers' professional skills and points of view.

Schools in the group designated as Emphasis I, however, subscribe to the idea that reading, to be taught successfully, must be regarded as a composite of skills that require a sequential development for which specially prepared materials are essential for all children. Other materials are used, but time and attention to them do not receive priority. The description of the other theories in practice will add further meaning to Emphasis I.

EMPHASIS II. READING'S SPRINGBOARD IN EXPERIENCE

The starting point for all teaching under the system we shall describe as Emphasis II is the focusing of attention on young children's ways of learning. The knowledge acquired from studies of preschool learning has supported the theory that children learn aptly through sharing in experiences. A child helping an adult with preparations for lunch learns to set the table, to help make sandwiches, and to tidy up after eating. In the course of the entire process, the child acquires not only many skills in manipulation, but also a large number of meaningful, essential words and common phrases. Vocabularies of five thousand or more words are easily acquired by children who, with conversational adults, watch houses being built, attend church festivals, play at outdoor picnics, observe road-construction crews, talk about television programs, and follow family chores with a watchful eye.

Children's Role in Planning Having a share in making plans for the day helps children acquire a feeling for that elusive quality, time. It also helps them anticipate what is coming next because they are closely involved in planning the sequence. They see the relationships of ideas and events. For example, gelatine dessert may be made in the morning so that it has time to set for an afternoon party; memos are written on the board as reminders of important jobs to be done; the story of an interesting trip is recorded in writing so that the youngsters can learn to read it at home to interested members of the family. Where such patterns are followed, the life of children is planned and has order and reasonableness.

Learning to read, too, is planned. Labels and name cards are placed to help children identify materials and their own property. Signs are posted as guides and reminders. Books are available for the enjoyment of those who wish to browse through them and for reading by those who already are able to do so. Words, their configuration, meaning, and phonic elements, are talked about because through such experiences children learn to recognize words and to read independently. Lists of books read, word-help needs, and signs of progress are recorded by the teacher to guide her in planning her future work. Children, too, start recording some items of accomplishment so that they can be more concretely aware of milestones in their progress.

Such experiences and countless more are a part of the active life of a first-grader who is sometimes exploring some new topic with the entire group, at other times working or playing in a small group, and at still other times working alone. Even when all share in some event of broad appeal, such as the story period, discussion of an important news event, listening to a visiting guest, or going on a trip, a wise teacher remains aware of the differing ways in which children react. Achieving an identical response from all may be necessary in some situations, but where a child's personal reactions and thinking should be developed, individual responses are encouraged.

Curriculum Content and Reading For a number of years, importance has been attached to children's learning through units, activities, or projects that they have helped to plan. The purposes for each study are examined first; then follows the planning of the work to be done; next, the plans are carried out; and finally, the work is evaluated or summarized. The studies are selected in the light of children's interests, the value of the studies to the children, and their readiness to pursue them. Through such studies, they learn much information and, in the process of gathering the required information, they become aware of the skills of reading, writing, and talking. When they face the need to develop additional skills in order to facilitate their work, they see the reason for gaining these added skills.

A teacher noted that in one week her first grade learned the following things essential to reading: when to use a library's card index to locate references on frogs, when to use the index of a cookbook to locate the page bearing a particular recipe, how to talk about the style of a book (pictorial or nonpictorial), how to look for variations in the difficulty of certain books. Reading, in this curriculum, quickly became an experience that led children to seek reference material and to use skills necessary in this process.

The topics or central themes of the Emphasis II studies are usually in the fields of social studies and science. Under this curriculum theory, children in first grade may study community helpers and life at home and at school; they may also make simple inquiries in the realm of science. The topics vary, and, as a rule, the broad area from which they are drawn is suggested for each grade to prevent duplication of content or omissions in the grades.

Motivation Through Sharing in Setting Goals In Emphasis I, preselected reading materials are placed before children. The separate-subject program does not make it essential for children to develop initiative, resourcefulness, and skills in finding and evaluating helpful materials. In Emphasis II, however, the children themselves, in setting purposes and goals for their work, develop interest in whatever learning tools they use, such as reporting, reading for information, and writing memos, and retain interest in the topics selected. They can describe what they are doing and why. This "involvement" of the children is an exceedingly important element in the educative process. It changes dutiful assignment-doers into active participants in all phases of their learning—a desirable outcome in educating children to become active participants in managing our affairs, from local areas to international life.

Learning to Read Through Recorded Experiences Let us take a look at how Emphasis II was put into practice in a rural area first grade in Nebraska. The children had talked at the beginning of the October day of how busy everyone in the family was. Several children mentioned the work that family members were doing. The teacher proposed they might study this work. She would write on charts what they found out.

In answer to her question, "Who works at your home?" they responded, "Mama, Daddy, hired help, Mr. Anderson, big brother, and me." Next, she asked, "Who works very hard?" Several proposed Daddy. The teacher wrote on the chart *"What does Daddy do?"* Some could read as she wrote. To her next question, "How can we find out what Daddy does?" they responded "When we go home we'll ask him." The following day, those who could remember and report mentioned such items as, "My Daddy works in town in his office"; "My Daddy calls us in the morning"; "My Daddy plows the fields"; "My Daddy is cutting our corn"; "My Daddy is selling some cows." The teacher wrote these items as children watched her and chimed in at times.

The account was called *A True Story About Our Daddies.* After several days of going over the story and adding more ideas in their morning discussions about work fathers do, the teacher asked if each would like a copy of this true story to learn to read and then take home. Of course, all wanted it. Each was given a copy of the story in a simple folded cover. Those who could wrote their own names on it. The teacher wrote out the names for the seven or eight who could not write their own.

At the teacher's suggestion, they looked at books in the classroom library for pictures that might show fathers at work. The pages were marked and the books brought to the next discussion period. In pictures, they found farmers who were feeding chickens, driving teams of horses, and greeting visitors. Later, they visited two fathers at work; one on a farm, the other in a general store in a nearby village. Through this experience, the word *work* took on many meanings. They also discovered that they got ideas from books. This was their first "reference" reading.

Their study continued with an examination of the work that mothers do. In their oral accounts, some words were used again and again. Once more the teacher told the children that their story was a true story—a real story. This idea seemed of great significance to them. Children at six are struggling with fact and fancy, truth and fiction. Therefore, this is an important time for them to read simple articles that are true, accounts of which they can sense the reality.

The theme of the kinds of work that various people do, as seen by six-year-olds, arose repeatedly in the discussions of this class. The world is opening up before children of this age; therefore, the teacher's guidance in studying work of those about them had specific value. In addition, these youngsters experienced the procedures involved in locating and reading some informational material that had real meaning for them, choosing the correct method of recording items, and extending their knowledge and awareness of the surrounding world.

Children may also dictate reports of important trips and unusual events. For example, a magician's performance at a Sussex County, New Jersey, school was described thus by first-graders:

He did tricks.
They were all magic.
He pulled a rabbit out of a hat and a big umbrella from his sleeve.
He let some kids come up and look in the hat to see if the rabbit was in it.
It wasn't.
Then the next thing we knew, he pulled it out.

The children in telling the teacher what to write used a vocabulary that came out of the experience—*magician, magic, pulled, rabbit, umbrella.* Children in Texarkana might not have had an experience with a magician. This story of magic may have little appeal or meaning for them. Children who first relate, then read stories of their own experiences find truly exciting motivation in this procedure.

The production of beginning reading materials based on the experiences of beginners has been in effect a number of years and has been developed rather satisfactorily in the hands of able teachers. Some of this production has fallen into the tainting influence of manipulation, as did this story found on a chart in a first-grade classroom:

We went to the farm.
We saw the farmer.
We saw a dog.
We saw a cow.
We saw chickens.

One can tell at a glance that the teacher in this situation was manipulating the children to get a previously determined vocabulary into the correct short-sentence form, with plenty of repetition, but with a lack of run-on quality, lilt, and humor.

Vocabulary Building The first step following such shared writing of a story is skill-building vocabulary work. The teacher decides which words should be earmarked for phonic analysis, which are nonphonic and need to be recognized by sight or by configuration, which are too incidental to call for drill, and which are already known by a number of children.

Secondly, a system of recording the vocabulary used as it accumulates, experience after experience, seems essential as a guide to the teacher. In a few schools each child keeps a list of *known* words in his own alphabetized notebook. He can give himself quick practice periods and reviews. The learning value of keeping the notebook up to date runs very high.

Thirdly, it is important to accumulate the written stories and reports in some durable form for each child to use as proof of his growing power and as satisfactory familiar material which he can reread. Anyone who sees a child revel in rereading a book he has already read can appreciate how rewarding an experience this is. It adds to the child's sense of accomplishment, it proves to him his power, and it is reading practice of the finest quality.

Creating a Contagious Reading Climate Such experiences can whet the eagerness of the slower to listen and to find out. Children can also be truly motivated to want to read that which has personal significance for them. They can see reasons for reading, for recording to remember, and for the use of books in a variety of ways. Although these learnings are elementary, they do point out the breadth of the concept of reading and the knowledge about selecting and producing materials that children can acquire. Practice with special words in both reading and spelling are a part of such experiences. Word-recognition skills are developed when they are essential to the work at hand and when some of the children are ready for them.

To a casual observer, such an experience, and others like it, may seem beyond the reading power of the children. For a small number of youngsters this may seem true, but by living in this climate they, too, blossom forth. The majority are ready to participate to some degree in planning, in recording, in noticing memos, and in seeing how those who are able to read refer to their plans. Many also see in new contexts some words they already know and learn others.

Some experiences demand wider use of reference books than others. For example, the first grade in a village school converted an unused sand table into a small "swamp." The youngsters went to the library to get books on snails, toads, and frogs for the teacher to read to them in order to help them make sure that their indoor swamp would be appropriate for the snails and frogs' eggs they placed in it. Some mature six-year-olds could browse through the books and acquire ideas of the appropriateness of the content from pictures. Many gathered information and, in addition, expanded their speaking vocabulary with such words as *moisture, temper-*

ature, bog, tadpole, and *mollusk,* just as through television and radio they had added *satellite, jet, pad,* and *rocket* to their language. But, in addition, for many it was a first experience of going to a library for books from which to gather important information. Also important was the fact that the school they attended made a point of discouraging the "headline reader" or "one-book answer man."

Developing Skills in Experience-Centered Programs While such activities are an integral part of each day's classroom schedule, regular class reading periods are also going on. In some schools this work may, in many respects, resemble the work previously described in Emphasis I. A basal system may be used for some children, one of the skill-building series for others, according to the special needs of the youngsters. In some schools the teacher plans all the reading work in relation to the curriculum, plus the children's individual reading, again using materials she believes suitable. The skill texts, or skill books, which resemble workbooks, contain graduated exercises, word-study helps, and tests. They require less time than do the more elaborate basal systems.

Some reading and curriculum specialists question the use of any preplanned material or basal or skill texts, but for some children the short page-by-page work may be extremely suitable. If selected to fit special cases, it is appropriate. Only if used indiscriminately does it violate the theory of fit-the-material-to-the-child.

In some programs, the skill development work and use of basal texts may have little or no relationship with social studies, science units, or other experiences that the youngsters may be meeting, thus crowding the child's schedule and unfortunately making necessary the omission of some valuable learnings. A child may not see the connections between some skills and their intended use. Those who pursue this dual reading plan fail to see the importance of reasonableness to the child in what he does.

In a classroom following an experience-curriculum theory, when children acquire sufficient skill in reading they are encouraged to become more active in the location of relevant materials. They bring in readers, books, and magazines from home and from the school library for ongoing classroom studies.

The focusing of attention on central themes demands large blocks of teaching time. Therefore, in many schools the language-arts work, particularly that of writing, spelling, and oral English, is taught in as close a relationship to the special project as possible, thereby reducing the number of separate periods and obviating some of the pressures of time evident in the more cut-up schedule. The daily program also includes story hours, discussion of books, and individual book-browsing. Each child receives a rich and varied reading diet.

Children's Understanding of Their Work A visit to a classroom operated according to Emphasis II theory presents surprises to those accustomed to Emphasis I teaching. The teacher's role is one of aiding, suggesting, and encouraging children to share ideas, to take responsibility, and to develop independent study skills. Children understand the daily program because they have shared in planning it; they also take part in periodic evaluations to see how well they are progressing in their studies. They are eager to describe their work and able to do so. The boundary between home life and school life is less pronounced. As a youngster becomes excited over a study, he brings in ideas and material from home and neighborhood that he believes will be helpful. Stories and short pieces of informational material written in school, clippings of news events, and appealing books are taken home so that his family may enjoy them and keep informed through him of his work at school. Parents often comment on how much they learn from the child's description of his school work, and they also respect the ability he is acquiring in his reporting to them.

In addition to the broad scope of information a child acquires in such a richly varied reading program, he is also growing in that invaluable power, the use of language. His vocabulary becomes enlarged and more precise, and his ability to test out his thinking in conversation is stretched. Many of these points cannot be evaluated by simple tests but only by careful observation and detailed records. However, an alert parent and teacher can make simple checks from time to time and observe individual progress.

EMPHASIS III. INDIVIDUALIZING READING

Similar to Emphasis II, yet different in one important respect, is the point of view of a group of school leaders and reading specialists who accept the broadly based curriculum in which children share in planning units in social studies and science, but who stress the teaching of all reading and skill development on an individualized basis. The emphasis on the individual approach rests upon a two-fold purpose: (1) guiding young children at the outset to be selective—to choose from books and other materials that which appeals to them; and (2) meeting the variation of ability among readers by a personally guided program. In this program, each child receives the help he needs from reading the books he personally selects and from the individual help the teacher gives him in developing his skills. The common practice of dividing a class into small groups in order to approximate most accurately each child's reading needs is vigorously rejected by those who hold this third point of view.

Facing Individual Differences Among the most persistent problems in teaching, from kindergarten through college, is the difficulty of meeting the differences within large, and even small, groups of pupils in terms of their ability, past experience, and variety of interests. Some pupils literally zoom ahead; others progress in slow small steps. The glibly expressed hope of "bringing all up to grade" is based upon a lack of knowledge of this variation.

The greatest effort to give individual help is required in teaching the skills—reading, writing, spelling, and arithmetic computation. In fact, to many competent observers, the measure of a good school, no matter what the expressed curriculum theory, is the degree of study and concern given to this ever-present and pervasive teaching need. In a school where this is an active concern, even teachers with large classes include individual-help periods.

The writer experienced the imperativeness of the need for individual help in the skills while teaching a third grade composed of thirty-six eight-year-olds. The class included one boy who could read everything, "including Shakespeare," and three who could read nothing independently. Of these three, one was a gifted child who, with little effort, grew into a competent, independent reader. The other two plodded along with day-after-day individual help required; one of the two was robust, all-boy, jerky, and impatient, while the other was an extremely shy girl. Both had to be given aid individually.

In the individualized program of Emphasis III, ample materials are provided to fit the highly personal needs of the children. A variety of library books is kept in the classroom—texts and practice materials to fit those just beginning, as well as those able to read books commonly enjoyed by children several years older. A good school library is essential to satisfy the classroom demands for such quantity and variety of materials. In a program under wise teacher guidance, some young readers may read fifty to several hundred books during their first-grade year.

Basing Evaluation on Individual Growth Evaluation of reading growth in a program based on Emphasis III is tailored to fit this plan. The child's growth in his ability to keep records of his own reading is an important part of such evaluation. He selects the books, he gets help when needed, and he keeps a record of the books he has read. The teacher's evaluation and record of the child's progress is based on his work with and observation of each child. Both informal and standardized tests are used in some schools as an additional check and an amplification of the individual evaluation. Teachers and administrators who have tested the effectiveness of the reading program based on teaching with individual emphasis have found favorable results.[1]

Losing Sight of the Group As the emphasis on individual reading has caught the imagination of educators, however, some, with insufficient understanding, have seized upon the idea almost as a panacea for all reading ills. This is likely to happen with any method or theory that acquires such an all-encompassing label as "individual." (Semanticists caution against the use of labels because they tend to short-circuit understanding.)

[1] Philip J. Acenapiera, *A Comparative Study of the Results of Two Instructional Reading Programs* (unpublished Ed.D. thesis). Teachers College, Columbia University, 1959.

In a few classrooms all reading activities are on an entirely individual basis; thus some fine group-learning opportunities are barred. On certain occasions and at strategic times, members of an entire group, with their many variations, can share profitably from common experiences. For example, a first grade of thirty-four youngsters in Connecticut, whose teacher was applying an individual method of teaching reading, listened avidly to an account by a Chinese graduate student of how Chinese first-grade books are made and how Chinese children read their books back-to-front.

There are many possibilities for challenging the interests of an entire group on topics that are particularly appealing to young children and do not demand a wide background of information. Whole classes often can profit from such experiences as movies, trips, and easily managed work and play opportunities. Children are also greatly helped in working together in small compatible groups. In fact, learning can be increased by group work. Reading specialists, who have exerted great influence in the direction of helping children individually, have not suggested the exclusion of all group work. They also understand the value of rich group experiences which evoke the exchange of ideas by children.

Basic Requirement: The Teacher's Understanding Encouraging teachers to explore new ideas in teaching is highly desirable, but it is also desirable to see the new in perspective with the old. Today's child needs the most competent and visionary teaching possible in order to become the functional, critical reader that our world demands at this time in its history. True, the child is concerned with the here and now, but his direction in future living is developed by day-after-day guidance, much of it the subtle influence of the teacher. Therefore, the *meaning* that reading has to the teacher will be passed on to the child.

Furthermore, the more we learn about how children function and the more we examine their thinking and their ways of working, the more we notice that what seems logical to us may leave them unaffected, and what seems sensible and logical to them often leaves us in a quandary. Getting closer to children by offering individual help and by observing them for clues to their thinking may not make a precise, inclusive pattern or system, but it does make a sensible approach to teaching them. Therefore, the upsurge in emphasis on individualizing reading should yield promising results.

In an accidental way, the "individualized approach" to teaching reading has caused another effect upon the curriculum. By emphasizing the selecting, reading, and recording of books chosen individually, attention to reading related to curriculum studies has been reduced in many classrooms. Where this happens, the child's growth in broad, functional reading and in the acquisition of study skills is held back or weakened. Both positions, the attention to each child as a unique reader and the study of curriculum experiences, are essential to the proper education of today's child as a reader.

THE BIG PROBLEM

No matter what position school leaders, specialists, and teachers take about teaching first-graders to read, several important observations can readily be made. The first of these is that children, up to the present time, *have learned to read* and that the majority have become successful readers. Second, one may observe that in some schools up to twenty-five per cent have failed to make a good start on reading in the first grade, no matter what the theory, basal system, or emphasis used. Third, bright youngsters may find first-grade materials boring and the teaching pace too slow for them.

Handling Individual Differences What to do with those who are considered failures, as well as with those who are ready to leap ahead, is faced in a wide range of ways. Some schools that rely heavily on uniform basal books and test results regard retaining the poor achiever in the first grade for another year as the best solution. Some of the high achievers may be advanced a year, but such advancement is not a widespread policy.

In schools with marked respect for individual differences, methods and materials in succeeding grades are adapted to all levels of reading accomplishment. The threat to the child of failing or of being labeled a failure is carefully avoided. Studies of failure have shown that children not only fail to improve by repeating a grade, but may even regress. Occasionally a child does repeat the first-grade work, but the decision to have him do so is based upon a broader set of facts than consideration of reading accomplishment only and is not considered his failure. Adjusting the program the following year to meet the slower reader's specific needs is considered better than exposing the child to the effects of failure. This plan makes sense because it aids all children, while it hurts none.

This one problem alone—recognition of the facts of individual differences—keeps conscientious teachers, administrators, and parents struggling year after year to find the most helpful ideas and materials with which to meet the challenge. All realize that exactly as we will never be able to design a suit or dress that would fit all six-year-olds precisely, so, too, we will never be able to find the one all-fitting reading program that all of any given age can meet with equal intellectual stimulation and learning success.

Testing New Theories and Proposals Researches from time to time present leads and clues favoring now one approach, then another. Extravagant claims and accusations are not uncommon. In an area as important as a child's introduction to the skills required for good reading, from which he will acquire satisfactions for his entire life, certainly extended research to evaluate these approaches is still needed. With all the data already available on the many variables that go to make up each youngster, and with the recognition of all the conflicting influences that a child meets before he puts a foot across the first-grade threshold, no speedy acceptance of sweeping generalizations will advance the teaching of reading. Extreme procedures and sweeping claims for a given method should be tested by clear thinking and sound logic.

Emphasis on any method, to be sound, must include the respect for the ideas a child is acquiring about reading and his attitudes toward the promises for him inherent in reading. Despite the bulk of material related to the teaching of reading in the first grade, a wise school encourages teachers to explore new, promising ideas and materials with children, to keep careful notes for evaluation, and to keep all avenues of information open for further adventures.

PLANNING FIRST-GRADE READING PROGRAMS

The child's year in first grade is so important that every elementary-school staff should and can, through careful planning, assure each child of a successful year for him. In up-to-date schools across the nation, time is spent in regular staff meetings for this purpose. It is safe to assume that in schools under the influence of professional principals, curriculum workers, and teacher associations this important school year for children is given appropriate consideration.

The following activities may help the school staff in planning reading programs in the first grade:

1. An examination of ways in which a teacher can study children in a classroom under everyday teaching conditions. All too often teachers are advised to "study your children," but are not helped to do this intelligently. Specialists, teachers, and principals who have studied child development recently should share their books, pamphlets, and notes with teachers.

2. The creation of a simple, usable form or method for keeping individual records for the teacher's personal use. From Point 1 above, ideas of what to record will develop. Busy teachers may need added help to keep important data available for use.

3. A briefing on books, pamphlets, and articles on the teaching of beginning reading. After a short, intensive study period so that teachers and staff can be brought up to date, some plan should be made for keeping all apprised of emerging important publications.

4. A plan for keeping informed of new materials—books, magazines, games, teaching aids, and the like—for children's use. A busy teacher cannot browse widely enough to follow today's extensive literary output in the reading field. The once-a-year study of books at teachers' conventions or during Book Week will not suffice. Through help from libraries and by sharing information, some simple system may be devised.

Parents may share in the activities described in Points 3 and 4 with profit for all. Many parents make a point of keeping informed and can be invaluable aids to the staff and parent groups. Many others are eager to keep informed. Teachers in a cooperative study plan will not meet the embarrassing situation caused when the well-read parent informs the not-so-well-read teacher.

5. A carefully considered guideline for the first-grade reading program to be applied in the daily routine. Points given in Chapter 1 might be used as a springboard. Many schools have worked out

curriculum guides that include specific goals for first-grade reading. These need to be re-evaluated periodically. Schools that have not yet progressed to this point are wise if they start with careful study and test their plans for adequacy. By so doing, they avoid falling into the common error of drawing up good plans but failing to put them into practice in day-to-day teaching.

6. Adoption of one or several definite steps in teaching, as an experiment, and plans for evaluating these activities. Teachers quite naturally find former practices comfortable and easy to rely upon. Experimental changes, planned and tested out, are invaluable in their livening effect. Creative teaching draws dynamic force from trying out new ideas.

7. A careful plan for evaluating each child's growth in the total reading program. To plan an exciting, rich reading program with attention to stimulating children's taste and ability to talk about books, only to fall back upon "the same old testing program," is as discouraging to teachers as it is unenlightening. Tests can offer limited data at first-grade level. Observations and recordings of children's work and samples of their writing and art add valuable evidences of learning.

To yield best results, all work that flows from study by teachers and staff must be kept within reasonable time limits out of respect for teachers' time and energy. The end results will be apparent in the everyday reading growth of the children.

A deeper insight into children's behavior will continue to be a goal for those who live and work with them and surely for those who devise plans to educate them. The former casual regard for the significance of early years has now been replaced with a new and wholesome respect for their importance. Kindergarten and first-grade years are strategic, not only in what a child learns in knowledge and the basic skills, but also in the inner feelings and attitudes he acquires about himself as a learner. The old idea of presenting him with an opportunity to learn and then "making him learn" is professionally as sound as the old practice of applying leeches to the soles of the feet as a cure for tuberculosis. One hopes that all those who design new programs for beginning reading have the time and opportunity to inform themselves of the new insights into the behavior of young children and their development of meaningful vocabularies. This last point is a major challenge of particular concern to those working with first-graders. The next chapter is devoted to vocabulary selection practices now commonly used.

SUGGESTED READINGS ON FIRST-GRADE READING

ALMY, MILLIE. *Children's Experience Prior to First Grade and Success in Beginning Reading.* New York: Bureau of Publications, Teachers College, Columbia University, 1949.

The findings in this study reinforce respect for everyday experiences at home as a help to the child in first-grade beginning reading.

BROGAN, PEGGY, and FOX, LORENE K. *Helping Children Read.* New York: Holt, Rinehart and Winston, 1961. Part I, Chapter 2, and Part II, Chapter 5.

Description of beginning reading and skill development in a reading program, with emphasis on the individual approach to the teaching of reading.

GANS, ROMA. *Guiding Children's Reading Through Experiences.* New York: Bureau of Publications, Teachers College, Columbia University, 1941.

The development of each phase of reading power through home and school activities rather than through basal materials is the focus of this monograph. Many examples used to illustrate key points.

GANS, ROMA, STENDLER, CELIA, and ALMY, MILLIE C. *Teaching Young Children.* Yonkers-on-the-Hudson: World Book Company, 1952. Part III, Chapter 7.

An account of children's growth as readers from the beginning to independent reading power, with the emphasis on a personal-experience-centered approach.

LAZAR, M., DRAPER, M., and SCHWIETERT, L. *A Practical Guide to Individualized Reading.* Board of Education of the City of New York, Bureau of Educational Records, 1960. Chapters 5 and 6.

Suggestions appropriate for schools in urban areas, with real help for teaching slow beginners. Many examples from classrooms.

MCKIM, MARGARET G. *Guiding Growth in Reading.* New York: The Macmillan Company, 1955. Part II, Chapters 3, 4, and 5; Part III, Chapters 6 and 9.

Suggestions for teachers on many phases of teaching beginning reading, particularly in a basal reading program.

MIEL, ALICE, ed. *Individualizing Reading Practice.* New York: Bureau of Publications, Teachers College, Columbia University, 1958.

A description of the steps essential in establishing a program of reading, with emphasis on the individual approach. Particularly helpful for first-grade teachers. Easy-to-read style.

MILNER, ESTHER. "A Study of the Relationship between Reading Readiness in Grade One School Children and Patterns of Parent-Child Interaction." *Child Development,* XXII, June 1951, pp. 95-112.

The results of this study indicated that children with opportunities to have close, satisfying experiences with parents at home tended to succeed in beginning reading. Breadth of experiences for beginning readers rather than too closely centered learning-to-read work was recommended by the author of this study. Technical, but heartening reading for parents and teachers.

VAN ALLEN, R., and HALVORSEN, GLADYS C. *The Language-Experience Approach to Reading Instruction.* Boston: Ginn and Company, 1961.
The entire book is a rich resource for teachers working toward an experience-centered reading program.

CHAPTER 7

Today's Talking Child with Yesterday's Reading Vocabulary

The impact of television, radio, movies and a mobile life on the vocabulary of children is unbelievable to one who is not within daily listening range of a young child. The strongest influence seems to come from television. No sooner is there a new beverage—let's call it Zingo—than a young sprout will say to his mother, "Let's get some." He promptly learns the accompanying commercial jingle as he expands his vocabulary to include the new trade name, Zingo.

VOCABULARY EXPANSION—EARLY AND RAPID

Brighter threes, fours, and fives are discriminating cereal selectors in the self-service markets by means of the packages and often, as they buy, chant the jingle that goes with the brand name. Biz, Whir, Kringles, Push-pops, and Gooz may seem like new and strange names to us, and we may never sing their jingles on key, but not so with today's child. He is growing up in this advertising age in which products are paraded via catchy names and tunes, some of which may not stir our adult interest or buying desires but do intrigue our young listener, who is at a key learning age.

Not only are these young citizens stretching their vocabularies with advertising names and phrases, but they are also acquiring ideas from news broadcasts. *Tornado, blizzard,* and *hurricane* have entered many young vocabularies. If you talk with youngsters after they have spent a brief period listening to a news broadcast, you discover that they are gaining a language with which to think.

Today's youngsters not only know the words that catch the ear, such as *blizzard,* but they gather enough meaning to have basic concepts of some words on which to build. "When are we getting a blizzard here so I can see big trucks push the snow?" asked young Mary of her grandmother in balmy South Carolina after both had just seen pictures of a big blizzard in Buffalo, New York. Through many such listening and talking moments, today's children sound very different from youngsters of a previous era.

Later this same child, Mary, reported that she could point out the ocean during the course of an automobile ride, but that there were "no whales near Charleston." Then she added, "I saw them harpoon a big whale on television. He was as big as our house." Yes, this was an alert child who would enter the first grade within two years and there read "See, see, oh-see" primers.

Slower youngsters may not react in the same manner. They may remember fewer names and may not start to sing an entire jingle or even a part of one until they are older, but they too reveal the effects of mass media. The teacher of a slow kindergarten group discovered this when she showed her pupils pictures of wild animals that she had mounted on large cards. She was amazed at the speed with which they correctly recognized the animals. Several pointed out the giraffe, elephant, monkey, and lion. Not one had been to a circus or zoo. Some had seen animals in books. When asked, "How did you know this was a giraffe, Edgar?" a child replied, "I see on television." If more of these youngsters came from a talking-family life, more effects would be registered. Their slowness undoubtedly would be less noticeable.

Looking, Listening, and Learning Traveling about in this age of winking neon signs has also influenced the growth of today's young children. Preschoolers who have had good conversational relationships with their families startle us on trips with the number of signs they notice and the way in which they use some signs. Have you ever suggested to a child while riding with him that you would stop to get him an ice cream bar as soon as you saw a place where ice cream was sold and then waited to see if he would spot such a place? Our modern children are keyed to looking, listening, remembering, and using ideas, particularly those that appeal to them. They learn much, all in a seemingly effortless way, merely by being around us in our kind of world.

We can glean much by listening to their dramatic play. Three four-year-old girls playing house beside a porch on which the adult listener sat unnoticed referred to their various tasks. "Come and help me put this mixer together." "I can't come now. First I have to burp the baby, then I have to find the key to my roller skate." "Honey, will you help me?" "How can I help you? That's an old broken mixer." "Well, we can pretend it's a blender and make some sherbet." "No, you don't make sherbet, you get it out of your deep freeze. We do." Into their dramatic play come our modern equipment, daily duties, and language. Observing play experiences of this sort offers teachers and families excellent opportunities to see how closely interwoven with today's life a free young child is and how faithfully his vocabulary and ideas reflect current times.

The high mobility of families can add much to such learning. A good teacher of older age groups becomes acquainted with a new class in September by finding out where the members have lived before, what places they have visited, what foreign countries they know, and what means of travel they have used. Although we all say glibly that ours is an age of travel, it is in this type of conversation with a group of youngsters that the clearer reality of this bland generalization is brought into fuller appreciation.

DOES SCHOOL PUT THE BRAKES ON?

An extremely noticeable human characteristic, and perhaps the one that makes the human animal an interesting subject for study, is our genius for being inconsistent. We accept a change of fashions from season to season, we eagerly sample new, exotic foods, we move from household gadget to household gadget as quickly as the market displays the newer ones; but, when it comes to schools and the educational programs of children, then we may freeze into our nonexploratory moods and demand no changes but rather "business as usual."

The *status quo* attitude of the public affects the school's tempo of change. Here and there among a school staff one is sure to find a self-propelled, absolutely up-to-date educator, always on the lookout for helpful ideas and materials and ready to jog all the others along. In general, however, schools initiate changes very gradually.

This resistance to change, of course, reflects the public—the small but vocal "business as usual" public. We live in an age of strong influence by mass media on even very young children, and yet these same children at kindergarten age may enter schools that are the least changed institution they have met, unlike their homes, unlike their churches, certainly unlike the changing market areas of their early contacts.

To complicate matters more for the school, a marked change in attitude toward children has come about as the result of more knowledge about how children actually function. A large number of teachers, principals, curriculum experts, and others associated with schools, as well as parents, have devoted great efforts to incorporating in their teaching the information on child development that has been made available in recent years. The former method of planning a task carefully for children and then setting them to work at it has given way to increased concern for challenging their interests and taking leads from their reactions.

Professional organizations and in-service workshops have been a great aid in this genuine reconstruction of the profession. There has been a great shift from the former attitude toward children, and this shift is continuing, although it is by no means a fully accomplished fact. The go-slow attitude expressed by individuals and local groups and the pressures of adjusting to overcrowded classrooms and increased demand for able teachers have absorbed time and energy needed for up-dating the program more rapidly.

A CONSPICUOUS LAG

It seems, however, that one of the last places to be affected by increased understanding of how to help children grow through stimulation in living has been in the field of beginning reading. To one fully acquainted with the historical background of the controlled vocabulary trend, especially in primary books and supplementary materials, this comes as no surprise. Yet, to some, it may seem incredible.

The writer once taught an animated young teacher, Jenny M.,

whose entire personal school experience, including high school, had been in private schools in small classes. When traditional practices of the "old school" were described in her teacher-education course, she would ask with an expression of incredulity in face and voice, "How did a thing like that get started?" She hit her all-time high in doubt when vocabulary control came up for discussion.

Many veteran teachers in the same class had grown so accustomed to this influential practice that they had become almost immunized to it. To stimulate their awareness of the elements involved, two five-year-olds from a nearby kindergarten were brought in for a visit. These lively, talkative youngsters, Ellen and Mark, were unafraid to visit with the instructor and class members. "What are you making in the kindergarten these days?" they were asked by way of getting them started to talk, and this conversation followed:

"Oh, we are building a fence for dogs. Once in a while we have dogs that come to visit. They aren't supposed to run around in school, so we are building a fence." "Is it almost finished?" "Not quite, because we need hinges for a gate. It's very high because one of my friends has a golden retriever and he can jump over low fences." "Are you working on the fence too, Ellen?" "No, I'm not much good at building, but we've been washing and ironing all the doll clothes and packing them into a new doll's suitcase. We are almost finished."

When asked their favorite TV programs they mentioned "Kukla, Fran and Ollie" and "The Dave Garroway Show." They liked watching "puppets, chimps, and tough guys" on television.

Imagine one year later these two standing before a group of their peers reading "Oh see! Oh oh, see! See Tom. See Judy." No wonder Jenny M. could not believe some things she heard. To understand them, one must examine the logic that gave birth to what can properly be termed the *Controlled-Vocabulary Era* and examine it in some of its historical setting.

WORD COUNTING AND THE CONTROLLED-VOCABULARY ERA

Following World War I, when group intelligence tests (the Army Alpha and the Army Beta) made their debut, a wave of ambition in research surged in the United States. Reading, because of its great importance to learning, naturally became the focus of literally thousands of inquiries, some minor, some major in value.

The number of failures in reading quite properly came under the researchful eyes of many noted educators, and, as a result, changes were made in both methods and materials. In methods, more silent reading and less oral reading was emphasized because studies indicated that excessive use of oral reading slowed silent reading. Oral reading in unison, which in some schools had a delightful voice-choir quality and through which some of the timid actually grasped the essence of reading, was *verboten.*

The Scientifically Constructed Book Equally large changes came about in materials. The former accumulative tales, such as *This is the House That Jack Built* and *The Old Woman and Her Pig,* were replaced with stories of present-day Jacks and Jills. But these primers and first readers, unlike the old type, were *scientifically* constructed. This was the burgeoning age of science and all things of importance, such as seating equipment, lights, and books, needed to carry the hallowed description "scientifically made."

Primary books were written with vocabularies based on lists of words most frequently found in readers, other books for young children, and several other sources. During the period from 1920 to 1930, word counting was one of the big occupations in graduate schools. It was not surprising to find the word *the* high on the frequency list; *one* is given as the noun highest in use on a much-used frequency study.

Words such as *an, once, no, now, not*—glue words that bind the content together—naturally ranked high. One can neither speak nor write without them. Most of the words high on the lists were of this character, meaningless by themselves, therefore nondramatic to young children; many also were flat in appearance. If a word were high in usage, it was important in primary materials. From this idea, by some twist in logic, many erroneously deduced that *high frequency* words were, *ipso facto, easy words.*

Any adult who has not sensed the dilemma posed to young beginning readers by this error in thinking can quickly sample it, but with his adult advantages, by taking a list of ten words that rate high on any vocabulary list, having them translated into Swedish,

Russian, or any unknown tongue, and practicing pronouncing them and giving their English meaning. This adult experimenter will discover at once that he has so little in content or meaning to clutch at as a hint to his memory that the task is surprisingly difficult.

Let us unravel this matter somewhat further. Additional research found that children could assimilate a limited number of words per page that were new to them in reading. Such limitation controlled the introduction of words essential to meanings, or the chewy stuff, for which we want children to read. For example, if we wanted to write a short dramatic incident—*Jack fell off his bike*—a check on the words might reveal that *fell, off,* and *bike* would be new words, too many to include on one page. To overcome this problem, a picture of a boy falling off his bike and below it the caption *Jack fell* could be used. That would meet the controlled vocabulary standards by placing perhaps only one new word, *fell,* on the page (the assumption being that *Jack* had previously been introduced). It would also get rid of another real problem, the word *bike,* which is too far down on any word list to encourage its use in a beginner's book.

There followed additional researches that showed the advantage of short sentences over the longer, more involved. As a result the well-known short, staccato primer style came into being. In addition came research establishing the number of times it was necessary to repeat a word to aid the child in recognizing it with more certainty: the end result was the "oh-oh-oh, see-see-see" insulting style in primers, preprimers, and primary books. Most of us have heard the effect of this style when a beginning reader takes a deep breath and in unrhythmic gusts reads, "Oh, oh! Oh, look! Look, look."

"Common Experience" Content To complete the picture, one other factor was of genuine concern to primary book producers—the type of experience on which the reading content was to be based. True, the vocabulary was limited to words on lists, but words unique to experiences had to be used in limited number in order to have "stories" or "accounts" or "incidents." The books were planned to be sold across our land, in rural as well as urban

areas, to widely experienced children as well as to children with circumscribed backgrounds, to the north and south, east and west, Negro and white.

The question properly posed became: What subjects will have appeal to all children regardless of location and conditions of growing up? The answer is found in the content: All children know boys and girls, brothers and sisters, fathers and mothers, grandparents, and pets. Although some critics have correctly challenged the writers that these ideas were common, conclusions were practical. But by the time the standards determined by research were applied in writing the books and illustrations of "average" American children and their families were included, the books took on qualities unreal and unalive for the children for whom they were first produced. With the increased use of television and travel, they have grown increasingly less appropriate.

The misfitting qualities are not due to carelessness or incompetence on the part of authors and producers. Indeed, they exercised great care and consistency within the framework set for the job before them. It was the whole concept of research-based "scientific" production and the then acceptable child psychology that were responsible.

Some criticism of the content of beginning books also reflects the fact that changes in our land, not only in psychological insights but also in our social conscience, are constantly developing. In line with this view, the inclusion of Anglo-Saxon, prim, well-groomed children only and no Negroes is frequently mentioned, as well as the exclusive use of children and family situations typifying our middle- to upper-class economic life. More immediate, however, to the first-grader's concern is the lack of come-hither quality for him in the content and pictures. This unfortunately would be difficult to produce within the vocabulary limits prescribed.

Burgeoning of Basal Systems In the late 1920's, basal systems were produced with record speed to include the latest in reading research both in the materials for children's use and also in suggested methods for teaching reading. No place was more up to date, except for the reading specialist's office, than the office of the editor of a basal reading system. And perhaps the most effective teacher and administrator education to permeate the country came from the sales representatives of basal systems. One may question some of their efforts, but the net result for schools as a whole was good and in spots even outstanding.

The combination of emphasis upon "scientific" materials and the redirecting of teaching methods resulted in deeply rooted ideas about beginning reading and classroom practices. It is not surprising, then, that strong adherence to these ideas lingers on today. In fact, it is surprising that the frequency and intensity of challenges should already be so prominent.

One important contribution from these early efforts in vocabulary control and the scientific writing of books for beginners remains a genuinely valuable legacy. These innovaters took some real steps forward in bookmaking for young children. The size of type was increased, and the style was simplified. Serifs were removed from letters, and fonts that bordered on the flowery were discarded. Books were put in attractive covers, and pictures took on real color. All in all, the controlled-vocabulary books for beginners were an improvement over the old drab ones in many ways. Their main lack lay in the psychological poverty of content and style for the understanding of young children.

The Need for a Change Yet, to those who have kept close to the pulse of young children's living, who have noticed their enjoyment of good books and imaginative toys, who have listened to their dramatic play and to their use of the latest language from television and adult happenings, the vocabulary-controlled language and ideas of primary materials are long overdue for a change.

The newer knowledge of how children learn is now being carefully examined for use in devising new materials and methods. Literary writers for children have much to offer here because they have for so long written with an understanding of their young reading audiences. The changes, if adequately faced, will need to be extensive, and they are far from easy to create and put into widespread use. A look at what is entailed will add further significance to this last statement.

WHAT WE HAVE LEARNED ABOUT LEARNING

In an age before young children's feelings had come under careful study, there was a common belief that little children had "little feelings" and, in fact, no feelings at all about many things in life. The myth of "happy early childhood" was still popular. Such ideas were as sound as the then popular belief that all fat men had jovial, nerve-free constitutions. Slowly but surely, careful studies have given us a deeper insight into children's ways of feeling and reacting. It needs to be stated, however, that there have always been warm, intuitive parents and teachers, commonly described as "having a way with children" or being "born parents or teachers." Without benefit of any study of child psychology they seem to use good ways of "bringing out the best" in children. Today's depth psychology throws light on such rare persons, too.

Children's Urge to Learn What are some of the characteristics of children's behavior that should influence the teaching of reading? In previous parts of this book, especially in Chapters 2 and 3, references are made to the ease and eagerness with which young children propel themselves in learning. If they are mentally and physically well—and this concept includes their emotional health also—they are zestful after the new, yet they also cling to the already mastered and the familiar. A new story is followed with wide-open eyes and ears, and an old story is fairly purred over. They need no lessons that prescribe for them what to do, no time schedules, no grades, no marks, yet they are genuinely motivated learners. Of course they can receive more individual attention at home than in nursery school, kindergarten, and first-grade, and the fortunate ones live in a home situation that is planned about their needs and comforts as much as it is about the concerns of adults.

In this early living and learning, no matter whether it be in English, Spanish, or Polish, they master difficult tasks. They learn to speak the family language with proper inflections, idioms, and gestures. They achieve this, first, by being interested; second, by listening and observing; third, by practicing. Language growth for some is extremely rapid. They may take time to learn a few words—*car, milk, dog*—then suddenly they launch into *see car, want milk, see dog.* Many two-year-olds speak clearly and in short sentences. By the time children who have verbal inclinations are five, they speak in compound and complex sentences. Such mature speech is, of course, delayed in slower or less verbal children; it is also delayed in bright children who grow up with too little attention or who are left to themselves too much of the time.

One significant observation belongs here. The language style of preprimers and primers is the short-sentence stage of growth for many at approximately two years of age. These books have another quality out of keeping with talkative five- and six-year-olds. Young children who grow up in a normal, busy family life have rhythmic patterns of speaking. Their first tales have genuine literary quality. Note Judy's report of an incident she had just seen:

> "A boy was zipping along on his scooter
> and his mother called him
> Stop! Stop!
> and he didn't stop
> until he got to the corner."

As a rule their tales have a run-on quality and often a good resounding ending. They have lilt in style as well as drama in content. Some of the old tales, such as *The Rutabaga Woman,* had these qualities too.

Their Versatility in Learning. All the while young children are learning to speak they are also acquiring countless other skills: learning to ride tricycles, carts, and scooters; to walk on balancing beams and sidewalk cracks; to climb, to jump, and to push and pull anything that is loose. They also learn how to socialize, how to gain possession of the one-of-a-kind scoop shovel, how to steel oneself against a competitor, and how to stall at bedtime. They learn how to fight and how to make up. They also learn which adult means business when he gives instructions and which adult is "just talking."

The surprising fact to many who relished Lilliputian concepts of young children is that children feel big—most of the time. Even as early as three and three-and-a-half, the child before us is a *girl,* not a tot. She needs to feel big and adequate and wishes to sound that way, too. "Little ideas" for "little people" are not for her. Neither are "kiddy" words. The new refrigerator is a Frigidaire, the car is an Oldsmobile, and her new dress is a "piqué party dress." Unlike the image previously held of young children, they are highly sensitive to their status; therefore, their desire for us to respect their bigness deserves our careful attention.

They also enjoy the exciting, the unusual, and the colorful. This is observable in the way they quickly attach new words to their vocabulary. For example, Mr. Anders, in the presence of his four-year-old son Tommy, reported to his wife one evening, just after he had come home from work, that Mr. K., their neighbor, had been arrested. "Not arrested!" gasped Mrs. Anders. Immediately, Tommy caught the stir of the unusual and asked, "What's arrested?" Both Mr. and Mrs. Anders assured Tommy that it was "not much, just stopping from work a while." But Tommy was not fooled. The following day he told Mrs. K. that her husband had been arrested. The lesson is not only that adults should be cautious because little pitchers have big ears, but also that if one wants children to learn, one must offer them some spark and excitement from time to time.

Young children not only are alert to sudden sparks in language but are masters of one-word exclamations. Many parents have found it difficult to cope with their youngsters' excursions into toilet talk and other highly personal matters. One father, to save his family's reputation in the neighborhood into which they had just moved, suggested to his four-year-old son Bill that the *worst* name to call anyone was a *sprat,* but not to use it unless he was "really mad." This technique worked successfully. It is a tribute to the power and persistence of young children that they can bring a word into popular usage almost simultaneously across the United States. They did precisely this with *stinker,* did they not?

Learning in Spurts When we examine the manner in which children space their learning, we note that they have sudden flashes; there is excitement, and then there may be pauses of seeming neglect and a wandering off to another field of interest. At a later time we may note a return to the former experience and the practice related to it. Usually, they keep one iron hot at a time. When learning to climb, they use every piece of furniture, even chests of drawers, as pieces of climbing apparatus. When they explore some new type of play in socializing with chums, this form of play is carried on both morning and afternoon for several days. They really work at new adventures—but these new adventures must contain an element that appeals.

Not only do young children specialize in their learning process, concentrating usually on one thing at a time, but they also need to have more complicated learnings broken down so that they can proceed one step at a time. A four-year-old with his first jigsaw puzzle was noticed dumping it out on a table, then replacing the pieces right side up but with no attempt at proper placement. Only then, after these first experiments, did he begin to place two pieces together.

Interest Span Young children also space themselves between high activity and rest, or a change of activity. The tempo of this spacing varies with the child and with the activity. Studies of interest spans in the very young have presented some generalizations, but in working with young children, including those in primary grades, discerning teachers have estimated the interest span of the children by watching them in action. For example, a substitute teacher in a kindergarten with thirty-four five-year-olds was hard pushed to find some way of containing their restless energies until noon dismissal. So far, during the morning, they had concentrated on no single experience for more than a few minutes. She found a large box of scraps of colored construction paper and hit upon the idea of pasting. "Youngsters do love to paste," she said, "but I thought of each sitting quietly at his table and putting pieces of paper together." Instead, one child in a clowning gesture pasted a long green strip on the blackboard. The teacher remarked approvingly, "That's a good idea, because that blackboard does look so homely with no color on it." A mass production ensued. All the youngsters pasted colored pieces all over the entire board, using chairs to reach the higher section.

When suddenly the dismissal bell rang, the children uttered a protest. They were not ready to quit the project. As the teacher reported, "I myself couldn't believe it was eleven forty-five, the time flew so fast. And those wiggly little rebels had worked at this with no fights, waiting for their turns, for more than thirty minutes."

In general, the attention span of these very young children is shorter than thirty minutes, but they are capable of staying for longer periods with what fascinates them. Kindergartens and primary schools have been extremely conscientious on this point. Seldom does one visit a group of young children who are held at work or play for a period of time that is unduly long for them; as a result they are spared boredom and the problems created by lack of interest.

Increasing Learning Efforts Through Satisfaction Of great importance to note is their need for success in their efforts. Watch a child with a new toy. If he can manipulate it in a way that is satisfying to him, he plays with it. If he exhausts its possibilities and can improvise no other way of playing with it, he discards it. If it yields to him in no way, he ignores it at once. The feeling he seems to convey for himself is: I must wiggle, manage, use. When something resists this need, to urge him to continue is to threaten his fun of learning.

Occasionally, an understanding person can give him the just-right hint or proper touch. The child then pushes off the aid to see how far he can go on his own. Every healthy youngster, as a part of this powerful drive to add up to a competent human being, needs to increase his independence. As discussed in Chapter 2, these developing creatures want to be on their own, and in preschool years they demonstrate this by taking on important jobs of self-management such as eating unaided, dressing and undressing, and getting about safe places in the neighborhood unattended.

Success in pushing out the boundaries of what they know and what they can do is naturally linked with their need to display their powers and to win approval—and, occasionally, to raise eyebrows. To a child at ease with himself, the need for such display is not showing off in the undesirable sense but more nearly akin to giving a progress report. It is similar to the desire of a hostess to serve an absolutely perfect lemon meringue pie of her own baking or the natural tendency for a young professional man to call attention to "a nice piece about me in the press." It is when the need for praise and attention tends to stop the joyful side of activity and when approval is sought for almost every piece of activity that a youngster needs to be helped to find more satisfaction in the doing and not so much in the reactions. Other reasons for such behavior too should be considered.

Young But Strong Personalities Finally, a quality which is always a delight to recognize but one which causes many of the dilemmas in teaching youngsters to read is their strong individuality. Although we may talk about the "sassy fours" and the "restless fives," they themselves refuse to be grouped, averaged, or typed. Each, in his way, must get attention.

This outstanding quality was brought home with force to a former teacher of junior-high-school mathematics who argued against a single salary schedule, saying, "Imagine, paying a person as much to teach kindergarten as to teach math! Why, all a kindergarten teacher needs to do with those little bunnies is to push them around." Then, in her own words, she let the elementary-school principal "twist her arm to just hold school" in the kindergarten one wintry day when the regular teacher was ill.

She accepted, and at noon that day she gave an account of the gift five-year-olds have for being able to exasperate. She had never experienced such power in a junior-high-school mathematics class. "If they don't want to do something, they just don't. That little Emma sat there and wouldn't budge. Imagine! And they say she's not very bright. Well, she didn't have to be to get my goat."

It is easy to gather similar evidence of the strong individualities these children possess. Ask anyone who works with them.

SEEKING BETTER WAYS TO TEACH READING

These descriptions of preschoolers or prereaders are simple to understand and accept. Application of this knowledge in teaching them to read is a more serious matter. For years this has been a recognized need, but recognized also as an extremely difficult one. W. H. Auden's surprise that we presume to teach young children to learn to read in groups, rather than individually, as he was tutored, is warranted.

The fact that young children, strong individualists as they are, accept group instruction and profit by it is surprising. Evidence now available revealing that our schools have done so well in the past few years, and under circumstances that could be highly inhibiting, is a testimonial of their professional strength and competence. It also reflects favorably on the value of the reading materials used.

The focus of the present quest is to eliminate the failures that still occur and to produce even stronger, more able readers with our current knowledge than we were able to do before. Valiant efforts have been in process, but more new ground needs to be broken. From the foregoing description of preschool qualities, certain guidelines for beginning reading materials seem to emerge.

The Fallacy of All-Purpose Books One can see that, in the light of our newer knowledge of child development, beginning reading materials can never be made to fit all needs merely by modifying them. For example, it is doubtful that any one book will ever be precisely right as a preprimer for all the sprouting readers of this land. Universality in materials—particularly for beginners—is incongruous with the facts. One can immediately follow within the logic of this idea to the next: namely, that the block-buying or adopting of beginning books for basic use is no more feasible than is the attempt to produce a book that will be just right for every child.

Another side of the problem must be dealt with equally ruthlessly. The project of producing, through limiting vocabulary and repeating words, a book that will be right for the limited reading power of the beginner and still be a *book* has proved to have insurmountable difficulties. Either the content has appeal and literary quality but an "unscientific" vocabulary, or the vocabulary and word count are acceptable but the content cannot truly be called a book. The aim to make a book its own teaching device, even with the addition of elaborate aids, seems not only futile, but a travesty of children's wholesome preschool knowledge and enjoyment of books.

A child, to become a reader, must come to grips with recognizing letters, phonograms, words, and their sounds, with the left-to-right process of reading English, with the careful reading to follow the author's ideas, and so on. The idea that the core of such learning must be woven around a basal book forms the nub of the problem to be challenged by those who feel a better way must be found to launch beginners.

These two long-existing practices, attempting to fit one book to the backgrounds and interests of *all* children and attempting to devise a controlled-vocabulary book with genuine book merit, seem out of step with children and how they learn. The result for far too many children has been a book that had the *oh, see, look* drivel, an affront to their respectability. It also may have altered the respect they already had acquired for good books from early experiences.

LIFTING OUR SIGHTS FOR BEGINNING READERS

The contrast between a preschool child's exploratory enjoyment of books and the almost wooden method and materials of his preprimer and primer reading period has been lessening over the years. However, the evidences of progress and true insights have been more frequently found in forward-looking schools and in enlightened classrooms than in large countrywide movements. An exception has been the two theories discussed in the previous chapter, one emphasizing the experience approach to reading and the other the individual method. Both are within the potential frame of promise for newer and even better approaches to teaching young children to read.

Fortunately, there are about us many alert educators and lay citizens who respect the fact that the field of education, like the fields of science and medicine, is a live, growing field. We add to our knowledge, and this in turn causes us to alter certain of our customs, discard others, while retaining some. Tomorrow's readers will be able to achieve greater reading power than even our best have done, if we continue to seek for sounder, more helpful, and more inspiring ways of building their first approach to reading consistent with their way of learning.

SUGGESTED READINGS ON VOCABULARY

FOX, LORENE K., and BROGAN, PEGGY. *Helping Children Read.* New York: Holt, Rinehart and Winston, Inc., 1961.
The emphasis is upon developing selective and independent reading through individualizing the use of books.

GANS, ROMA. *Guiding Children's Reading Through Experiences.* New York: Bureau of Publications, Teachers College, Columbia University, 1941.
Experiences in beginning reading at home and at school, with nonrestricted vocabulary described.

HUNNICUTT, C. W., and IVERSON, WILLIAM J. *Research in the Three R's.* New York: Harper & Brothers, 1958. Chapters 4 and 7.
Outstanding researches in readability and vocabulary control are briefed. A good starting point for one interested in research in this field.

MOORE, ELEANORA HAEGELE. *Fives at School.* New York: G. P. Putnam's Sons, 1959. Chapter 7.
Description of a kindergarten program for urban children that extends children's vocabularies and shows relationship between background and reading readiness. Good for parents and teachers.

SMITH, MARY KATHERINE. *Measurement of the Size of General English Vocabulary Through the Elementary Grades and High School.* Genetic Psychology Monographs, 24, November 1941. Pp. 311-345.
This study found that some children at the end of the first grade had a vocabulary of 35,000 words. (This was before the advent of television.) Technical style.

CHAPTER 8

Making Gains in Independent Reading Power

The child's years in the second and third grades seem to be calm in contrast with the beleaguered first-grade year. People at home and school seem relieved and exultant when six-year-olds manage to go through the first grade and emerge from it. The pervasive concern among adults over phonics in particular and beginning-reading methods in general is not as evident after first grade.

With the entrance to second and third grades also comes a noticeable shift from day-after-day encouragement and work on beginning reading to a more inclusive emphasis on all the skills, particularly arithmetic and spelling, and on the continuation of social studies, science, and the arts. The teacher rightfully assumes that the majority of pupils are on the road to success in reading skills and are ready to push ahead in other phases of the curriculum, along with their continuing growth as readers.

The same curriculum emphases that affect the program in the first grade are usually present in second and third grades and, in most schools, throughout all the elementary years. The pressures noticeably felt about the teaching of reading in the first grade, although less evident in second grade, may reappear to some extent in the third, especially in reference to the slow learners. Both parent and teacher concerns quicken if a child in the third grade persists in demonstrating less nimble learning patterns than many of his contemporaries. Youngsters not successful in reading may by now become articulate about their lack of enthusiasm for school. At the ages of seven and eight, they begin to be aware of their status within a group, and they become more conscious of being achievers or nonachievers. Some acquire techniques of evasion to hide from teacher and classmates their difficulties with learning.

CONTINUING TO FOSTER INDIVIDUAL SKILL IN READING

Beginning-of-the-Year Inventory Assessment of each child's progress by the teacher at the beginning of the year is commonly practiced throughout the schools of the United States. A sensible teacher recognizes the immediate need for becoming acquainted with each member of the total group. What is his state in reading? How adequately does he express himself? How does he write? What are the evidences that he applies phonics in spelling? Is he a worker, showing the beginnings of good independent study? What interests does he display? How eager is he to tackle new adventures in learning? How dogged and persistent is he? Does he seem well, vigorous, and happy?

The answers to many of these and similar questions are acquired by the teacher much as any person getting acquainted with newcomers "sizes them up." An observant teacher gathers much information even in one week's time. Answer to some questions are obtained by analyzing responses on tests (standardized, basal-book, or teacher-constructed), especially in schools where emphasis on individual skill development is stressed. Records of the previous year and transcripts from other schools are also scanned for added information.

Some schools keep bleak records that yield little information to an inquiring teacher. Others maintain anecdotal records, which are found more helpful. Some teachers question the desirability of recording anything other than the minimum facts, lest the child's next teacher be prejudiced by certain data. A sage Pennsylvania principal handled the matter of avoiding prejudicial recording by making the following statement to the teachers each year: "First, aim to *like* each pupil; second, gather all the information you can about each one. If you work on the first point, the second will take care of itself."

Common Goals in Second and Third Grades The goals articulated and followed by schools vary, but guiding the seven- and eight-year-olds to become increasingly independent in reading is one purpose accepted in all classrooms. For children to become independent, continuing growth in word-recognition skills must be nurtured. Help is continued in the study of phonics and phonemes, in structural analysis of words, and in knowing and applying rules for word pronunciation. Checks on comprehension include instructions and questions more complicated than those used in first grade. Increased emphasis on spelling and writing add to the child's reading skills and also offer the teacher evidence of a child's achievement. Beginning with the second grade, additional textbooks are introduced. Spellers and simple number workbooks are used in most schools. Some schools defer additional textbooks, however, to third grade, because they prefer to teach the development of early skills in relation to curriculum experiences.

THE GRADE-LEVEL TEXT DILEMMA

A common textbook for all class members presents one of the most serious problems in today's classrooms. For a number of the children, sometimes as many as fifty per cent, the textbooks add to their reading problem. For the least advanced, the books may be utterly useless; for others, much personal help from the teacher, even where the book is in limited use, is essential. Often youngsters find an arithmetic text too difficult for their reading power as well as for their mathematics skills. They need simpler books and other materials, closely related to their experiences. Therefore, some schools do not use a common text in any subject in second and third grades. Such schools are in the minority, however.

To any reasonable person, the problem created by supplying all children in any given grade with identical textbooks is clear. Within a year variations between those who take all learning, especially reading growth, in stride, and those who make little or no discernible progress are grossly evident. It is not uncommon on reading tests to find the range in second grade from zero or low first-grade ability to fourth-grade and even higher ability. Such variation does not reflect on children, on their parents, or on the school. The well-established fact is that children of any given grade are not identical in learning tendencies; in many ways, they are not even similar. The quality of responsible leadership of schools can be judged by the methods used in facing the differences among children, which not only persist from kindergarten through their entire school career, but grow more involved and complicated as children grow older. Of real concern should be not only the waste of money on inappropriate, even useless, books, but more especially the crippling frustration felt by the less mature child because the texts are too difficult, and the boredom and loss in learning felt by the more able reader because of the lack of challenge.

Fortunately fewer and fewer schools persist in using a single text in the early grades. Instead there is a growing trend to provide a variety of books, workbooks, and all manner of teaching materials and library resources, with a wide range of difficulty as well as broad variation in content, and to encourage their use. The importance of an ample supply of materials cannot be overemphasized. Where the supply of materials is inadequate, a competent teacher is denied the essential tools for teaching and often more than half the students are being denied their right to helpful, rather than harmful, education.

Anyone can readily deduce from the foregoing that in schools where goals are expressed in terms of work on grade-level texts, an in-service program of education is sorely needed. No matter how skillful and conscientious the teacher, some children cannot develop the degree of ability needed to derive any value from the grade-level text. Some of us can still remember classmates who were compelled to sit with an open book before them and simulate interest while the teacher called upon the lucky ones who, chiefly by the good fortune of being born with learning power, could decipher the correct answers from the book without pausing to think. Much effort in teaching has been wasted by teachers who tried, through all manner of techniques, to help slower readers "catch up" in reading ability in order to read the common text book. Basic to this practice was the belief that a child's learning opportunities were limited to what he could draw from the grade-level texts. Although these narrow ideas of a child's learning and of the curriculum content have not been completely discarded, only in retarded school situations are they in operation.

Reaching the Individual Child via Group Work A wide variety of methods for dealing with the widening range of abilities of pupils is now in use. Perhaps the most common practice is to divide the class into three or more groups, depending upon ability. Materials appropriate to each group are then provided to facilitate their learning. A common current method is to purchase six to ten copies of a variety of texts rather than whole sets of one book.

As a child's reading power grows, he is able to help himself more and more. Good teaching not only utilizes the child's self-management ability but also is directed toward increasing it. Story and information books that he can read independently further his reading interest and success. Skill-building materials are also pertinent, because many include simple instructions for doing a given exercise and also self-checking techniques for the child to use independently of the teacher's aid. Some give the scores considered normal for the exercise so that he can evaluate his own work.

Three groups, and sometimes more, may be guided simultaneously. The teacher goes from group to group, giving help and support as needed. Some teachers prefer to arrange their schedules so that only one group at a time is working on reading, while other pupils are at work on individual reading or other studies, dramatic play, painting, or activities of a relatively quiet nature. Obviously those with least independence need more assistance than do those with greater power. However, no matter how carefully the dispersal of aid is planned, able teachers lament the limits of time and the burdens created for such young, immature children by classes larger than twenty-five.

Time for the Individual Plodders and Speeders Frequently, especially in the second grade, several youngsters are still so much in need of individual help in reading that the teacher works with them individually while the others are engaged in groups. The mature, rapid learners also need individual help to keep them forging ahead. Devotion of adequate time and uninterrupted attention to the needs of both types of children demands high-level classroom management. Many truly professional teachers indicate that the lack of sufficient time for work with youngsters on an individual basis is one of their greatest frustrations. So sincere is the concern of responsible educators for the success of every child's reading that many schools with meager budgets have extended their services to include specialists in guidance and in reading. Grateful tributes should be paid to those schools for demonstrating their faithfulness to duty: to do all that is possible to give each child the best education possible for him.

Meeting the needs of the plodders has progressed more rapidly than meeting the needs of the sprightly learners. Due regard for individual potentiality reveals the double-barreled need to help not only the slow reader but also those avid readers who "eat up" books, exercises, and learning projects of all kinds. As one teacher aptly put it, "I no sooner get the advanced group at work and turn to my next group than I hear the chairman of the first group call out 'We're finished.' " Planning for such youngsters demands that they share in outlining their next reading pursuits, which should be extensive enough to continue beyond one day. Short, sketchy lessons prevent these children from developing their full potentiality. They flourish in a curriculum planned with respect for their increasing powers.

Focusing on plans for a reading program that encourages attention to the individual, both as an individual and as a member of a group, produces the most satisfactory ways and rates of children's learning. It is safe to conjecture that in the future more materials and means of using them for skill development, not only in reading but in all other skills, will fill an ever-widening school demand.

PROBING NEW DEPTHS IN COMPREHENSION

At the ages of seven and eight, boys and girls are ready to sprout in comprehension beyond the timid or hesitant manner of earlier years. They show pride in "thinking things out" for themselves. Intellectually, they reveal a process of cutting the apron string which, with proper guidance, represents an important growth for them. Discussion of their reading offers many opportunities for the teacher to encourage them to think independently and test out their own feelings and ideas.

Encouragement of independent intellectual reactions to reading requires attention to comprehension—that is, the ability to understand what is read. A child needs the inducement to react for himself, to grow in sensing what he likes or does not like, and—at times—to understand why. He also needs opportunities to bring his previous knowledge to bear on some items he reads and to react in light of his knowledge. For example, a second-grader who read a story about the farmer feeding his cows commented, "That farmer couldn't be living on a ranch because on my uncle's ranch the cows feed themselves."

Discussions shared by the whole class on questions of common interest and discussions by smaller groups or by several individuals on special interests lead children to struggle with ideas and learn to think for themselves. The usual comprehension tests that ask for true-false, yes-no, or other short answers serve as a check of a child's ability to understand points and relationships expressed in the content. This ability is basic for true understanding of what is read. A child must be able to grasp the specifics in order to follow with his personal interpretation or reaction to what he has read.

Written reactions may often serve as an outlet for the older child's deeper understanding. Second- and third-grade children may not yet have acquired the skill in writing to express themselves explicitly. Therefore, for them, allowing them to talk things over is a teacher's more helpful technique. "We need a good story to read at story hour. When you find one that you would recommend, tell me about it"; and "You read our own report of our trip to the mountain cave. Read it again and see if we have put in all the points of the trip you think are important"; and "Look at the news items on the bulletin board. Decide which ones you think are still important to us and should be kept posted." These are characteristic of suggestions that stir children to read, to pause, and to think. Chapters 10 and 11 include further descriptions of important qualities of comprehension and ways of developing them. The primary grades can make a genuine contribution to each child in helping him become a thinking reader.

STUDY HABITS IN RELATION TO CURRICULUM THEORY

Able second- and third-grade readers can pursue reference reading, prepare materials, and develop skills we formerly thought possible only for older, more mature minds. Furthermore, these youngsters are able to work in teams or committees through which, at this early age, they increase their ability to give and take intellectually. Experience in planning their individual work and group curriculum studies with the teacher gives them a chance to see the purpose in their work. They develop the ability to look ahead, to plan next steps, and to be genuinely interested (therefore, motivated) in what they are doing. As a result, the word "study" takes on real meaning for them.

Formerly, the ability to study was treated as if it rested solely upon a child's willingness to sit quietly and carry out whatever happened to be the assignment. Then, as now, students were commonly described as having *good study habits* or *poor study habits.* With more adequate understanding of the complexity of this business of reading and the even greater complexity of the means by which a youngster understands what he is doing, direct teaching of study techniques has received more attention. The results have been promising.

Because reading is such an essential tool in study, helping youngsters to read properly in relation to studying has become an integral part of good reading programs. Such help starts with the beginning school years. From their work in the kindergarten, pupils learn to prepare their supplies for whatever they plan to do and to show and report on what they have done; they also learn to "clean up and put away." Anyone who has observed much older children sit down to study only to bob up again and again "to get my other book," or "to get the dictionary," or for any other reason is aware of the important learning that can be acquired in an effective kindergarten program.

There are some specific abilities in addition to some general skills that make it possible for a child to give full attention to his work. Many of these powers demand reading skills that cannot be assumed to sprout out of the ability to recognize words and to report or give back what has been read.

A teacher in an Illinois second grade became deeply interested in developing good work habits in her pupils. During the first two months of school, they had been taught by several substitutes. When she became their teacher late in October, they were restless and quick to dispatch any work assigned. She made a list of the study skills to be developed during the year. Among those she considered most essential for this group was learning to carry out a purpose in reading. In looking through second-grade readers on a shelf for Halloween stories, a committee of three browsed hurriedly and came up with the report, "Only one story." Upon further examination, with the teacher's help, they found four. On a number of occasions, in checking on an item in a story or rereading to see, "Did the author tell us what the time of year was?" or a similar question, the teacher noticed hasty, half-serious reading by able pupils.

Perhaps some of these brighter youngsters had already caught the why-do-more-than-necessary spirit characteristic not only of some older youths but unfortunately of many adult workers too. Reading, to be properly developed, must frequently be applied to some serious and even laborious purposes that demand staying with the work until the task has been carefully finished. To be sure that superficial, and often careless, habits do not become ingrained, primary teachers, like this teacher in Illinois, try to educate children to use reading in studying with care and with an attitude of responsibility.

Sprouting Study Skills Early Not many years ago teaching children techniques to help themselves began in the intermediate grades. The function of the primary grades was merely to give children the *tools with which to study*, to learn to read in particular; the youngsters would then be ready to use these tools in the intermediate grades.

At the time this emphasis was current, I observed three children in a family use that household encyclopedia, the Sears, Roebuck catalogue, to make up their list of requests for Christmas. The seven-year-old boy, the youngest of the trio, used the index to find *skates,* turned to the correct page, studied the content with great seriousness, then took up his pencil and wrote on a slip of paper the catalogue number of the skates and their price. Note the skills that this second-grader was exercising, from the use of an index to making a memorandum of essential data. He probably learned these essential study skills by himself through the family's mail-order curriculum.

Not all children have the initiative and opportunity to become so competent independently, but they can do it with teacher guidance. Before a child engages in study, he must be charged with interest and eagerness. The boy in the example given was sufficiently interested in the skates to want to undertake the work of looking up information, reading it, and writing down some essential data.

Basing Study on Comprehension The next essential for study is the child's ability to understand what is read. Many teachers and parents have seen a child "dig out" meaning from content they thought too difficult "because he wanted to know it." This is a key point to be kept in mind in careful teaching.

It is when one considers the varied uses to which reading is put that the real meaning of comprehension takes the center of the stage. So-called formal education in earlier times put great emphasis on one phase of comprehension, the ability to read and comprehend for recall. This one part of reading comprehension gave rise to the author's description of some reading programs as "spit-back" affairs.

To be able to read a short story or description in the first or the second grade, to be able to tell it, to remember the characters and incidents—these are absolutely essential aspects of comprehension. To stop with these abilities, however, is to stop short of the skills essential to the personal involvement of the reader, skills he is called upon to use in successful reading in everyday life.

Today, instead of regarding the development of the wide variety of reading functions as a by-product of the ability to pronounce more and more difficult words and to give accurate answers to short comprehension checks, teachers, starting in second and third grades, develop such functions as an integral part of the total reading program. Many schools have worked out guides for teachers to use in teaching children the multiple skills they are ready to master in the grades. Professional literature, manuals in reading systems, and skill texts also provide valuable help.

The scope and variety of techniques vary with the curriculum emphases. In schools that accent social studies and science, children are offered certain opportunities that may not commonly occur in a school that puts stress more exclusively on the "3 R's" in the primary grades. For example, the second-graders who studied "How the Post Office Helps Our School" had the following reading-study experiences:

1. Planning and writing the outline, or steps, of their study. This helped youngsters grow in sensing sequence, in planning next steps, and in testing out their ability to anticipate work to be done.
2. Sorting incoming school mail for a week as to whether it was *first class, second class, parcel post,* or *fourth class.*
3. Tabulating the data under (2).
4. Sorting outgoing school mail each day for a week as to *first class, second class, parcel post,* or *fourth class.*
5. Tabulating the data under (4).
6. Writing a report to keep as a record of their study.
7. Making a report to the other two second grades of the school.

The planning, organizing, tabulating, writing, and reporting demanded techniques used in careful study. The sorting and classifying of mail utilized careful reading for certain points. The teacher reported that this study seemed to alert children to observation of labels, methods of presenting data, and keeping records far beyond the ability she had commonly expected of second-graders. The work was done in teams so that all children—including slower readers—shared in some part.

Each project requires reading and work appropriate to the purposes of the activity, as the following experience reveals. A third grade in a rural county of New Jersey made a helpful study for the entire school. The class members had been discussing the plan for their topic in social studies, *Transportation: Then and Now.* At the start of this discussion, a new student was enrolled in the class. His father was a pilot for an international flight company. "Good," said a youngster, "he can tell us about up-to-date flying." Another added quickly, "And we can find out from books too."

In planning the work of this class, the teacher appointed a committee of three boys; one was the pilot's son, another a mature reader, and the third, Leon, a mild-mannered, slow worker who was just beginning to read simple books with some evidence of independence. These three were to find all available material in classroom and library books that was related to contemporary flying. Other committees were assigned to other parts of the study.

At the conclusion of the project, the committee members (1) described the books they had examined, including an encyclopedia and the classroom texts; (2) presented samples of stories and articles found on flying—none up to date (no jet mentioned); (3) showed pictures of planes found in various books, to indicate "the latest" available. Deeply involved in every part of the report was Leon. At the end of the report, he held up a third-grade reader, "with a good story about flying in it that I am working at."

Igniting the Spark of Critical Reading Powers In the experience just described, eight-year-olds were going beyond reading-to-understand. They were reading to assess in terms of a given criterion—up-to-dateness. They commented on the copyright dates of the readers in their room; none was new. They found the encyclopedia a "much too old" edition to have value on a subject as contemporary as modern flying. They also found the school library meager in the number of books that included any material on the topic of transportation. Richard, the mature reader, said, "We certainly found the tables of contents and indexes handy."

Evaluating materials in terms of their relatedness to a certain quest may not be considered reading comprehension by everyone. Some define the term *reading* as the recognition of the meanings of letters and phonemes in terms of their pronunciation. To others, comprehension is a literal matter, not extending as far as personal reaction and assessment in terms of use or even quality of content. Such matters are termed "thinking," as differentiated from reading.

This author's interpretation of comprehension includes the individual's reaction to his reading in relation to the wider context in which he is reading. A youngster in the New Jersey third grade described, for example, may understand every item of the story about an airplane but may be unable to understand or comprehend whether it does or does not give information on contemporary transportation.

To some, this entire point regarding comprehension may be academic. To the author, however, the point is central to the school's whole effort to teach readers whose comprehension fits them for the exacting reading of our time. In other words, comprehension is not merely an exercise in literal understanding of "what it says"; it is a fool-proofing process rooted in the proper concern for functional literates. The acceptance of this point of view must then be reflected in the reading program and the entire curriculum.

Some children as young as those in the second and third grades and even younger can develop the ability to keep to the purpose for which they are reading; others may need much help and frequent reminding. A challenging purpose for reading is a primary need for all. Keeping at the task and remembering the reason for doing the task is apparently easier for some than for others. The scatter-brained youngster who, if left unaided, becomes the scatter-brained adult needs much help to follow through on some set goals—perhaps help of a personal nature unrelated to reading ability. An invaluable contribution to a child's lifetime effectiveness is made by teachers who give adequate attention to developing purposeful readers. Through such efforts, children become persistent and conscientious students.

READING IN RELATION TO OTHER SUBJECTS

The nature of the material read determines some of the skills required in reading. Simple story materials have sequence, but the relationship of items in a story may not be as crucial as it is in reading even a simple problem in arithmetic. "Mary started to school. She took her books and a new pencil box. On the way to school she lost one of her books. She did not go to look for it. She wanted to get to school on time," has items to understand, a sequence, and connections between the items. These qualities are not of the same order, however, as, "Mary started to school with four things—three books and one pencil box. On the way to school she lost one book. How many things did Mary have when she got to school?"

Here, the whole point of reading is focused in the answer to one question. The accuracy of the answer depends on the child's ability to understand the items, to note the sequence, to relate them to one another in such a way that they indicate the answer to the question. Suggesting to young workers that they keep the question in mind or reread with the question in mind may be essential for many who are not able to manage the story containing the arithmetic problem without some help, although they can read the first story with accurate comprehension.

The various school subjects call forth innumerable reading skills that the teacher helps pupils develop. Many teaching materials address instructions for work directly to the children. This practice is common in arithmetic pamphlets, in workbooks, and in sections of some readers. However, written instructions, without which no modern-day cook could prepare a meal nor a do-it-yourself man assemble a lawn mower, demand certain responses from a reader. First, one must read carefully to understand what one is to do; second, one must proceed a step at a time, rechecking as often as necessary to be sure that the end product comes out right.

So too with children's instructions for how-to-do exercises. If such instructions are created and supervised by those who understand today's children, they can be extremely challenging and helpful. Many classroom situations arise that demand careful reading of instructions; instructions for mixing paints, cooking recipes, directions in a science book for using a compass, can all be used as learning opportunities. A teacher, if time permits, uses all situations of this kind to be sure that children become competent in this exacting reading.

The Power of Challenging At second- and third-grade age, the more independent reader is beginning to read informational materials that require skills he has not previously found necessary. A third-grade child, reading an account of "The Penny Shortage" that appeared in *My Weekly Reader* several years ago, finished reading the article to himself, thought for a moment, then said "How did all the kids get started to save all the pennies all at once?" The teacher, a sensitive person who gathered much information about children's thinking from such comments, said, "Your question is making me think, too. I didn't know there were so many penny-savers in the United States." From this exchange, they continued to discuss and react to this news story.

In this situation, it was not comprehension of the content that was the arresting skill but rather the child's power of challenging the plausibility of it. In reading on topics that interest them, alert youngsters may, at times, go beyond the context to raise questions. They begin to challenge authorship, date of writing, and other factors important to certain fields of information. Such reading experiences are implicit in teaching children to become mature readers according to goals stated in Chapter 2. Work in the second and third grades can do much to foster this growth.

The foregoing example calls to our attention an ability that many adults claim they need, the ability to accept or reject ideas read in light of their own background of experience and knowledge. Some of us would like to believe all we read; we see a neon halo over the printed word. Some children may be like that, too. If we read strong pro and strong con statements on a controversial topic, how do we react? Some of us might wish for *one* point of view only, forgetting that in our land, thanks to our Bill of Rights, many viewpoints are freely discussed and written about, but that it is our privilege to accept or reject according to our own preferences. Had we been properly taught we might feel more at home in sifting the ideas we read, especially in controversial areas, before arriving at our decision.

Children, even in primary reading, run into ideas that make them ponder, which is right, this or that? Or they may react as did the third-grader who questioned the penny-saving dilemma. Even in the first grade, a question of *which is right?* may arise, as happened in a first grade near Philadelphia. A child brought in a version of *The Three Bears* story in which the bears welcomed Goldilocks when they found her in their house. A great protest was raised by another girl, who said she had that same story in a book at home; in her story, she said, Goldilocks did not receive such kind treatment from the bears and ran home "terribly scared."

The teacher, one of those dauntless souls who neither skips over the matter nor puts on her hearing dimmers when youngsters open up "sixty-four-dollar" questions, commented: "You're right. That's a different version. A version is one way of telling a story. In Judy's, the version is that the bears were glad to have Goldilocks. Your version is different. In yours, they were angry at Goldilocks, and she jumped out of the window and ran home."

News items from different presses may vary in details of local happenings. The weather is often a point of discussion, because the facts vary with the forecast. Early in life, under wise guidance, children can deal in their own way with these challenges in reading and grow so accustomed to them that, as adults, when they meet divergent views, they will not become irked and wish for a uniform, streamlined world. On the contrary, they will take time to become informed and thus formulate their own independent views.

BRANCHING OUT IN READING INTERESTS

Some reading skills are developed in relation to stories in books. Children are ready to notice plot, suspense, and sequence. Through wide reading of good books, they also become sensitive to other elements in literature. They acquire taste, some beginning preferences for stories of nature or technology, for true-to-life experiences of boys and girls or imaginative tales. They grow in their knowledge of poetry and, under the leadership of a good teacher, develop genuine satisfaction in getting to know A. A. Milne, Edward Lear, Dorothy Aldis, Robert Frost, and other poets.

Their ability to get to know and enjoy good books is burgeoning. In fact, it was the widespread expression of children's satisfaction with such books as *Millions of Cats,* by Wanda Gag, *The Story About Ping,* by Marjorie Flack, and *Mike Mulligan and His Steam Shovel,* by Virginia Lee Barton, that helped catapult these books into such popularity. Children who have ample chances to enjoy books in a good reading program can actually affect the book market and influence publishers and literary standards.

As the personal reading of books grows, children, of necessity, learn other essential techniques. After putting a book aside for a day or two, they learn to browse quickly to review what was previously read, before going on to the next part. They also experience the desire to read faster, in order to progress more rapidly with the story. Sometimes, like us, they skim, reading the high points to be sure to reach the end before the book must be returned to the library. Not all second- or third-grade readers may be this mature, but the majority are moving in this direction.

If a child is frustrated by an occasional vocabulary block but eager to proceed faster, the teacher can encourage him to improve the word-recognition skill needed. His discovery that reading is exciting and rewarding will motivate him to push himself to master the skill he needs.

Guiding and Evaluating the Child's Extensive Reading Children across the nation are reading more and more extensively. Much of this reading is inspired and encouraged in good school programs; but, although the school may be actively concerned only with curriculum reading, the appeal to children of some books that come to their attention is so strong that they "take" to book reading.

Saturday public-library programs during the school year and similar programs offered periodically during summer vacations have taught many children, otherwise not helped, to become readers of library books. Schools influenced by teachers and leaders who respect the value inherent in wide personal reading often introduce primary-grade children to the public library, help them to fill out admission cards, and encourage and even help them become regular users of the books in the children's book department.

Keeping Informed on Each Child's Extensive Reading Several quandaries plague teachers about children's extensive reading. Chiefly, these are: how to keep informed on what each child is reading, and how to check on the quality of the reading. Sensible solutions to these questions have been found. Children who are voluntary readers and who enjoy their reading are also able to keep an informal record of the titles of books read. Often all that is necessary to start this procedure is a suggestion from the teacher and help from her with some routine method of recording. Individual notebooks or simple manila folders have been found adequate for maintaining such records.

In some schools where charts are made with the number of books read by each child posted on them, and where stars or other awards are given to those who read the most, tendencies to cheat are, of course, noticed. When children are placed in that type of competitive learning situation, with special honors going to the most favored youngsters and embarrassing exposure to the least skillful, it is only natural for both the agile and the slow to report erroneously. Moreover, the real value, the enjoyment of reading, becomes displaced by the strong motivation for teacher approval and reward. Personal satisfaction in reading can readily be acquired by children if they are given uninterrupted time to browse through books and read those that make a specific appeal to them.

Obviously children should be accorded the same privileges we adults enjoy in reading; these include gleaning carefully ideas we like, skipping over passages at times, and putting back on the shelf, unfinished, books that fail to hold our interest. How carefully and how comprehendingly a child reads each book is not easy to discover, but a teacher gains much information about the quality of a child's reading by hearing him report informally on a book to the group or to her alone. When Charles said, "I read every word of that book on satellites, and I got my big brother to read it," the teacher knew he read sufficiently well to be excited by the ideas in the book. Alice's comment, "I read *All About Whales* and I'm going to read it again. It will be easier this time," evoked the question, "Did you like it?" from the teacher. "Yes," said Alice, "but some parts were very hard." "Bring the book up to my desk later on and read a hard part to me," was the teacher's suggestion. Alice was then able to reveal to the teacher her levels of easy and difficult reading.

Comprehension checks on all details, like those that follow selections in some texts, are neither possible nor desirable with children's voluntary reading. Any inquiry into the care with which they read books that interest them should in no way hamper their eagerness or fill them with uneasiness. The assessment of reading skills in comprehending and remembering details can more readily be made in the regular reading connected with various aspects of school work.

Sustaining Interest Once a child has passed the challenge of identifying words, and the glamor that surrounds becoming a reader has been dimmed, the application of reading power that demands more mature skills rekindles the youngster's interest. A live, up-to-date curriculum maintains stimulation and rekindles the dwindling eagerness to read for those few who grow bored when insufficiently challenged.

For the reference type of reading required by curriculum studies, a school library is essential. A classroom library, even if carefully stocked with books related to topics commonly studied and also supplemented with books borrowed from the public library, cannot meet the demands of even primary-grade children bent on gathering information. Proper evaluation of a school's reading program can be made in part by studying the function of the school library. If there is no library or the library cannot be fully utilized because the staff does not include a librarian, teachers can develop good reference reading only with much planning for use of school and public-library resources. Independent reading by children is thwarted if such necessary materials as reference books, maps, pictures, and encyclopedias are inaccessible. A good library is an essential resource of the school.

THE CHILD WHO LEARNS AT A SLOW PACE

What about the plodder or the very slow child who enters the second grade with only meager beginnings in reading? What happens to him in the third grade? Some such children, even if retained in first grade for two years, remain slow in all work involving letters, figures, or any use of symbols that demand thinking. The second- and third-grade years are crucial for them. These children must receive enough personal help and encouragement to keep up their interest and to aid them in continuing to grow at a rate that is consistent for them. Home, as well as school, plays an important role in this helping process. Each child needs to know that his interests and his efforts mark him as a *good* student, no matter how slow his learning tempo. Such assurance is particularly important in a family where children are close in age but show wide variations in learning power. Imagine the threat to the ego of a seven-year-old whose younger sister is ahead of him in reading.

Encouragement and vocally expressed respect for this slow-paced child are an important responsibility of both teacher and parent. In conferences with parents, teachers often discuss their methods of offering reassurance. Conversely, parents reveal to them supportive techniques they have found helpful. But in addition to the reassurance that "Your reading is developing slowly, but you are working well and are a good student," the child needs specific help properly calculated to fit his state of learning. Responsibility for providing this aid can be taxing for a teacher but also rewarding.

The Educational Value of Good Games An excellent teacher in a North Carolina second grade of thirty-three children, more than half from homes too poor to have books, papers, or games, was successful in helping each of the slower ones. She showed them how to play a matching game of eight cards. One set of cards was called *Boys-Girls.* It included the names Joe, Mary, May, Alice, Jim, Sonny, Sue, Red. The child arranged the cards on his desk in two columns, one column of boys' names, the other of girls' names. Once he mastered this game of separating the cards into the proper categories, he traded with another child who might have an *Animal-Sound* game: dog, cat, cow, woof, moo, bird, cheep, meow.

Excellent materials of this nature are published and should be made available to the teacher. Games giving special drill on phonic elements were made by the North Carolina teacher. The game was called *Find the Joker.* The teacher placed seven cards in an envelope. The word on each of six cards started with the *s* sound; the word on one did not. The object of the game was to place the six *s* cards in a column, and the seventh to the side. To add excitement to the use of these games, each child, after mastering a game, wrote its name on his personal "Reading Chart." Children could talk specifically of what they knew, the number of games they had mastered, and the game on which they were working.

The games were short and simple enough for children to play with a minimum of teacher supervision. The requirements were specific. Thus the child acquired a sense of accomplishment essential to building up his morale. And as he successfully matched more and more sets of cards, he could feel himself progress. Slow learners need to see evidence of their growth. To say "Fine," or "You are getting better," may make no impression at all on a struggling child.

The Proper Goal: A Respect for Work At this time in the child's life, his attitude toward his worthiness is being formed. Therefore teachers, as well as parents, may need help in learning how to reassure a child and help him grow into a healthy, constructive student. If he is treated with respect, he will retain respect for himself. Obviously, such treatment demands classroom and home emphasis on the child's work habits, his efforts, his willingness to struggle, his pride in his progress. Corollary to this emphasis is the "playing down" or minimizing of emphasis on fast achievement and advanced learning; without this minimization, the bright child, with little or no effort, wins approval, while the hard-working, slower child is slighted. The quick worker, too, needs to acquire respect for serious effort rather than to be content with "snap" accomplishment.

In a classroom where emphasis is placed on how far ahead some are—and there is ample opportunity to observe this practice—the bright child cruises, gets by with minimum effort, and acquires careless work habits. He may also acquire a snobbish attitude toward less alert children in the group. The slow learner senses that he is the second-class citizen of his group and begins to anticipate the day when he can be *finished* with school.

We have for so long placed our emphasis on the *end product* and on grade level achievement that to avoid this stress we must take great effort to alter our attitudes and even our language. A parent with two boys, one quick, the other slow and resistant, became aware of the frequency with which she made comparisons between the two. Once she was aware that she did so, she made an effort to stop the practice. "But," she lamented, "you don't change yourself overnight." True; and a teacher, in whom many routines become almost built-in, may find it equally difficult to shift. Effort is required merely to avoid saying "the better readers," or "the slow group," or "those up to grade level." Our language has become filled with phrases that stress comparisons, yet we can readily realize how sensitive we ourselves as adults would feel if placed on a line of gradation from top to bottom, especially if, in the comparison of an important quality, we are found "slow," or "below grade," "average," or the "common garden variety."

READING GROWTH IN MANY DIRECTIONS

Accompanying the variation in reading ability that stretches from grade to grade comes also a variation in interests and marked differences in individual ventures. The number of books read by able readers may vary widely, because some are polishing up other interests in sports, in club work, in neighborhood play, in viewing television, and so on. As children reach this age, they are increasingly able to manage wider neighborhood travel and to tap more sources for things to do. An alert third-grade teacher takes account of outside pressures but encourages reading as one of the child's continuing interests. Those children with a capacity to sprout many interests may enjoy reading but may not maintain as wide a breadth in it as some less aggressive venturers.

Both home and school influences leave their mark on children's extension of some skills independent of the school group. Alice, a third-grader, became skillful with the dictionary because her brother, a fifth-grader, was helping her in language skills. Arthur was developing ability in the use of an atlas borrowed from an upper grade because his father traveled for a government agency and sent letters to Arthur from various foreign fields. Polly was growing in library techniques, particularly alphabetizing, through working after school with her sister, a paid assistant in the school library. The possibilities for unusual growth in certain skills, particularly at third-grade age, indicate the potentialities within this age and the importance of cutting the curriculum cloth so that each child is provided with ample space in which to stretch.

ACQUIRING READING GROWTH THROUGH SPELLING AND WRITING

Further help to reading growth in second and third grades comes through consistent work in spelling and writing. The variety of writing occasions increases in second and third grades because children are older and, if given help and inspiration, want to write more. They continue to help plan curriculum work while the teacher records their plans. They write short stories and news items, and many write letters and notes. The use of proper paper and attractive form in writing adds dignity to the child's writing and encourages the writer. As in first grade, children may still resort to copying whatever the teacher records on a chart or on individual papers for them. This copying is their way of testing out their competence and also improving their skill by self-selected practice.

Help in forming the letters may no longer be needed, except by a few, but most need regular periods of help in acquiring skill and ease in writing. Manuscript form, widely used in kindergarten and first grades, is continued in second grade. Frequently the transition to cursive writing is made toward the end of the second grade or at the beginning of the third. In some localities, no shift is made; children establish their own writing form and pursue it through the grades. Practice books or writing workbooks are used in some communities, but in many schools no commercial materials are used, the letter forms and practice helps being planned by the teacher.

The careful selection of words and phrases and the general organization of content as children write feeds back into their reading. Similarly, their reading content influences their writing. Some already write in sentences, using a capital for the beginning word of the sentence and ending with a period. They begin to *feel* sentence structure.

And, of course, from their own writing, they begin to grow in awareness of their spelling or their spelling needs. Although spelling books and lists of words per grade are extant, in many schools children keep records of the words they have used in writing and have learned to spell or need to learn. In one second grade, an eager writer had a list of four hundred and sixty words in a notebook labeled, "Words I Used in Writing," and could spell each one. In a classroom where writing and spelling are recognized as factors contributing to reading, children move from one skill to the other with ease and apply learnings from one to the other.

EVALUATION OF SECOND- AND THIRD-GRADE LEARNING

The growth of most youngsters from the beginning of the second grade to the end of the third may be inadequately described by scores on standardized or other tests. Actually, many have grown from the independent recognition of about one hundred words to a workable reading knowledge, through use of all word-recognition skills, phonics, structural analysis, context clues, and even an introductory use of the dictionary. They have added to their knowledge of books and the manner in which books are organized. They have become acquainted with a wider variety of printed materials. They have opened the door to reference reading. They have added to their awareness of their own preferences. And they have begun to employ the essential techniques of critical reading. Only in a broad, inclusive type of reading assessment can the growth of these youngsters be properly evaluated. Many of the slower pupils have shared in the experiences of the nimbler and have gained some insight while continuing to work on materials and techniques tailored to fit their needs.

The educational philosophy of the school will, of course, influence the quality of the assessment. Obviously, a school with emphasis on skill development in close relationship with grade norms will be sure to inquire into such accomplishment. A school that sets as one of its goals the development of selective and critical readers will need to check on the degree of success they have met. Curriculum variations leave their mark not only on the manner in which goals for reading are expressed but also on the plan for evaluating the subsequent achievement of the children. The entire process of planning-teaching-evaluating is essential for helping children to do good work in the second and third grades. The process is equally necessary for guiding youngsters in intermediate grades but becomes increasingly difficult with older children.

From the description of practices in teaching reading and the potentialities of the children in second and third grades, one can readily see the close and important influence on reading created by the type of curriculum accepted.

Suggestions for Examining Reading Programs To offset a tendency to assume that second and third grades are the less important years between the important first grade and the more serious intermediate grades, a study of the quality of reading in these grades will assure each child of continued growth and will stimulate changes in classroom practices and curriculum point of view. Such examinations as the following, if forthrightly undertaken, will be helpful to staff and ultimately to the children:

1. An inquiry into the acceptance of each child at any level of ability. Teachers who make a studied effort to understand the quick and restless, the slow but serious, the indifferent, and the discouraged will become more sympathetic and helpful to each.
2. An inventory of each child's reading skill, through tests, individual interviews, and observations; and an inventory of each child's voluntary reading as revealed by home reading and classroom use of reading. Parents may be asked for their estimate of a child's attitude toward reading.
3. An examination of the opportunities offered children by the curriculum to select, discuss, and evaluate materials. Once a selective eager reader is stimulated by challenging questions and interesting topics, materials that suit his quest and his reading ability must be available. In situations favorable in these respects, a self-propelling reader is being developed.
4. A study of Points 1, 2, and 3 naturally leads to an examination of goals set for the reading program and also an examination of the influence of the goals in practice.
5. Serious considerations of one or several of the foregoing points will stimulate interest in examining the curriculum theory in action. If, for example, a staff selects as a desirable goal the development of children's ability to read informational material with increasing independence, then the curriculum must help cre-

ate the challenge and the specific needs to do so. The school must provide the necessary reference materials.

6. Evaluation of a year's growth in light of each child's potentialities and in harmony with the accepted goals will become a necessary part of the staff's concern.

SUGGESTED READINGS ON PRIMARY GRADES

BROGAN, PEGGY, and FOX, LORENE K. *Helping Children Read.* New York: Holt, Rinehart and Winston, Inc., 1961. Chapters 1 and 2.
Teachers' reports of how they worked individually with children to extend the youngsters' skills in reading, at the same time developing a wider choice of books in their reading. The entire book is helpful for those interested in moving toward an individualized reading program.

HEFFERNAN, HELEN, ed., Committee of the California School Supervisors Association. *Guiding the Young Child.* Boston: D. C. Heath and Company, 1959.
The function of reading as an integral part of the whole primary program is described. Examples include ways of meeting varying rates of reading growth in the program. Entire book keeps readers close to children in classrooms.

FRANK, JOSETTE. *Your Child's Reading Today.* Garden City, New York: Doubleday & Co., Inc., 1960. Chapters 6 and 9.
Excellent suggestions for reluctant readers and for stimulating independent book reading. Much information about books for children. Although written primarily for parents, it has real value for teachers.

MCKIM, MARGARET G. *Guiding Growth in Reading.* New York: The Macmillan Company, 1955. Part III.
Entire section devoted to reading program and methods of teaching in the primary grades. Particularly helpful for teachers who are eager for specific how-to-do suggestions.

MORSE, ARTHUR D. *Schools of Tomorrow—Today.* A Report on Educational Experiments, New York State Education Department. Garden City, New York: Doubleday & Co., Inc., 1960. Pp. 176-178.
List of schools experimenting with ungraded classes in the primary grades with a brief description of the plan of each school.

RUCKER, W. RAY. *Curriculum Development in the Elementary School.* New York: Harper & Brothers, 1960. Chapters 9 and 10.
Detailed accounts by teachers of their methods of planning work with children. Accounts reveal wide variety of reading skills children acquire and their growth in organizing ideas.

STENDLER, CELIA B. *Teaching in the Elementary School.* New York: Harcourt, Brace & Co., 1958. Chapter 4.
Very good confrontation of difficulties of meeting individual differences in reading and other areas of learning as they emerge in the classroom, with concrete help suggested. Entire book has merit for teachers.

STRICKLAND, RUTH. *The Language Arts.* Boston: D. C. Heath and Company, 1957. Chapters 7 and 11.

These chapters describe the relation of all language arts to a child's growth and the sequential development of reading from prereading stage to mature reading. Information of value to an understanding of primary-age children's reading.

CHAPTER 9

The Expanding Function and Power of Reading in the Intermediate Grades

Many of today's adults can still remember that when they attended the fourth, fifth, and sixth grades, the teachers assumed that all who were in the given grade were able to read. In those days, further help in becoming a reader was not given. Most of the less able readers had been retained in the third grade "because they would not be able to meet the heavy textbook demands of the intermediate grades." Today's schools, however, face realistically the fact that growth in reading skills must be fostered in every grade, and, for many pupils, even in high school. Even mature readers require teaching help in meeting some reading skills that may be demanded of them by more advanced work.

For those who grasp reading slowly, the intermediate grades comprise an important period for receiving special help in areas where they need a "boost." Such help, recognized at this period by some as "face-saving," is frequently asked for by the children themselves. They recognize not only the esteem shown at school and at home for those who progress with their reading, but also the important role that reading plays in their entire success at school. If they have had stimulating curriculum experiences and are developing interests, they sense the value reading could have for them. If they have had proper personal experiences in the primary grades, they have come to recognize that asking for help whenever it is needed is not only acceptable but commendable. As a result of the modern school's concern for each individual's reading growth, current teaching seeks, even in the fourth, fifth, and sixth grades, to meet the many levels of reading skills found in the school population and to increase each child's total reading power. A time is commonly set aside daily for such assistance.

THE LIFE OF CHILDREN IN THE INTERMEDIATE GRADES

Let us look at the youngsters of intermediate age. They are between nine and twelve years old, or perhaps thirteen. As they reach fourth grade, some marked differences between them and primary-grade children become apparent. They are growing in out-of-school interests. They have a facility for knowing what is going on in their neighborhood, in the lives of their friends, and in the community. They are beginning to share with adults such interests as sports, movies, comics, and news events.

Children in the intermediate grades are continuing to cut the family apron strings and are relying increasingly on the advice of friends and their peers (sometimes in preference to parents). Anyone in a lower grade is considered immature, "babyish."

They are acquiring new physical skills through organized games, skating, folk dancing, and physical exercises demanding special techniques. Scouting and other organizational or club activities offer important programs for them, and informal or unorganized groups compete for large portions of their time and meet important needs in their social life.

During this phase of growth, they are aware to a considerable degree of their own adequacy, the quality of their performance in their multiple school responsibilities, and the extent of their talents and their lacks. In many localities, children in the intermediate grades may feign an air of "It's smart to hate school." Nevertheless, school interests are often their main topic of conversation and events at school are of primary concern to them. The majority, despite gestures of disdain toward school, are deeply interested in their own growth and work diligently to progress in their tasks. That they take their education seriously at a time when they are deluged with so many other absorbing activities deserves a tribute not only to their good sense, but also to fine teaching and parental guidance.

Their drive, energy, and ability to keep many irons in the fire constantly amaze an onlooker. "It tires me just to think about what these kids do," commented a young teacher who himself led a very active life both in and out of school. Many of us have made similar observations. In fact, some sensible adults ask whether children of this age and even younger, particularly in suburban areas, are not currently leading too crowded and too tightly scheduled lives. Not only are they living under the pressure of time, but they are being deprived of important family contacts. Good parents complain of this, and rightly so.

MULTIPLE READING FUNCTIONS AND INDIVIDUAL DIFFERENCES

Beginning with the fourth grade, the school program puts heavier emphasis than in earlier grades on the content areas: social studies (or history and geography), science, arithmetic (now frequently termed mathematics), writing, art, and music. In recent years instrumental music has gained in popularity. Sometimes as many as ninety per cent of the children in a class are developing the ability to play an instrument.

The reading work of the intermediate grades falls rather clearly into three categories, all using certain common skills but differing widely in function. These categories are: (1) extending skills; (2) reading in the content areas; and (3) personal reading. No matter what the maturity in reading of the fourth-, fifth-, or sixth-grader, he needs wise guidance in all three categories.

Facing Wide Variations in Skills in Reading In the first category, skill-building, the teacher must face the responsibility of meeting the wide range of reading power within the group. Classroom work needs to be organized and scheduled so as to permit group and individual help and encouragement. The planning required to meet just this one responsibility taxes the teacher's ingenuity heavily.

Consider the range of ability in a class where some are still not far along in word-recognition independence while others are able to read with adequate understanding books, newspapers, and magazines on the general adult level. Good teachers seek not only to meet each child at the point of his emerging power but also to keep each one feeling both responsible and respectable; neither "uppity" nor "down-in-the-mouth" attitudes are encouraged. It is essential that any hurt experienced by a child through previous difficulties in learning be corrected before he grows older.

For those least mature in independence, daily work planned to increase their knowledge of phonics, structural analysis of words, and sight recognition of nonphonic common words may be essential. The less independent youngsters may also need more experience in comprehension checks based on relatively easy stories that deal with topics of interest to this age group. In this connection, teachers commonly rely on basal readers, skill texts, and similar materials. It is wise to use material that is both new and appealing to the youngsters. Reusing materials from the lower grades that children identify as "the same old stuff," or "baby dope," is obviously unhelpful, certainly without respect for a child's need to be challenged and won back to reading effort.

The present policy in schools headed by alert leaders is to provide teachers with a rich variety of materials upon which to draw. The practice of encouraging children themselves to aid in the selection of books, exercises, and games they wish to try out "for size" has been found rewarding. All ways of teaching are invaluable that give not only bit-by-bit help but also personal encouragement to youngsters for whom learning to read may continue to be a struggle.

For those who can comfortably read the books of the grade level, continued skill-development work necessary in the pursuit of their studies follows. Teachers often use grade-level workbooks, readers, and skill texts as guides and as sources of ideas. Whatever lacks are found in individuals are faced. Some children may have come from a school where they have had no previous library experience or reference-reading work; others may have had no dictionary or encyclopedia experience. Some may have had no opportunity to react personally to their reading. Many of today's children travel about with their mobile families, and it is natural to expect that they may have missed acquisition of some skills others have gained in the school they are currently attending.

The assumption that all youngsters progress from kindergarten through the grades as a continuing group in the same school has long been abandoned as untenable in this age. Also gone is the idea that those who enter a class in the fall will attend all year. In some areas less than fifty per cent who register in the fall may be in attendance throughout the year. Entrance and departure are day-in and day-out affairs. This point is relevant here because it increases the difficulty teachers meet in planning the skill-development program, particularly in the intermediate grades, in order to tailor the reading program to fit each child's needs.

Getting Acquainted with Differences in Backgrounds and Skills
In a Florida fourth-grade class of twenty-nine, for example, the teacher made a study of dictionary experiences. Seven children reported on their exploration of the unabridged dictionary in the third grade under the guidance of a truly exciting teacher. To prove their knowledge, they borrowed the unabridged dictionary from the library and demonstrated the elaborate definitions of such a simple word as *can*. They compared the amount of information devoted to *can* in the unabridged volume with the amount in their classroom dictionaries, doubtlessly leaning heavily on what they had learned the year before. Others in the group who had had the same experience recalled little, if any, of it. Nine class members said they had had no previous work involving dictionaries; six claimed never to have seen a dictionary until they entered the fourth grade.

In this same group, an informal test was given requiring the children to place a column of words in alphabetical order. The results ranged from eleven who received a perfect score to three who obviously did not know the alphabet in sequence. Those three became fascinated with learning to alphabetize. With encouragement from the teacher, they also spent rewarding time testing their speed in locating words in the classroom dictionaries.

Similar methods are used by many teachers in locating individual variations in other skills. Able youngsters in some schools gain their first experiences in outlining in the third grade. This important skill in organizing ideas becomes an essential need in planning reports and taking notes on reading in all intermediate grades. However, some fourth-graders may need help on finding key points and main topics of the material they are reading. They may still need much help before they can manage even the simplest form of outline.

The "middle group" in skill development may form the nucleus from which a teacher branches out to those below and those beyond. Work in small groups and individual help is then planned accordingly. Those lay observers who oversimplify the work of teaching should pause to examine the responsibility a teacher faces in skill development alone. When we add to this the other multiple teaching, guiding, and classroom-management responsibilities of teachers we appropriately ask, "How do they manage to do so well?"

All Hands Needed Such an appraisal of a teacher's responsibilities reveals also the understanding and tolerance pupils need in a busy classroom. Individual help from the teacher is not always available. Adults who are not close to children in daily life do not always realize why parents and older family members play such an important role in the education of children. We want for each child every kind of personal assistance, but, unfortunately, each may share one teacher with more than thirty other eager workers who also need personal aid. Even with parents, teachers, and children working on the highest efficiency level, some important learning opportunities may be overlooked. Perhaps we are not realistic when it comes to the education of children. Perhaps we —that is, responsible parents, dedicated teachers, and knowledgeable citizens—are idealistic. But then, no harm can come from reaching up to lofty heights.

CONTINUING DEVELOPMENT IN ABLE READERS

A vital problem that today's schools are facing is the guidance of those youngsters who are beyond the need of word-recognition skills and comprehension checks based on individual items or simple meanings. Alert teachers recognize the boredom caused by the lack of challenge these youngsters feel if they are required to do work below their level of ability. Most of the grade-level reading materials in the intermediate grades are too easy for them. The more docile will respond dutifully and may make perfect test scores without actually having been challenged. They may also fall into a pattern of expecting all work to be a "snap," something they can do with little or no effort. Many parade their power by finishing ahead of the group.

Teachers can cite many such examples. A sixth-grade boy was sent to the reading specialist for diagnosis of the reason for his failure in a school new to him. The child reported quite frankly that he had been the best pupil in his former school and that he had done all the work with ease. In the new situation, the teacher included him in a small group of high achievers who worked on "harder stuff that took so much time it made me mad." Fortunately for this child, his negative attitude toward the new, challenging learning was discovered early enough to be corrected.

Common Methods for Meeting the Needs of Rapid Learners
Even a small group of avid workers can keep a teacher busy planning with them, for, as is so often said of them, "They literally eat up work." Segregating them in classes under homogeneous grouping does not seem to be the answer to their needs. Advancing these youngsters to higher grades, although viewed favorably by some parents and teachers, is also open to serious question. A ten-year-old needs the companionship of others close to him in age. Providing work that is appropriate for him even while he remains in a regular class can be achieved, but it demands considerable planning on the part of the teacher. In a curriculum where children share in planning units of work that are larger than a daily lesson, the alert can plan specific responsibilities for small groups and occasionally for individuals. The teacher can tailor the nature of each part of the work to fit individual personal abilities. Utilizing individual intellectual hobbies in relation to the curriculum also is effective in motivating the able workers to continue their growth.

In former years, and perhaps in some localities even today, the mature readers were given books on the adult level. One often heard then and hears occasionally now of a "fourth-grade child so bright he's reading Shakespeare." Sensible parents and teachers respect the wholesome concern of adults in keeping a nimble child interested in his work and in building continually on his ability. Brightness and experience are not synonymous, however. An extremely bright child of ten or eleven or, for that matter, of any age has lived the experiences of his given number of years. A child may be able to read Shakespeare or Thomas Wolfe—or even John Dewey. But a young child has not yet acquired the insight that an understanding reader should bring to the meanings of such adult content. With so much material available that possesses both stimulating content and literary value for children, they can enjoy challenging reading appropriate to their age. Otherwise, they are being encouraged to read on one age level while they live on another.

Possible Gains from Deeper Study of Our Language Advanced word-study and vocabulary-development work offer such children an opportunity to gain important knowledge of our language and add to their power in making fine distinctions in meaning. A sixth-grade group made a study of words often interchanged, such as *peculiar* and *different,* with a resulting distortion or confusion of meaning. They maintained a list of words and phrases they found intriguing in the course of their own reading. Their vocabulary studies continued throughout the year and demonstrated their ability to develop increasing competence. Through these studies, both their written work and their depth of comprehension were enhanced.

In the intermediate grades, some schools include the study of reading with language arts. Textbooks of English include much work that gives specific help in relation to reading and writing. They include further work in using a dictionary among suggestions for extending independence in reading. The mature readers are ready for regular use of an unabridged dictionary or one designed for high-school students. Children in the intermediate grades are at an age when a dictionary becomes a prized personal possession. Even where schools furnish dictionaries, the child enjoys owning one for himself.

A Word About Writing The function of writing expands as children draw on the ideas they gain from school work and from the outside environment. Their skill in writing often amazes us because of their apt choice of words and refreshing integrity. As they write their own accounts of information gleaned from reference books, reports of an excursion to obtain firsthand data about a factory, or an introductory study of the history of their own community, they become acquainted with such items as introductory remarks, topic sentences, and paragraph unity. This newly acquired information is, in turn, related to their reading and adds to their awareness of the unity of ideas presented. Here again, bright youngsters often reveal power far beyond normal grade expectancy. Sometimes they shock us by their awareness of points in their reading that we may have overlooked.

Many creative writers feel that good writing by children is squelched by an emphasis on structure, form, correct English usage, and other standards. This has undoubtedly been true and may often still occur. However, the adult who works comfortably with youngsters in this age group, who is aware of their low tolerance for too tight direction, but who is also aware of their powers, imagination, creative ability, and unsophisticated integrity, needs only to encourage them and remain available for giving help. Children bent on writing that they are eager to do will ask for the kind of help that some of our literati consider too restricting and confining. The important factor is their respect for using their own power to do their own work. Where the adults who work with them have created a wholesome, honest climate, this factor will serve as a balance wheel between the too strict study of form and the careless acceptance of sloppy production.

Supplying New Skills to Meet New Demands Each field of study places a responsibility on the skill-growth of the reader, some unique to the particular field. In reading concise and abbreviated directions for construction, for science experiments, or for arithmetic problems, a child must employ a reading technique different from the loping speed he applies in reading an interesting story, or even a news account. Unlike familiar words that he can recognize at a glance, numbers must be read with attention to each figure and to its location with reference to the others. The word *still* may be identified by the fifth-grade reader with "half an eye," but the number *1973* must be read number by number in careful sequence.

A class of sixth-graders in a suburban area reputed to have good schools was preparing to discuss China with a Chinese-born member of the community who had left China before the start of the Communist era there. In preparing themselves to meet him, the youngsters did two things: they read about China in geographies, encyclopedias, and several pamphlets secured from the library; they also formulated the questions they wished to ask their guest. Among the questions rather widely accepted by the group was, "How does the climate of China compare with ours?" The class scribe wrote the question on the board. The teacher then commented, "You have been reading about China. Have you read anything that makes you wonder if we should ask this question? Think before you volunteer." (This teacher was emphasizing the need to "stop-and-think before restlessly waving your hands.")

Some of the youngsters most eager to answer accepted the question as a good one; others, not so hasty, began the critical appraisal. "China is huge; some parts are very cold while others are warm." "The United States has frozen weather in North Dakota while people are sunbathing in Florida."

This discussion was followed by a further study-discussion by the group to help formulate cautions for future reading and discussion-preparation: (1) the need to relate specific information to questions at hand; and (2) the need to examine omnibus terms such as climate, China, and United States. After one such experience many were able to apply both points in future work; others needed many more such experiences.

A good teacher such as the one described in the foregoing situation is a blessing to each child during this important period of his education, because, in the years ahead, the skills he acquires in these three years will truly nourish his learning. For further amplification of skills, we need to examine some of the ways in which reading functions during this period.

REFERENCE READING—A MUST FOR ALL

The second category of reading in the fourth, fifth, and sixth grades is closely related to the nature of the curriculum. Broadly based projects that continue from several days to several weeks offer excellent possibilities for growth in mature reading skills. Among other new experiences, youngsters learn to keep in mind the focus of the study; to take responsibility for keeping notes, appraising what is relevant and important, and determining what questions or topics need further inquiry; and, lastly, to summarize important knowledge acquired. In a narrow curriculum where the teacher sets out the daily lessons to be learned, these important skills cannot be acquired.

Gaining Experience as a Reference Reader Examine the variety of skills called into use by the following curriculum experience: A fifth-grade class in a Connecticut community made a study of the early industries of that area, which bordered on Long Island Sound. In planning the study, they first settled upon its focus: What were the industries in this town during the period from approximately 1700 to 1850? Next, they listed sources of information and organized committees to be responsible for reading these sources and gathering the information contained there. The following sources were listed:

1. Textbooks and reference books that devoted some pages to this period in Connecticut—from school room, from school library, and from homes.
2. Books, on youth or adult level, about the state of Connecticut —from school library, public library, and homes.
3. Interviews with long-term residents, especially their own grandparents, great-uncles, and great-aunts.
4. Materials from the Connecticut Historical Society.
5. Any books in public and school libraries with stories referring to this period.

They planned the ways in which they would use the materials. A list of regulations for taking notes was posted on the blackboard, and each child wrote them down for his own use. The items included: (1) whole title of book, or pamphlet; (2) where located; (3) name of author and publisher; (4) date of copyright; (5) outline of important points on which to report.

For most of these children, this was their first experience in genuine historical research. The teacher, an able one indeed, described to them the differences between primary and secondary sources. Some quickly understood the differences. By the time the reading was fully planned, each child had a reference to seek out and read. Each was responsible for keeping notes and for subsequent reporting.

The study was in process for about two weeks. Daily progress reports were given, and the teacher provided help for those who seemed bogged down. For example, one of the committees (which included two of the less agile readers, who were examining books for relevant material) found a story of pioneer life in New England. No occupations other than farming and household duties were given. One committee member felt that because the book was *about* pioneer life (the dates were not given) and the story was set in New England, it should be listed as a source of information.

The entire class entered into a discussion of this story. Through discussion all were made aware of an important factor—relevance. If this question of relevance were raised again and again, not only in judging reference material but also in adhering to a topic under discussion, a major contribution would be made to the straight thinking of these young learners.

Experiences such as these, some simpler, some more elaborate, form the basis of the social-studies program in many schools. Through them, a child not only acquires essential study skills but also matures as a "reference" reader. Children ready for more involved responsibilities and more critical assessment of a wider array of materials can forage wider for their content than can the less able, but all profit from this approach. Through this sort of serious study in science, social studies, and current affairs, interests are developed that lead some youngsters into hobbies and years of satisfying inquiry.

Anyone who has taught college youth, even graduate students, has observed the wide variation in ability to pursue a study independently of teacher help. In schools where youngsters learn reference work as soon as they have enough independence in reading, a more mature, responsible, and competent reader is developed.

The Reason for Developing Research Skills Unless skills beyond word recognition and simple comprehension are pursued in connection with ongoing studies, able young readers reach a plateau at the age of eight or nine; at this point they either engage in deeper pursuits on their own or cruise and fail to grow into their full potentiality. An intellectual maturing takes place at intermediate-grade age. Boys and girls begin to see relationships in ideas, to notice what is important, what is minor. As a result, in these grades marked growth is achieved in the ability to organize independent oral and written work. The youngsters now also begin to analyze information read and to keep notes on readings related to ongoing studies. Heretofore they have selected the important points from a story and have noticed general topics and supporting details. They are now ready to develop and carry out more elaborate plans for their own writing. In some of the experiences through which they acquire this added power, it is impossible to tell which phase is *reading*, which is *writing*, and which is *thinking*; all are interwoven in the total process.

Enter Charts, Graphs, Maps, and Figures Some reading may require that the reader look away from the text to examine illustrations, charts, maps, graphs, and designs. To read and interpret these requires specific reading skills. Every youngster must become capable of interpreting them with ease and confidence and using them to add to the meanings of readings in which they appear. At first, a child may skip them or, at best, be bothered by them as distractions in his reading. Once he learns to use them and sees their value to the content, he can grow to use them and derive fuller profit from his reading.

Graphic presentations of data quite naturally bring about a temporary slowing down in reading speed and also require eye movements other than the left-to-right sweep of regular line-after-line reading. Such departures from regular reading demand patient effort and the kind of "know-how" that some adults indicate they failed to receive in their reading guidance. Indicative is the comment of a graduate of a respectable college, "Anything with a chart or column of figures in it, I skip. I just can't manage that kind of stuff." This frank admission is of especial significance because in our concern for evaluating the reading of today's child, we are inclined to overlook the reading of today's adult—who was taught in "the good old days."

The Good School Library Helps Build Reading Maturity Great facility in library skills is acquired by a few in the fourth grade and by more and more in the fifth and sixth grades. In some schools, children of the intermediate grades take turns serving as "library assistants." In an excellent school-library situation in Putnam County, New York, for example, the librarian has given many of the fifth- and sixth-graders mature library responsibility.

One can sense, of course, that such skills sprout through a program that stimulates their need and then fosters it. First, the school must have a curriculum that requires library supplies. Granted this basic framework, the primary requisite is a library, well stocked, open for use all through the school day and every day. Such a library is not required in a school whose curriculum stresses day-to-day short lessons or assignments, mostly limited to the use of a single text. Even suggestions for extended study, such as are now included in various textbooks, readers, and books related to the social studies and science, are passed over in narrow teaching programs.

HOMEWORK AT THIS STAGE OF SKILL DEVELOPMENT

In the primary grades, it is not common school policy to encourage homework. Many educators, aware of the pressures placed on the modern child by numerous outside group and club activities in addition to their regular schooling, discourage teacher-assigned homework in the intermediate grades.

The conventional assigned homework has been one of the genuine hardships of childhood. Tired children, if dutiful, did it drudgingly. Conscientious parents were often caught between the desire to lift the burden from a weary youngster and the fear to invade the province of the school. Many a child learned his distaste for school through pressures of homework. At intermediate-grade age, children need opportunities to socialize and to plan and work on out-of-school projects. They need a change of routine—a school day saps their energy as it does that of the teachers. Parents who urge more homework as a way of keeping children "busy and easier to keep track of after school" give tragic evidence of lack of insight, or poor regard for good learning, or, even more serious, an inadequate respect for the child as a person.

The away-from-school continuation of study by the child whose interest has been sparked is not only proper but highly desirable. At intermediate-grade age he is beginning to cut free from his close reliance upon parental assistance; he is, therefore, readier to assume more responsibility for independent studies, hobbies, and self-selected reading interests. Such work is personally motivated homework.

Such efforts can be enhanced or stymied, depending upon home factors. A school administration sensitive to the home conditions that contribute to or militate against a child's desire to continue his learning at home keeps in mind such factors. Some of the best teachers observed by the author made a point of challenging youngsters with their work to such a degree that out-of-school work—and this does not mean here prescribed homework—grew out of the interest stimulated and was teacher-inspired but not teacher-directed. The few who were not yet "inspired" to work independently in or out of school were given specific suggestions in such a way that they grew nearer and nearer to planning the work and setting themselves to the job of doing it.

Where homes are not suitable places for individual work, in-school time for independent study and relaxed reading should be made available to the children. Many schools encourage teachers to plan each day so that every youngster may have a quiet, uninterrupted period for such personal use. The important aspect of individual, quiet work time during these years is the opportunity it gives the child to grow in independent reading of study materials, texts, and reference books. The more a child manages to propel himself at work, away from teacher or parental help, the better his education. He is growing away from the spoon-feeding process and becoming a full-fledged, powerful person.

READING AS A PERSONAL PURSUIT

The third category of reading, the individual's personal reading, is carried on completely aside from work in school studies. It is the kind of reading we hope all youngsters will pursue during their school years *and* throughout life. For many, it has its beginnings in preschool years at home; for some, in nursery schools, where they listen to stories read to them, look at books, begin to own and cherish books, and glean some first hints about how to read. If properly nourished thereafter, they continue to like books, draw books from school and public libraries, and make the next book to be read an important plan in their busy lives. Good schools and helpful homes foster a continuing interest in personal reading.

Trusting the Child's Personal Reading Some school administrations, mindful that the child needs to read individually and should have the right to do so, began library work as a part of the reading program; but, feeling uneasy about the child's ability, or integrity, or both, they devised checks and "catches." Teachers, whose reading time was limited, found it necessary to limit the books from which children could choose to those that they themselves had read and for which they could prepare checks. Often, checks were used to discover not only how carefully the child had read but also whether he had completed the book. A book selected was to be read from beginning to end and a review prepared. As a result, some children avoided drawing books from the library in order to avoid the checks and the required completion of a book.

Such practices are an invasion of a child's right to privacy in his personal reading. They discourage the less able or uncertain readers, encourage the frustrated readers to cheat, and remove the zest from what should be a real delight in reading. Free comments made by children (similar to adults' conversations on books) and informal chats with individuals will reveal to the teacher facts about a child's satisfactions in reading. If he is a normal child, he will skip parts of a book and at times return books unfinished. These facts are important only when many other behavorial signs tell us a child is not enjoying his reading—and perhaps none of his other work.

Guarding the Child's Time to Read A child who wishes to sit back and relish some reading invariably must make a choice between reading and some other activity. If, in addition to reading stories, comics, and magazines that he likes, he also is to become a reader who continues to rely on reading for keeping himself informed, growing professionally, and making decisions based on competent understanding, then parents, as well as teachers from kindergarten through college, must nurture and protect such eagerness to read, despite pressures to the contrary.

The importance of reading for personal satisfaction grows increasingly in our era of hectic living. Today, personal reading may provide the only serene moment available to a child or even to an adult. Personal reading must, therefore, not be crowded out by a too-busy life. The importance to adults of reading for gaining competence in meeting daily obligations is also apparent. Its inclusion in a busy life must, therefore, not be left to chance.

Sometimes children's personal reading is crowded out by other assignments. At peak times, such as examination periods, this is understandable. However, there are schools even today, such as that attended by young Francis, where personal reading is considered a luxury to be indulged in only if there is nothing else "important" to do. This eleven-year-old considered summertime the really privileged part of his life, "because I dare take time to read library books then."

At a meeting of summer camp directors, several reported the great eagerness of some youngsters to read books during the "quiet time" after lunch. Many youngsters revealed to them that they had too much homework to permit personal reading during the school year or that home life was too hectic to permit any semblance of a quiet atmosphere for reading.

Instead of registering regret at the poor showing some children make in reading, we should register amazement and gratitude over their persistence. It would seem that some schools develop the power to read and whet the appetites of youngsters for reading but by their conduct actually imply, "Try and do it!" Fortunately, those who encourage and aid the important growth in reading ability through personal reading are increasing in number. Common sense should tell us, in this day of far too many pressures on our time, that a child needs the encouraging and supporting efforts of school and home to grow into the kind of adult reader we need.

When Children Encourage Parents to Read So important was personal reading considered for the members of an elementary school in an economically underprivileged area of a large Eastern city that the last forty minutes of class time in all grades, from the second grade on, were devoted to uninterrupted personal reading. The school principal and staff, with great effort, established an excellent school library. Youngsters were encouraged to take home books "parents might like to look at and read." The loss of books or faulty care of them in transit was declared "minimum" in contrast with the values for tired, deprived parents who, perhaps, were enjoying their first associations with good books. Not the least valuable element consisted of the parent-child bonds built around sharing books.

In preparing for a book fair to be held for parents at a school in New York City, children helped teachers to organize the book display for their own grade groups. A stranger approached one of the fourth-grade display tables as a man still in working clothes laughed heartily. He turned to the stranger and said, "Look at this! My kid wants this for Christmas!" It was Bemelmans' *Madeline*. "Kids today have a chance at books I never had," he added. "I read all the books my kids bring home." This was a workman on the city subway system who felt he "had to quit a few hours early to get to see these books or my kid would never forgive me."

This incident shows vividly how a good reading program can spill over into family reading and pleasure. It gives dramatic testimony of a child's love of personal reading, of a school's influence on reading, and of a father's relationship to his child.

An Essential Check on Reading Programs In a previous chapter it was suggested that evaluation of adults' reading is necessary in order to measure the effectiveness of children's reading programs. Where reading is taught for school purposes only, as in the author's childhood, then no matter what the attested achievement of the pupils, those who become understanding, persistent readers do so independently, not from inspiration by the school. This third category of reading for personal use raises the question of how adequately a school meets the goal of creating functional adult readers. It also highlights the appropriateness of scheduling in-school time for all types of personal reading to assure each child a quiet time and place for pursuing his reading.

An informal study made with parent help in a Minnesota school brought to light the widespread regular reading of adult newspapers and magazines by intermediate-age boys and girls. Some of this reading was stimulated by the school's current-events program, which was a regular part of the work in social studies. Some of the reading was focused primarily on sports and on comics. Several sixth-grade girls were building a recipe file from recipes that seemed appealing among those published in a daily newspaper. The manager of a newspaper and magazine store reported that "do-it-yourself" magazines were bestsellers among early teenagers and were growing in popularity with fifth- and sixth-graders. Unless a similar sort of inquiry is made part of a school's evaluation program, teachers may be somewhat in the dark about the progress of their students as functional readers.

Personal outside reading, if encouraged and recognized for its real value—and if fed through school, home, and public library—becomes a rich addition to the child's education. The school's influence on children's reading can easily be observed. A librarian at a New York City branch library reported the following incident at a civic meeting: "Our library had few cardholders among children, and our children's section was the least used part of our library when, suddenly, a booming business began in that department. We then discovered that a new principal had been appointed to the neighborhood school, a man who had in his office the motto, 'A Book Can Be a Man's Best Friend.' He evidently knows how to influence teachers and children." Progress in solving reading problems would be greatly enhanced if such principals could be multiplied by thousands and located across the nation.

ADDITIONAL SIGNS OF MATURING AS A READER

Variations in Personal Reading Interests Along with the use of wider independent reading in the intermediate grades, other signs of reading maturity become evident. Noticeable personal preferences appear. Some of these preferences persist for several months, even several years, and become abiding interests. One fifth-grader not only read all he could find related to the Civil War—history texts, encyclopedias, stories—but announced that for summer reading he planned to work his way through *Gone with the Wind*. Some, perhaps not as independent or agile, enjoy short stories and may even cherish all old school readers. Many are broad in their preferences and, like ten-year-old Dick, go with ease from the comics in the daily press to a paperback book about animals. The amount of time spent on reading, provided homework is not too time-consuming, waxes and wanes with the demands of sports and other activities. When the pressure period is over, if the youngsters enjoy reading, it again comes to the fore as an important pursuit.

It is normal for youngsters of this age to work hard at whatever is the ongoing thing to do. It may be roller skating, softball, science experiments, cooking, or knitting. Reading gets sandwiched in between the day's activities or is assigned a sizable amount of time over a weekend of inclement weather or during a minor illness. The degree to which it is carried on is noted by good teachers when they evaluate each child's reading progress. If personal reading happens very seldom, they work to whet the appetite. Exposing the child to attractive new books within the range of his reading power is often all that is needed.

The Effect of Personal Reading on Speed Speed is acquired by many youngsters during these three intermediate years. What better motivation is there for gaining speed than to have a book you are eager to read but must return to the library when it is due?

A discerning teacher helps youngsters understand speed in relation to the many factors that are involved in reading. This relationship is discussed with the group from time to time. Some materials must be read slowly in order to get their real meaning. The too-rapid reading of an arithmetic problem or the directions for cutting out a bird house may result in a serious mistake. The story of early whaling, if read too rapidly, may fail to reveal to the child relevant items for which he is reading. In contrast, the last chapter of an exciting story may fairly pull the reader rapidly along the lines because of his eagerness to learn the outcome.

Learning to gauge speed in relation to the purpose of reading, the ability of the reader, the nature of the content, and other such influencing factors, including time, is a technique some young readers acquire on their own. Many, however, need guidance in this process. We adults can cite examples of the too-rapid reading of important matter that led to a serious error; perhaps we, ourselves, have had to wrestle to overcome what we often call "careless" or "compulsive" reading.

Reading and Personality Factors Some youngsters have personal qualities that affect their reading. Understanding teachers recognize those characteristics, as did Miss Ellis in a Missouri school: "Jerry is a very bright boy, but he is so nervous he can't read carefully. He wants to zip through everything. Julie is a most methodical child. She does everything dutifully, slowly and carefully, but she never looks up and off and sizes up the whole thing."

Speed, caution, and other qualities can be influenced by the kind of child each youngster happens to be. Wollner's[1] study of children's voluntary reading reveals clearly the array of personality factors affecting the amount of reading and the motivation for it.

Reading Promoted by Children The gregarious impulses characteristic of this period in child life are clearly reflected in the way many youngsters use their reading experiences. A book found enjoyable by one class member is "promoted" or "sold" to the others. A robust boy who became fascinated with books after three years of indifference to them bounded excitedly into his fourth-grade room one morning to announce, "I found the best book in our attic that I ever read. It's called *Little Eagle*, and it's a true story about an Indian boy." He showed marked satisfaction when classmates displayed interest and asked to borrow the book. A girl who loved horses and had just read *Smoky* for the second

[1] Mary Hayden Bowen Wollner, *Children's Voluntary Reading as an Expression of Individuality*. New York: Bureau of Publications, Teachers College, Columbia University, 1949.

time said with real feeling, "You just have to read this story. It's an old book but it's so good."

Books and magazines, including comics, are boosted, borrowed, and swapped at this age. Some of the less ardent readers are thus given the "boost" neither parents nor teachers were able to achieve, and they too get excited about books. They may begin to read more merely to "keep up with the crowd," but they may become won over to reading through association with satisfying books.

Becoming Book Owners and Magazine Subscribers Youngsters in the intermediate grades are also quite definite about the books they want to own, preferring to suggest which ones might be given them as gifts. Often they take great pride in a growing collection of books on one subject or hobby. Boys and girls of this age also enjoy magazines published for those of their level. One child in a neighborhood who talks about the latest addition to his book collection or the new magazine to which he has subscribed sparks his friends with similar desires. In some ways parents find the preteen-age contagion a problem, but when it spurs a deeper interest in books, they should feel pleasure, even if the expenditure involved must be kept minimal.

Oral Reading for This Age Oral reading, quite common with beginning readers for practice purposes and enjoyed by them as a proof of waxing power, is also enjoyed during the intermediate years—if properly handled. Some youngsters at an early age become entertaining readers. At times, their friends in class prefer to listen to them read than to the teacher. It is a fortunate group where reading longer, interesting stories aloud is a regular part of the daily school program. Youngsters may share in this reading. Many also read excerpts from books and news articles as their way of contributing to certain topics under consideration.

A teacher who respects the satisfaction available to both the reader and the audience discovers many opportunities for oral reading. Always, however, there must be a genuine purpose for oral reading and an interested audience. The time-worn spiritless oral reading to a bored group under the direction of an unimaginative teacher has almost faded from the contemporary scene. Its deadening influence is still reflected, however, in some adults who find it distasteful to listen to even a good oral reading.

The Great Strides Evidenced in Intermediate Grades Through further aid on skills, through wider reading in the various content areas, through the use of library skills and resources, and through much unassigned, personally selected reading of books, newspapers, and magazines, a tremendous stride in reading power occurs in the three years of the intermediate grades. The majority of students enter the fourth grade as young, eager, growing readers. They leave the sixth grade approaching a type of functional reading maturity that may put some beyond the reading power of the average adult newspaper reader. Tests, informal and standardized, reveal how far each has grown in this time span, but only a careful observation of the life in school and the extent of reading out of school tell the whole story.

Growing in Ability to Read More Difficult Content As independence in reading grows and the ability to read rapidly increases, a youngster's reading becomes not only more extensive but also more difficult. At this stage, the child must face the necessity for organizing ideas and putting them into their proper relationships. The need to face conflicting ideas and more than one point of view may also occur at this age.

In beginning reading, first steps in aiding the growth of comprehension included checks on the simple items read and their sequence. Stories and articles prepared for young readers are written with their ability to comprehend in mind. In the intermediate grades, some organized way of dealing with longer articles and more difficult reading content becomes essential. Simple outlining of content in the material read is taught to some in the fourth grade, to most in fifth and sixth. Comprehension checks that require more involved thinking are used, although short-answer tests, resembling those used in primary grades, are still employed from time to time. Also included are thought-provoking questions that make the child go deeper into the meanings than heretofore and some that help him organize ideas properly in his mind. Questions that ask *why* and *how* are used by teachers to help boys and girls reread, examine, and reflect on those points in their reading that require more than a hasty thought.

Developing Deeper Comprehension By Means of Discussion A good discussion led by a teacher who understands discussion leadership can help youngsters make great strides in straight thinking about complicated reading. This type of guided discussion, aimed at deepening comprehension, is one that is crying out for more attention, however, and one in which teachers admit they need assistance. In a good discussion, children need to learn to listen to the comments made by others and then, when possible, relate their own comments to those previously offered. All too often in classrooms there is one reciter and one listener—the teacher. Anyone who thinks this is a practice peculiar to an elementary school needs to listen carefully to adults "discuss." More frequently than not, many talk but few listen. No thread seems to link the various comments. No wonder a fifth-grade boy who attended a father-son luncheon discussion reported, "everybody was talking about something different all the time."

The following chapter will examine more closely the responsibility of developing the type of comprehending reader who can safely select from, and browse through, today's materials. More reference will also be made to developing techniques of discussion. Fourth-, fifth-, and sixth-graders are ready for additional assistance in the critical assessment of what they read. They are also ready for some of the intellectual disciplines of straight thinking.

SUGGESTED READINGS ON INTERMEDIATE-GRADE READING

BURROWS, ALVINA TREUT. *Teaching Children in the Intermediate Grades.* Boston: D. C. Heath and Company, 1952. Chapters 9, 10, and 11.

Excellent suggestions for the entire reading program in the intermediate grades. Special attention to individualizing reading instruction given in Chapter 10. An excellent reference book for experienced and inexperienced teachers.

LARRICK, NANCY. *A Parents' Guide to Children's Reading.* Garden City, New York: Doubleday & Co., Inc., 1958.
Particularly helpful for parents eager to encourage children's reading interests through home influence with the aid of well-chosen books. A handy resource for teachers in schools with no librarian.

MCKIM, MARGARET G. *Guiding Growth in Reading.* New York: The Macmillan Company, 1955. Part IV.
Recognition of specific skills in reading that are developed in the intermediate grades with help on increasing reading power in content areas of the curriculum.

MICHAELIS, JOHN U. *Social Studies for Children in a Democracy.* Englewood Cliffs, N. J.: Prentice-Hall, Inc., 1956. Chapter 5.
A unit in social studies is presented and indicates the skills in reference reading children acquire as an integral part of a good school program.

RUCKER, W. RAY. *Curriculum Development in the Elementary School.* New York: Harper & Brothers, 1960. Chapters 12, 13, 14.
The experiences of fourth, fifth, and sixth grades are described in detail and reveal the day-by-day variety of uses of reading and writing. Methods of competent teachers in developing personal responsibility on the part of maturing readers are included.

CHAPTER 10

Comprehension – Probing with Reasons

In the previous chapter references were made to reading comprehension, and examples were given that imply a deficiency in the concept of comprehension that is the basis for much present-day teaching. The major focus in teaching comprehension has for decades been: "What does it say?" The child who could give back a satisfactory answer was considered a comprehending reader. Gradually, teachers became aware that a child who answered by repeating the words of the book might not understand but might merely be parroting words. The child was then asked to "tell in *your own words*." Many youngsters were thus brought closer to dealing with the meaning of what they had read, obviously an essential step in comprehension. The technique did not go far enough in terms of a child's growth as a thinking—at times even a reflective—reader.

The teaching that transforms the child into a comprehending reader should go beyond the "what does it say?" level. It should include training in the ability to probe, for which preteeners are intellectually ready. It should also include more of the preparation necessary to keep our oncoming young citizens from perpetuating some of the glaring errors so often made in our adult society. Both elements, their readiness and society's need, must be used as guidelines in the reading program of these intermediate-grade years. If these young people are guided to become thinking readers, our land will more surely maintain its lofty ideals of freedom.

RECOGNIZING ENVIRONMENTAL INFLUENCES

Boys and girls at intermediate-grade age, as indicated in Chapter 9, are beginning to assert themselves more independently at home and in school. They prize friends. They need the assurance of acceptance that comes from being included in clubs and various community and school groups. They reach out in all directions for their reading—school and public library, family newspapers and magazines, and book racks at the neighborhood store. They follow along with adults many of the radio and television programs in sports and news events. At times they show marked maturity; at other times they are noticeably young children.

A characteristic of this group, as revealed by research, is that they are becoming influenced by some of the symbols and conditions in our life. They are beginning to classify people as rich or not so rich, as influential or inconsequential, as in the right group or not in it. Materials are judged as up to date or fossilized, as approved by friends or not approved. Youngsters at this time seem to be testing out the ability to make up their own minds, much as they formerly did with the new-found power of riding a two-wheeler or going to the shopping area unaccompanied. They give signs of stretching their thinking in more adult ways. This, then, is an important time for the school to make a conscious effort in guiding their thinking so that they make worthy choices.

Too often we have thought of youngsters of this age as too young to be aware of adult influences, or at least to be seriously affected by them. On the contrary, at this age they catch the spirit of the climate about them and relate themselves to social influences in ways that may be good or harmful for themselves and for society. These are the years in which guidance of the young twigs must be wise in order to be more certain of the straightness of the trees.

The child acquires from early years attitudes toward himself and others that affect his conduct, and he is affected by the world outside and the people about him. These influences cannot be boxed into tidy, separate packages in teaching and guiding him. For example, we cannot slice off the effect of shoddy values in his home life from his evaluation of a book or movie about family life.

The story of a pioneer risking life to add to the comforts of his wife and children may evoke from an unfortunately influenced child, "He's a dope." The parents and teachers who hear a bizarre report of a community incident and who comment to young listeners, "We'd better be careful. Before believing this report we must get more facts," are influencing children to "get the facts first."

The field of reading has long suffered from being piecemealed into seemingly tidy compartments and isolated from other fields. For too long, comprehension was treated as a technical skill in reading, while thinking was sliced off as an important part of the realm of psychology. As a result, the education of thinking, deeply comprehending readers was neglected. With more adequate insight available to aid educators and parents, we can now face the responsibility of teaching children more effectively. The wisdom of studying children in relation to factors that influence them is now accepted.

COMMON ERRORS ADULTS MAKE IN THEIR THINKING

Once one becomes alert to the quality of thinking in which we adults indulge, new ideas about teaching children to transcend our weaknesses seem to pour in upon us. Those who share the author's concern in educating children for their intellectual and moral safety will see the connection between children's thinking and their safety as unsupervised readers.

The following errors in thinking are, unfortunately, a part of our everyday climate. If accepted by children, these errors will have a negative effect upon the ability of children to read competently and critically and will also affect the quality of their personal life.

Error 1: The Short-Answer Habit. Extremely common among these unfortunate factors found among adults is that which has been dubbed the *short-answer mentality.* We know that many of the problems we meet cannot be solved in one-word answers—yes-or-no, right-or-wrong, do-or-don't. Yet many adults are impatient. They want a quick answer, as in the case of the parent who, during a conference about her son, said to a fifth-grade teacher, "Tell me in one word what's the matter with him. Is he dumb, or lazy, or what?" (The child, incidentally, was an overweight boy with little athletic skill, whose twin sister was a star in all school sports.)

We might appropriately ask if the schools' extensive use of short-answer, true-false, yes-no tests and exercises have added to this impatience. We know that the anxieties of this age have surely developed much of it. Once teachers become aware of this practice of short-circuiting essential thinking, they may limit their own use of the techniques that encourage it and take more time to teach the qualities inherent in good thinking. Such questions as, "Can we answer this quickly or is this the kind of question that should take more time and more careful thinking?" and "Should we examine this point more carefully?" if frequently asked, will help children acquire a more thoughtful approach to serious matters. We can so teach them that their important decisions are less likely to be fraught with danger. One can imagine the results to the child if the teacher in the incident mentioned above were addicted to short-circuited thinking. If so, she might have said "Well, he's lazy," and the mother might have "seen to it" that the child put more energy into his work. Unfortunately we see all around us unwise decisions made upon the basis of such short-answer thinking.

Error 2: The Quackish Generalization. Equally erroneous and even more frequent are generalizations made without adequate data. Our reading materials are filled with them. Two widely read books critical of today's teaching of reading were studied for this error in thinking, and each example was underlined with red pencil. The books are a startling exhibition of red-lined pages. Such statements as "none of the children in our schools" and "all of the teachers in the schools" occur again and again. Imagine an author being so insensitive in his thinking as to overlook such a common error as making sweeping generalizations with insufficient facts.

One alert teacher started to correct this error in thinking when a boy, a newcomer to the school, came in to her first-grade classroom during morning recess crying. The teacher asked sympathetically, "What's the matter?" He said, "All the kids hit me." She said, "*All* the kids?" "All the boys," he answered. "All the boys?" "Four or five." When the children re-entered the room, she asked this youngster to point out the offenders. He looked around carefully, then said, pointing, "That one." The teacher then said, "This *one* boy hit you," and proceeded by her clarification to ease the situation.

Actually this six-year-old was no more erroneous in his sweeping statement of "All the kids" than are some of our so-called educated adults. Children in a fourth grade under excellent teacher guidance discussed a newspaper editorial in which the editor urged the police force to get busy and squelch "this North End behavior." Two boys from a section of town called the North End had thrown stones at passing cars. Some of the fourth-graders lived in the North End. They felt the sting of labeling the misdemeanor of two boys by the generalized term "North End behavior." The teacher commented that after the discussion of this condition, the children tended to check one another on their own statements and demonstrated genuine concern for greater accuracy in relating incidents.

Bias and all forms of prejudice flourish under this same brand of crooked thinking. Of course, once alerted as were the children in the fourth grade just described, a beginning is made in preventing this error. "You can't trust these foreigners," "Girls are no good in science," and "Teachers make poor parents," are flagrant examples of such erroneous thinking. The teacher who hears a child state a generalization of this variety and says, "Let's pause and examine this," is not only doing an essential job as a teacher of good thinking and of more adequate reading comprehension but also as a builder of a better citizen.

Error 3: I Don't Know, But My Mind Is Made Up. Another evident quirk in thinking is the premature closing of minds to additional essential facts. We commonly regard people who make a practice of reacting in this way as opinionated. One of my sharp encounters with this type of reaction occurred years ago in Minnesota when voters were to decide upon the state's right to enter the field of paving highways. Heretofore this right had belonged to the city or the county. I chanced to meet an acquaintance, a one-time high-school valedictorian, who, I thought, would be enlightened on this issue. "Tell me about your views on the coming vote on the paving referendum," I asked. "I assume you've gone into the matter." Without a moment's pause he said, "No, I haven't gone into it, but my mind is made up. I'm voting against it."

A similar incident occurred at a meeting with teachers in a northern Pennsylvania community. State funds for schools were in question, and these teachers were concerned over whether or not they would receive their next salary checks. "What do you think of a sales tax as a way for the State of Pennsylvania to increase its funds for schools?" I asked. The spokesman said, "I myself know nothing about taxes, but I do know I'm against the sales tax." This type of person, who admits knowing nothing on an important subject on which he will help shape decisions affecting the future and who also admits having a closed mind, reveals not only an intellectual unreadiness to act as a responsible citizen but also an irresponsible attitude toward learning and future growth. If he were genuinely conscientious instead of morally numb, he would inform himself by reading and would seek interpretations from others.

Incidents of this type are met by fourth-, fifth-, and sixth-graders. These youngsters are ready to become aware of the errors of thinking inherent in these situations and are ready to be educated so that they will not follow in similar patterns. Here one must stop to ask: was any effort made in the education of such delinquent thinkers to direct them along proper, sensible ways of deciding what to believe? Did the gentleman in Minnesota become valedictorian by the spit-back method, giving back lesson assignments dutifully but never learning to think straight?

Error 4: Abdication from Thinking. The fourth type of error in thinking is revealed by the person who blandly admits his mind is not made up on a problem or issue, but that he is ready for someone to tell him what he should believe. No one today can be informed and competent enough to make decisions on all the everyday problems that confront us. Some of us, indeed, are so busy with lesser matters that we have little time for matters of importance. In some problem areas, we are in water too deep for us. When this occurs we are wise to seek advice, but it should be competent advice.

It is a matter of utmost concern when those who have had the privilege of high-school education and who occupy important adult roles abdicate from the responsibility of basing their thinking on a serious search for information. They are the ready pawns of the soothsayers, ward heelers, and patent panacea purveyors. Obviously in their own education they were not challenged to value their own ability and personal integrity. If they had been thus challenged, they would be willing to explore and assess ideas critically and then form their decisions.

Error 5: Inconsistence—the Mixed Mind. Another indulgence in crooked thinking is often so apparent that one wonders why it is not recognized by its generator. This is inconsistence. A recent example of startling inconsistence in thinking was given at a public hearing concerning the school budget in a Connecticut community. A speaker rose to state that the school budget was "getting out of hand . . . it must be trimmed." Later, this same person suggested two additions to the school budget: the addition of a French teacher so all children might profit from the early study of French; and liberalization of the school-bus policy by transporting children currently considered as living near enough to school to walk and by making more frequent stops to lessen walking distance for others. The desirability of the two proposals is not relevant here. It is of interest, however, that the speaker favored *cutting* the school budget but also favored *extending* it.

We frequently hear evidence of such careless thinking. The process seems to thrive on the topic of school finance. The Pennsylvania teachers described above who were uneasy about their paychecks later indicated they were against all taxes but were for higher salaries. Let us hope that today's well-taught, thinking children, hearing or reading inconsistent statements of this nature, will be strong enough in civic influence to modify or clarify such thinking.

Those who think inconsistently, although seeming to suffer from a type of intellectual indigestion, are apparently unable to diagnose their problems. One naturally asks, "Do those who are so confused detect conflicting points of view and contradictions in their reading? Were they given any help in school that would enable them to do so?" Obviously, one cannot treat thinking as though it flows from a spigot, turning on the tap while reading, yet turning it off in discussion. We may not always behave consistently, but in general, if we wish to be regarded as *strong personalities,* we should, and probably do, behave in this way.

Error 6: "Experting." The individual guilty of this next type of error is the so-called "big expert" who actually knows little. Each profession—medicine, law, education, religion—has its problems with incompetents who invade the field. Perhaps equally to be guarded against is the amateur, the self-styled expert. The person who assumes ability to advise but who actually may know little may be building a false front to cover a deep-seated feeling of inadequacy. Fortunately, these "quack" thinkers seldom have much influence.

Here, the following question is relevant: Did such individuals ever come under the influence of a teacher who, as a part of teaching comprehension, helped them to distinguish between a situation in which they knew a great deal about a topic and one in which they knew little? We all need to be sufficiently aware and emotionally strong enough to be able to say, at certain times, "On this subject, I am not informed." Unfortunately, the short-assignment study of fundamental topics in education may produce this inability to sense when one is or is not genuinely informed. The modern curriculum in a good school will counter this error. Children, in studying topics, learn to respect the amount of information available on many subjects and how much knowledge one needs to acquire in order to be able to say, "I know a little about this."

Error 7: Specializing in Snap Judgments. Not too unlike the "know-it-all" is the thinker who makes weighty decisions in the ticking off of seconds. There are many occasions when "snap" judgments are demanded, and they are often the only sort for which one has time. The truly wise person, however, if circumstances make it possible, takes the time needed to study, read, ponder, and, finally, to make a worthy judgment. Knowing when we should suspend a decision is in itself a major step in learning. Again, evidences of teaching this concept as policy can be found in fine educational environments.

Pausing to think may seem to run counter to our swift-paced age. Yet the seriousness of the decisions required of us should argue that for our own safety we must make deliberation in decision-making a routine practice. The place to acquire this practice in the course of our normal living is in the elementary school, especially in the intermediate grades.

Error 8: Fear to Stand up and Be Counted. Some of the severest critics of present-day American ways of life have charged the adults in our land with a sheeplike tendency. We are told that we are afraid to hold views that diverge from popular attitudes and that we lean toward whatever the majority favors. Such conformity is evident in the rapid rise in popularity of gadgets, styles, sayings, and even books. We run with the pack, then rationalize our reasons for our conduct with the pat statement, "Everybody does."

Such conduct not only denies to society the ideas of persons who could be constructive, creative thinkers but, even worse, deprives each such person of a large share of his individual integrity. The story of young Dwight (a third-grader), who disliked a particular book and was being told by his classmates of their acceptance of it, bears repeating here. With unhesitant directness he said, "I don't care if the whole world likes this book, I don't." As young children so often do, he still possessed great personal integrity. The wider world had not rubbed it out.

Many reasons are given to explain why thinking power is discarded in order to run with the herd. The important point here is that children who are encouraged to express themselves freely and who acquire tastes for certain books as well as for making selections and judgments regarding aspects of life are being taught to counter the "herd" trend. If, in addition, children are helped to have the courage to differ with the group, the result is the development of a strong, honest character, a child with real integrity who can and will stand up and express his thoughts honestly.

COMPREHENSION AND THE DEMOCRATIC SOCIETY

The reader, contemplating the eight thinking errors just presented, may question their relevance to this chapter on comprehension. If the schools were teaching a generation of individuals who were to grow into a nonvoting group living under a dictatorship, these points would be irrelevant to the theme of comprehension. Once reading and thinking are censored, learning how to accept replaces learning how to comprehend. We, however, are educating children who will be decision-makers, children who will need to grow up to read conscientiously before making weighty decisions, and who, by strength of conviction undergirded by real knowledge, may blaze new trails of loftier freedoms not only in the future of America but for other nations. Concern, therefore, with how today's youth turns his thinking ability toward comprehending vital reading matter is appropriate for educational leaders.

Furthermore, the ability to think is a learning that has a pervasive power. It is not fenced into a given time, permitting us to think, for example, from nine o'clock to eleven o'clock each day. It spills over into the before and after hours. One becomes a *thinking person*. During the important years of the intermediate grades, observant teachers have helped youngsters develop into thinking children, children who can pause to consider and reconsider, revise earlier answers, hold off judgments, and use many other techniques of good thinkers. If youngsters are being well taught, they are being called upon to use the qualities of good thinking in reading while studying.

Experienced teachers who have consciously sought to guide children into the habit of good reading by drawing upon good thinking are convinced that the full power of children has scarcely been developed. With increased effort and more knowledge of how to bring forth these powers, great new advances in education can be achieved. Help from researchers in children's thinking and from specialists in group dynamics is becoming increasingly available to teachers, curriculum workers, and reading specialists. Such help will continue to influence educational practices, especially in teaching children to become comprehending, foolproofed readers.

THREE BASIC STEPS IN GAINING READING COMPREHENSION

Reading comprehension can be analyzed in many ways. It seems relevant here, in light of the foregoing descriptions of common problems in clear thinking, to examine reading comprehension in terms of the thinking abilities the reader is asked to use in common types of reading.

Step I: Understanding Items and Their Relationships Step I is essential in carrying on every type of reading. The reader must be able not only to recognize the meaning of items within a story or article but also to understand the relationships among these items—from the beginning to the end of the reading. This process is the first step in achieving comprehension. A child's ability to carry out this procedure is examined by a teacher in asking a pupil to tell what he has read. For example, in an account of why water, when it freezes, breaks a covered glass, the pupil needs to recognize such words as *covered, freeze,* and *expand* and to perceive the causal relationships among the items.

Step II: Reacting to What Is Read Step II is, of course, a highly personal process. A child may respond to reading by liking, not liking, accepting, or rejecting, by being challenged to think further or by being indifferent and giving the content no further thought. His reaction will depend partly upon the kind of child he is. Much reading is not remembered because it is not considered important.

Both children and adults often use these two steps in reading stories and accounts of incidents. Following the reading, they could pass a test on the items included. They have understood in a cursory way the ideas the author conveyed, but they are not sufficiently interested to give the ideas further thought.

Step III: Probing Deeper Step III is applied to reading that we assess as important. Teaching in this area of the reading process may suffer because of lack of classroom time or adequate regard for its importance, or because the teacher is unsure of her ability to pursue it.

Step III requires many abilities. These vary with the individual's purposes in reading, the nature of the material, and the reader himself. In some readings, he must be concerned with the competence of the author: who is the author; what is his background; what qualifies him to write on the subject? A group of fourth-graders, reading a book about the South Pole in which polar bears were mentioned, raised such questions. They had studied explorations of the South Pole and had read that there were no polar bears at the South Pole.

At other times, implications, shades of meaning, and emotionally colored words must be recognized for what they are. The fourth-graders who resented the implication regarding North End behavior were applying this ability to their reading. In each case, a child must have the ability to get at the meanings inherent in the lines *per se*; then he must seek beyond the lines for deeper meanings in order to comprehend them fully.

To sum up the three steps essential to gaining comprehension, the reader must first apply the primary skills of word recognition and identification of meanings of words, phrases, sentences, and larger units. Next, in Step II, he must be able to sense when the careful reading of Step III needs application. His knowledge and background of experience play an important role in helping him at this point. More attention to these three steps in reading comprehension follows.

STEP I INVOLVES "READING THE LINES"

When a young child sees a sign, he asks, "What does it say?" A mature questioner asks, "What does the author say?" To be able to relate, retell, or give back the content is an essential reading power derived from a composite of skills that a reader must tap, no matter what other steps follow.

Much help has been given teachers in guiding youngsters toward acquiring this element of comprehension. Practice material is included in workbooks, texts, and supplementary materials. Comprehension at this stage is easily checked by yes-no, true-false, multiple-choice, or similar tests. The majority of questions contained in such tests permit only one correct answer and are therefore useful in building standardized tests that may be corrected via machine. Teaching and testing this step of comprehension lend themselves easily to the use of machines and programmed education.

The very nature of such tests makes them helpful in evaluating large groups, because the personal element in this stage of comprehension is intentionally restricted. A young child might read:

> Gordon had the biggest dog in town. The dog had big, floppy ears but no tail. His name was Oscar. When Gordon called, "Here, Oscar," his dog would come running. But if his mother called Oscar, or his father, or his sister, Oscar would not come.

Checks on the story might be:

1. Who owned the dog?
2. What size was the dog?
3. What was his name?
4. What kind of ears did he have?
5. What did he do when Gordon called?
6. What did Oscar do when Gordon's mother called?

A child in rural Kansas who seldom saw a television program and a New York City child who watched two or three hours of television daily might answer such questions identically. They might offer identical answers, even if one knew much about dogs and the other knew little. The same would be true of reporting back a chapter read on ranch life in the Western states or Edison's discovery of the electric light bulb. All the items, given in sequence and woven together, have a common meaning for the wide variety of young readers, no matter what their background of experience.

STEP II REQUIRES GOING BEYOND THE LINES

Step II brings into the reading process personal variations in comprehension. A child's reactions toward a story might be a rather general feeling: "I like this"; "A good story"; "This doesn't appeal to me"; or "Not much of a story." Toward some informational material the reaction might be: "This is new to me. Good stuff"; "This is very important"; or "I've known this. Not very important." Reacting calls upon the background and experiences of the individual. Reading the story of Oscar, a boy who knows how to train dogs might be intrigued by that dog's behavior. A youngster who has no dog but longs for one may resent the story slightly because it touches upon his deep yearning. One who has no dogs in his background may see nothing unusual in the story and consider it a trivial one.

Much of what a child reads is taken in lightly and scarcely remembered. But if a child is unable to come to grips with anything he reads, then the child is in need of help, or the situation requires examination. Is the material *worthy* of the child's interests? Is he free enough emotionally to think about what he reads? Is he so involved with the mere recognition of words that identifying them is his sole concern? Where a reading problem of such intensity occurs, individual diagnosis is needed.

Developing Individual Reactions Through this basic type of comprehension, the selective powers of children get their impetus and children's taste is encouraged. A teacher interested in probing taste, preferences, or individual reactions periodically takes time to discuss stories and articles that several of the group have read. This discussion, to have value to both teacher and pupils, must be guided in such a way that individual youngsters not only feel free to react but wish to do so and will do so honestly. The teacher's overt expression of respect for each child's view and the teacher's manner of stating it will evoke such honesty.

One wonders, harking back to the frequent criticism of United States adults who reveal sheeplike tendencies not only in styles of clothes and homes but also in their reading, how much effort was invested in making yesterday's children—today's adults—independent in preferences. One might also question whether there was an ample supply of widely varied materials to challenge all tastes, and whether there were many occasions for browsing, sampling, and discussing. A reading diet of identical texts scarcely stimulates individual reaction.

Some teachers may need help in creating a climate that encourages children to express honest reaction. Some may have to grow in stature to be ready to accept children's honestly expressed ideas.

A classroom in which the teacher asks for opinions and gets them in unison is not a wholesome place in which to develop independent thinkers. This is a typical "yes" atmosphere in which individuality, integrity, and thinking are soft-pedaled.

Time and Courage to Think Time is an important factor in developing reading comprehension. To ask, "What do you think about this news item?" of a group of alert children who are developing the power to react demands that the teacher allot time to listen to three or four comments, some of which may be unfolded slowly. A fifth-grade girl, in commenting on what was wrong with her school, said, "I don't get time to think. Nobody does. We are all too busy."

In addition to having time to think, each individual needs the courage to do so. As one examines carefully the way in which a comprehending reader is educated to bring his personal feelings and attitudes into the process of appraising and selecting and to voice these feelings, one sees immediately the relationship of this stage of reading growth to the increase of the child's integrity and moral strength. It is not easy, even in an excellent classroom situation, to state a personal assessment of reading matter. For example, one girl gave her view of a popular natural science series that was appearing in the local daily paper. "I don't like these science stories," she declared. She then gave her reasons: animals talked; essential data were omitted. The articles were "dressed-up science fiction." Not all her fellow students were in agreement. A teacher, aware of the strong pro and con attitudes that even very young children develop, must be ready to help youngsters in such situations to respect the speaker's forthrightness and courage. Those who do not agree with the divergent viewpoint may be encouraged to analyze their reasons for differing and to state them.

It is a privileged classroom, indeed, be it a kindergarten or an upper grade, in which "This I like" or "This I don't like" are honored statements. In the "everybody does" program in which one-hundred-per-cent agreement is sought on most matters, children are being denied the chance to develop taste, the chance to learn how to read before arriving at convictions and outlooks, and the chance to become honest, wholesome, strong personalities. They are being denied an opportunity to test themselves out in standing up for what they believe; instead, they are being encouraged to ape our Caspar Milquetoasts of standard design.

Problems in Developing Genuine Reactions There are reasons why widespread teaching of this reaction phase of comprehension seems to lag. As has been stated, such teaching takes time—perhaps only five to ten minutes, but in today's crowded school schedule a teacher may feel too hurried to give even this scant attention to it. Unlike Step I, Step II does not lend itself to silent comprehension checks. Essay answers from each child are not always helpful. Value seems to be lost when reactions are written rather than given orally. A strong, independent thinker exerts a contagiously wholesome influence on the group, an influence that is missed in writing.

The finality of a written check or test prevents the less courageous from recording honestly. Jack, a third-grader, related at home that his teacher was making a study of how youngsters liked their new library books. After a child read a book he was to record "Like" or "Don't like" on a chart. Jack told the family that he had read three books to date, had liked two, had not liked the third, but had recorded "Like" for all three. "Why did you do that?" asked his mother. "Because I didn't want to hurt my teacher's feelings." Without special guidance from the teacher in expressing his opinions freely, this boy would have found it equally difficult to express his reactions orally.

Many other influencing factors are present in classrooms. A fifth-grade boy, for example, when asked how he liked the new social-studies book, responded, "Who cares? We've got thirty of them now."

The development of growth in ability and honesty in reacting is not a simple matter to achieve. For example, placing halos over certain books by labeling them basic may prevent readers from examining them carefully. Teachers, therefore, should be given real help and much encouragement and recognition for their efforts in building these qualities into readers.

STEP III INVOLVES READING BETWEEN THE LINES

The techniques involved in the third stage of reading comprehension are of the utmost importance to the child's competent and safe use of reading. Once a child decides that a story or an article or a part of a book is important enough to merit thought, what he thinks and how he pursues his point are of real value to his growth. In Steps I and II he calls upon his experiences and his memory in utilizing the tools of reading to follow a thread of ideas with their interrelationships and to react sufficiently to his reading to determine whether he should probe deeper. To go more deeply into the meanings of some of his reading, however, he must engage in more complex thinking than is required for Steps I and II. Most of the responses in Step I are made to the stated or implied question, "What did it say?" In Step II the child responds to, "What is your immediate reaction?" Step III requires the reader to go into a variety of deeper ways of thinking, some of which may take time and further study.

Making Discoveries About Motivation The sort of challenge involved is revealed by the experience of a group of spirited fifth-graders. This group had been studying weather, the method by which it is forecast, the function of forecasts, the use of radar in forecasting, and the use of new machines in the forecasting process. They had gathered their information by reading pamphlets, references in their science textbooks, and descriptive material they had received from a nearby weather station.

One of the boys brought in a newspaper article in which it was stated that "the *Farmer's Almanac* is a more dependable weather guide than all these new-fangled methods." The article, which was brief, was read to the class. The teacher, a young man in his second year of teaching, asked, "Is this important enough to discuss?" All but three students said, "Yes." One of the dissenters said, "Nothing in that paper is ever worth talking about." This judgment, after some exploration, was found to be unfounded. The class then decided to examine the article but try to limit the time spent.

The first task set was to list the questions or topics that were to guide discussion of the article. The questions were:

Who wrote the article? How much does he know about weather?

Why did he write this?

Had the writer been misled and inconvenienced by a report of the weather?

Then followed a plan for the next step:

How can we find the answers to these questions?

It was agreed that the writer of the article must be located for a personal interview in order to secure the answers to some of the questions. The study was assigned to a committee of three, which was to report back to the class.

Within three days the committee members presented their report: The article was not written by anyone at the weekly newspaper from which it had been taken. The material contained in it had been culled from articles sent to rural weeklies as space fillers. Rural weeklies subscribed for this material, which included short items considered of general interest, such as the weather item. The content of the article had been selected for this particular paper by the editor, who was "getting fed up with the use of machines to do everything. Next they'll have them eating for us." The editor admitted that he had never studied weather.

After the committee had made its report, the teacher commented: "We have used some important points in reading this article. We have examined the authorship and the editor's motivation. 'Who wrote this and how informed is he' are questions a good reader answers before he appraises the value of some of the informational material he reads."

Later, these same youngsters brought in an unsigned handbill headed "Why You Should Vote *No* on the School Bond Issue." Their first question was, "Now who wrote that?" It was quickly followed by a second question, "Why?"

Asking Questions About Newspaper Stories Today's children can find their way among informative articles that include conflicting data and viewpoints. Several children in a New Jersey sixth grade brought to school news accounts of an issue that had arisen in one of New Jersey's largest cities over the right of individuals to pass out pamphlets regarding a strike. One news story indicated that "the policemen cracked down on the distributors." A second paper gave a more complete story, indicating that the police officers had stopped distribution of the pamphlets and had taken the names and addresses of the distributors, but also that the distributors claimed that prevention of their distribution of the pamphlets was a violation of the Bill of Rights.

These New Jersey youngsters were in the process of studying famous documents of the United States, including the Bill of Rights. They became involved in a serious discussion of the two news clippings. The teacher, a veteran of almost thirty years of teaching, said it was the best discussion and the finest teaching and learning experience of her career. Youngsters found themselves facing, for the first time, the slanting of news by emotionally colored words and by omission of important facts. Awards are made annually to newspapers that demonstrate competence combined with ethics in reporting the news. Few of today's adults were guided in their early education to appreciate the high canons of journalism to which our best newspapers are dedicated. Here were sixth-grade boys and girls receiving their first lesson in this fundamental area that is closely interwoven with critical reading and essential to their use of reading as informed citizens.

Budding readers not only are capable of growing in critical assessment of content but are also able to gain insight into the use of "color" words and to probe authors' motives. Some may even sense the deep psychological reasons that lead some authors to write as they do. In the case of the editor who included a criticism of gathering weather data, the young interviewers were unable to express in psychological terms the influence of the editor's emotions on the content, but they were able to notice that he "had a grudge against machines," and that this grudge influenced his selection of the particular article for his paper.

Guidance in such comprehension is appropriately called the foolproofing process. Critical readers are developed through experience after experience in assessing readings in terms of fitness or appropriateness for acceptance. At times the up-to-dateness of the content may be the point in question; on other occasions, the motive of the author. In some cases the competence of the author, based on ascertainable facts pertaining to his background, may determine the final reaction. As boys and girls acquire more information, they can challenge the accuracy of facts in light of their previously acquired knowledge.

Danger: Reader Not Foolproofed One can easily see that interpreting or *comprehending* reading to this depth requires careful thinking. Not all occasions demand such great care in reading. As youngsters grow capable of wider and more independent reading, however, such need increases. Far too many tend to accept ideas they read without knowing why; others reject them out of ignorance. The common adage "I see by the paper" was used as the caption for a daily news column in a Midwestern state. The half-educated reader (and one who reads but is not foolproofed is such) may extend this adage by concluding, "so I believe it." In an age when every variety of material is readily available, from the finest to the shoddiest, and much of what is available is propaganda calculated to misinform, the only defensible concept of comprehension is one that is as inclusive as the growing reader requires to read with full understanding of the content and its implications.

Deeper Comprehension Starts Early and Grows Slowly It is fascinating to observe the beginning of the difficult and complicated intellectual process of comprehending. In a kindergarten one morning the teacher read a preprimer to the group. The story told of twins who grew bigger and bigger. Pictures showed the twins at various ages and, finally, as they celebrated their first birthday with a cake bearing one candle in its center. After listening to the first comments that followed the reading of the story, the teacher asked, "Why do you think I read you this story?" One youngster responded quickly, "Because you have twins and you like twins." Another chimed in, "How old are your twins?" The teacher, who was the mother of twins and had told the kindergarten group about them, said, "I think you can almost guess." Some responses came quickly, "They are one year old. And today is their birthday." Young as they were, the kindergartners had sensed the teacher's liking for the story because of factors in her personal life.

Even very young children will also tell why they do or do not like a story. "I don't like stories where big people are mean to little kids." "I like stories when everybody is happy." "I like surprises and I wish I'd get more surprises." Such comments from first-graders indicate that some six-year-olds are already able to know and articulate their preferences. A few years later, they will begin to understand even more adequately why they have such likes and dislikes. As they read and discuss stories, teachers help them to become interested in the lives and other writings of some of the authors. This adds to their enjoyment and understanding. Once they grow excited about their own independent information-gathering and are able to pursue interests through reading, new facets of comprehension will be developed. The entire process of becoming a comprehending reader must be a matter of years.

It is obvious that some, of whatever age, who are growing in thinking, will grasp the principle of critical reading sooner and more adequately than others. We should all proceed cautiously, however, in judging a child's potential growth as a thinker. Some studies have revealed that youngsters who rate highest on reading tests are not necessarily the soundest in deeper comprehension. This matter of measuring thinking ability by standardized reading tests is another important area in the teaching of reading that needs more research. The author's own research has raised serious questions as to the typing of children's thinking ability according to their reading ability as measured by some standardized tests. High scores on reading tests did not correlate highly with the ability to select materials helpful to solving proposed problems.

Stimulating and Evaluating the Application of Step III The three levels of reading comprehension are called upon in many parts of the school curriculum and in many out-of-school experiences. All three are pertinent to such fields as social studies (including current events), science, and those aspects of the curriculum dealing with health. The more challenging the child finds his work in school, the more will his fullest comprehending abilities be developed.

Testing the ability of an entire grade in Step III—critical reading—is not as simple as measuring the first stage of comprehension. Some tests do approach this need, and good schools consciously select reading tests that call for more reflective responses than those based on short recall. But an observing teacher must gather information concerning each child's thinking-in-reading abilities from his day-after-day work in school in order to evaluate growth in deep comprehension.

PREREQUISITES FOR DEVELOPING THINKING READERS

Basic to teaching today's child to become a critical reader are a number of prerequisites. Foremost is a thinking teacher who regards the development of thinking readers as the most essential goal in the teaching of reading. One teacher pursuing this major goal alone may run into obstacles; yet there are such valiant teachers. The teacher who functions in a school system where the entire staff aids and abets this major goal is fortunate. Luckily, there are many such schools.

Essential: A Teacher Who Is a Critical Reader Let us look more closely at the teacher and the teacher's role in reading. A teacher who is a critical reader and who is independent and honest in his reactions can be aware of reading situations arising in or out of school that call for guidance in children's understanding. A teacher who is not an astute, experienced reader can scarcely be regarded as being capable of helping children to become so. It should be stated quickly that this is not the fault of *teacher education per se*; it is, rather, the omission of focus on this need in all education, including the kind of education offered in many liberal-arts colleges. Many adults who have become alert critical readers have become so through their own powers. Some may have resorted to helpful books and pamphlets available on how to increase one's powers in thinking and improving comprehension.

In-service programs for educators have helped lift the sights of teachers in careful evaluation of methods to improve teaching. Many schools have incorporated excellent methods into the total program as a result of the study of teaching science. The "scientific" approach to studies has added greatly to an emphasis on abilities demanded in real comprehension.

Importance of Guided Discussion A second essential prerequisite to developing mature comprehenders is the teacher's ability in guiding discussion. In good discussion a child examines ideas carefully, reacts to the thinking of others, and reintegrates ideas in such a way that he stretches his own comprehension powers. He is not told *what* to think or *how* to come to a fixed conclusion; rather, he enters into a process of mind-meeting-mind, idea-linking-with-idea, or idea-altering-idea. The technique of guiding discussion appropriate to the age of children is so strategic to children's growth that the next chapter of this book is devoted to the subject.

The Right to Think Honestly For many years children have been taught that "Teacher knows best" or "Adults know, but children don't." This attitude is closely interwoven with another, that children should respect their elders. Both ideas have valid bases for application, but both, if misapplied, can prevent children from growing educationally. The problem is double-edged: adults need to learn they must not hamper the right of children to learn to think logically, and children need to learn when adults are due their confidence and respect.

This is a complicated assignment for both, but the burden of responsibility rests with the adults, who are, or should be, the more mature. A classroom in which the teacher permits her ideas to be challenged by the students is an excellent place for essential learning. This teacher clearly reveals respect for children's thinking and does not feel threatened by their ability to challenge her. A teacher strong enough to say, "I overlooked that in my reading," "I am not informed on this point," or "You may be a better judge of this story about football than I," is emotionally ready to teach children to think independently.

Learning How to Challenge and How to Differ While the school must play an important role in encouraging a child to think independently, it also has a closely related responsibility. A child growing into new phases of thinking may not yet have become "polished" in his method of challenging an adult. Under wise teacher guidance, he learns polite techniques. In his less informed state, he may venture forth to challenge his mother or father. In some homes this challenging of parental authoritativeness might be misinterpreted as showing a loss of respect for parents. A school can avoid such misunderstanding and add to a child's growth through helpful meetings with parents on such a theme as, "When Children Question Your Knowledge." Helping parents to understand the important new growth that this process implies—and many parents do appreciate it—eases worries and also prepares them to enter into discussions with greater understanding. Such home contacts via discussion can have far-reaching consequences in building or sustaining good parent-child bonds.

Increasing the Child's Respect for Himself Where a give-and-take spirit exists between teacher and children and between parents and children, another vital by-product is created. A child senses that his views are listened to, that he is accorded as much respect as adults are. He is thus given a tremendous boost in self-confidence and belief in himself. He, therefore, is readier to put greater effort into his work. If, once in a while, he seems a trifle too brash, this brashness will fade if the adults continue to honor him with a respected place in discussion.

Learning Self-Control in Discussion A school in which children share in planning curriculum studies to be undertaken and in which there is much discussion of reference reading is a school ripe for many important opportunities to stimulate careful thinking and to guide dignified ways of discussion.

On many occasions, children will meet opposing views held by informed people. When current events hold an important place in the curriculum, difficult problems with high learning values arise. Youngsters may read news articles from good journals and find them contradictory. The important ability to feel at ease in controversy and the know-how to manage one's share in discussion with emotional calm and intellectual poise can be acquired under the direction of the teacher in situations where such incidents occur. It is vital that the educated citizen possess these abilities, but even college-educated adults often reveal complete inability in this area.

To attribute lacks in this field to emotionalism only is too easy a solution. Educating today's children to transcend the present adult generation in thinking powers and in techniques essential for probing a wide range of problems is not an unrealistic ambition. The promise lies in large part in our willingness to struggle with our own comprehension so that we may help the elementary-school child with his. It is to be hoped that, in the years immediately ahead, much greater attention will be focused on the development of this type of astute reader throughout the school years.

In the next chapter, a description of techniques essential to guiding discussion is included for those teachers and parents eager to take bolder strides in this direction.

SUGGESTED READINGS ON COMPREHENSION AND CRITICAL READING

CHASE, STUART. *Guides to Straight Thinking.* New York: Harper & Brothers, 1956.
The entire book alerts a reader to thirteen errors common in adults' thinking. Growth in reading comprehension demands growth in straight thinking. This book, therefore, will stimulate teachers to guide children in applying techniques of sound thinking in their reading. A pertinent book for lay readers. Highly readable style.

GANS, ROMA. *Critical Reading Comprehension in the Intermediate Grades.* New York: Bureau of Publications, Teachers College, Columbia University, 1940.
A study of the ability of intermediate-grade children to select and reject materials relevant to problems presented. Readers who were able according to standardized tests did not reflect similar ability in this phase of reference reading. A technical study.

RUCKER, W. RAY. *Curriculum Development in the Elementary School.* New York: Harper & Brothers. Chapter 3.
A description of steps in the problem-solving process. Excellent suggestions for reference reading. A "log of a problem project" included in detail. Teachers and lay persons can acquire increased respect for the role reading plays in a good school program and a more inclusive concept of reading comprehension than is commonly accepted.

WILES, KIMBALL. *Teaching for Better Schools.* 2nd ed. Englewood Cliffs, N. J.: Prentice-Hall, Inc., 1959. Chapter 12.
Classroom climate and methods conducive to making children responsible and intelligent in work that includes collecting data, keeping records, and self-evaluation. Useful suggestions of ways to include parents in judgment-making about children's progress.

CHAPTER 11

Learning to Extend Comprehension Through Discussion

Ideally, a classroom is a model of a good community. In it children tend to their major business of learning in a climate that fosters excellent learning conditions. In it they also learn the essential skills necessary to maintain helpful neighborly relations with some neighbors whom they enjoy and with others beside whom they can work and whom they respect, but with whom they do not socialize. They may tend to agree with some of their neighbors; they accept the fact that they differ with others. To some they look for help in their studies; to others they are able to give help.

Central to a good, neighborly classroom community of this sort are the ideas dealt with by the youngsters in it. On many points they may be in complete accord; on some they may differ and discuss their pros and cons. If properly guided, children in such a classroom will grow in their ability to accept the rights of others to hold their own views. This concept is basic to our American credo, in which we state our respect for man's right to his views. Only if this right is accepted can we declare our respect for his dignity. If these two inseparable ideals pervade the classroom, they give children an invaluable introduction to true democracy.

No experience calls for the application of these two essential rights more than does discussion. In applying good discussion techniques, a child has a chance to feel himself bloom as a thinker, a dealer in ideas in an oral language situation. He also has the opportunity to see his classmates do the same. The abilities he acquires in dealing with his own ideas and those of others in discussion he can then more readily apply to his understanding and his discussion of reading.

GUIDING CLASSROOM DISCUSSION

It is at this point that teacher education comes into focus. Every young candidate for the teaching profession should be given adequate help, not only in becoming a critical reader but also in understanding both general and specific techniques for guiding discussions with the age group he is preparing to teach. With such direct training he may join the ranks of that group of teachers who are able to guide youngsters not only into the full realm of reading comprehension, but also in the process of living up to our national ideals.

Techniques for guiding discussion have been developed recently by specialists in group dynamics. Anyone observing a group of intelligent adults engage in discussion under the direction of an able leader will readily see the common sense in teaching such techniques. Youngsters who are ready to profit from them now need not wait until adulthood to acquire them.

The readiness of children to utilize such help was brought home to the author by a sixth-grade group in which the pupils were following newspaper and magazine articles on the subject of nuclear-bomb shelters. A forthcoming television discussion on the topic was called to their attention, and two able students were asked to present a report of it. After a general appraisal of the program, they said, "Some new points for and against shelters, but it was not a good discussion. There were too many interruptions, and when one was talking, others were not listening."

These youngsters were not new to the field of discussion. Since their kindergarten days they had had experience in talking things over. For years at their school, informal discussion had been going on in all age groups, purposefully directed toward stimulating children to think independently and to gain skill in group discussions. These sixth-graders had become more mature in their techniques than were the adults whom they viewed on television.

BEGINNING TO TALK THINGS OVER

Discussion experiences should be planned to fit the age of the child. When children in kindergarten prepare for their first group trip by "talking over our rules for walking safely to the park across the street," a wise teacher recognizes that five-year-olds may not yet be accustomed to listening. A few may be ready participants; others are accepted as wiggling, nonlistening physical additions to the group. As daily five- to ten-minute sessions of "talking over" continue, more and more join in. The youngsters grow in their ability to listen while functioning as members of a group.

Another quality that characterizes these young "discussers" is their unreadiness to adhere to one topic. For example, in talking over the need for a safe rule for crossing streets, young Jerry piped up, "Our cat was gone a long time, and this morning there he was." The teacher did not know what stirred him to add this important news at this point, but she did recognize that the expression of a seemingly irrelevant comment is the way in which a particular child may enter into this kind of experience. Asking kindergarten children to hew to a topic is out of keeping with the readiness of the majority. Yet calling their attention to the need to talk things over eventually creates increased ability to listen, to speak up, and, for some, perhaps before the year ends, to be able to follow the main points.

Simple discussion techniques are frequently used in routine kindergarten life. Some children may not have been helped by previous home experiences to wait for their turn to speak. Learning to do so takes time and growth. Have most adults learned this? Some groups may be ready to have the teacher remind them of the topic from time to time by asking, "Who can tell us what we are talking about?" Have most adults learned this? Occasionally, after a cogent comment by one child, the teacher may ask, "What do you think of Ginny's idea?" in order to acquaint her young listeners with the process of reacting to ideas that come from others. Story time is an excellent time for youngsters to offer their personal reactions and to add related and unrelated ideas to the discussion. From many such friendly experiences, they acquire some understanding of the discussion process.

Working with Small Groups The foregoing discussions have referred to whole-group situations. It should here be added that, although fine learnings do come to some children in these whole-group meetings, for a real feeling of "belonging" to a group many need conversations with the teacher in smaller groups. Specialists in the techniques of group discussion consider eight adults a desirable number for good discussion.

The small-group quality can be achieved by a teacher who, for example, will stop briefly to remind a group of young builders using blocks of an important class rule. Such a contact is personal enough so that a child will hear, will listen, and will feel he is being spoken to. Going from lunch table to lunch table and reminding each group about street-crossing rules will often prove more effective in terms of later conduct than asking all the youngsters to sit and listen as members of a large group. Some children, in large-group situations, do not sense that the conversation includes them. Therefore, whenever possible, a teacher who understands kindergarten children uses small-group situations as occasions for making essential points.

The growth in sensing membership within a group and in being able to join in group-thinking processes varies, as do all other qualities of children's growth. We commonly expect too much of children in kindergarten and first and second grades by assuming they are able to attend to business in whole-class situations. Occasionally, lack of time requires them to make this effort. At other times, there is so much come-hither appeal in the nature of the experience that each one can take in what is happening. It may, however, be beyond the ability of many at six and of some even at seven and eight to listen to a teacher and to interact with her on an idea level in a total group situation. And these children may not be slow learners. Readiness for thinking in a group may involve many factors other than intellectual powers. Witness the conduct of some highly able individuals who do not appear to their advantage in discussions.

Beginning to Structure Discussion As children grow older, their discussions can be given more structure. Writing the topic or question under discussion on a chart or blackboard is extremely helpful in guiding discussion and is a technique widely used not only in elementary grades but also in adult discussion groups. Trying to keep closely to the point with children from six and seven years onward is helpful teaching. Raising questions, making additions to points, questioning some comments or parts of statements, asking for proof or references, citing authorities, bringing in countering data and other views—all these points occur in good discussion, and the use of these techniques may start in the primary grades under able teacher leadership. By the time children who have received group-discussion practice since their earlier years reach the sixth grade, they have become experienced in group discussion and perhaps, like those who reported on the television forum, able to sit in judgment on some adult discussions.

OVERCOMING HURDLES IN GUIDING DISCUSSION

At this point we must examine the relation of discussion to essential growth in the highest level of comprehension, described in Chapter 10 as Step III. In the more literal phase of comprehension, Step I, a teacher can both develop and test the skills needed by using prepared practice aids; youngsters can work on many of them individually and silently. A child who reads an account of the manner in which animals prepare for winter can be tested to see if he retains the outstanding major and minor items. If not, specific help to meet the nature of his need can be given.

Encouraging Personal Reacting In the second step or level of comprehension a teacher is eager to develop a child's ability to react personally to the ideas he has read. It may not be advisable to encourage youngsters to write their individual reactions, because most are still unable to express themselves adequately in writing. Then too, some may not be sure how they wish to react; they would prefer to wait and hear what others think. The shy and the less imaginative may lack the ability to speak up readily. Even though a teacher may be gifted in eliciting from children honest responses, pressures from within the group may unnerve otherwise eager participants. Many a fine teacher must work for months before some youngsters are ready to say, "This is what I think." The value of the end result is self-evident.

Facing Difficulties in Developing Critical Readers Other problems also beset the course of teaching youngsters to grow in critical appraisal of content. Children, like adults, are surrounded by a widely accepted code of behavior that can be quoted as, "Never mind if you don't agree, or if you have a question; the better part of valor is to keep still." In school-yard talk, this code adds up to, "Don't stick your neck out." The older and wiser youngsters teach this code to the younger. Therefore, the teacher who is eager to develop a group of placid accepters into critical readers must have the patience and skill to offset contrary influences.

One of the most important questions we can be asked is: What do you think? A discussion on the importance of this question with several high-school classes in a study hall at a certain school proved shocking to some teachers. Youngsters, many in their early teens, frankly admitted that they had learned to conceal their thinking on numerous occasions, particularly at school. Some commented, "You get into trouble if you tell what you think"; "You may be asked that, but grownups don't really want to know what you think"; "Before I answer I want to know why I'm asked that."

With such attitudes deeply ingrained, the difficulty confronting teachers who hope to guide youngsters in genuine thinking is obvious. How can these young people become forthright in discussing ideas gleaned from their reading? These youngsters were the victims of damaging influences, some no doubt in the school itself. Many able teachers are aware that these attitudes exist and, by daily evidence of their respect for personal integrity and by that integrity that they themselves reveal, are able to redirect pupils. This they must do if they are to be responsible for growth in reading comprehension.

Teachers in various sections of the United States found similar reactions among fifth- and sixth-graders and junior-high-school students. One sixth-grader said, "Sometimes we are safer if we don't think." In a discussion involving a news item on United States nuclear status, one child commented, "I wish we'd start a war with Russia and get it over with." That same day, the teacher received a telephone call from a parent, upset that the teacher *permitted* a child to make such a statement. Fortunately, this teacher could help the parent understand that a situation in which a child can reveal what he thinks is a wholesome one. Such frank comments by children make real guidance possible. The silent class is one the teacher can no more help than a doctor could help a patient whose condition he dared not examine.

It is reasonable to expect some teachers in anxious times to hesitate to discuss topics highly charged with controversy, yet this is one of the key educational needs. Obviously to guide thinking in all areas of life and, of course, in reading means we must be ready to deal with already warped attitudes when we meet them. Of first importance is the need to counter the influences that build such fear of honest thinking while children are in their formative years in the elementary school. The teachers who take this responsibility seriously must possess courage. A vital factor is the teacher's courage in accepting responsibility for what children say, either in seriousness or in an attempt to gain attention. Later in this chapter, guidelines for discussing difficult controversial topics are suggested.

Class Discussion and Behavior Problems Perhaps the most common problem in guiding any kind of whole-group discussion is to hold class members to orderly attention. Maintaining such control can be a serious problem in a class containing several highly volatile members. One hears all too often of groups with so many emotionally upset members that all teaching is jeopardized. Such conditions go beyond the question of curriculum and point directly to the need for effective school leadership and adequate guidance personnel. Help for seriously disturbed children should be available in all elementary schools for the sake of the youngsters and for the sake of learning conditions in the classroom. Given a responsible teacher and a normal group, the management of the group's conduct for discussion should be possible. It is the fear of disorder, however, that causes many teachers to avoid discussions and to rely upon the quieting influence of written work.

Many of us still reflect an attitude often implied in former times —namely, that discussion is *not* important; that it is not *learning*. How many of us have heard a teacher or chairman of a meeting say: "Now let's stop this discussion and get down to business." True, much discussion is neither learning nor business. Busy and sociable adults—and children—need the relaxation gained through many social contacts in which talking is not structured or guided according to a prearranged plan. Youngsters are ready, however, to learn the difference between *talking informally* and *discussing-to-learn.* The wrong attitude toward discussion requires correction by observation of good discussion and evaluation of the learnings encouraged in the process.

Experimenting with Small-Group Discussion In a visit to a second grade, the author told the youngsters of a new plan for working that they were going to try: the entire class of thirty-one was to be divided into reading groups; each group of four or five would meet together with their reading books (their teacher based her reading program on two grade-level readers); five groups were to use the first reader; three were to use the second reader. Each group was to choose a reporter; all groups were to discuss or talk over the following question: *Which story is about children most like us?* After a short period, all discussion was to stop, and each reporter was to report on his group's decision. If members of a group disagreed, the reporter was to report on the disagreement.

The question was written on the blackboard in writing large enough so that all could see. Midway in the discussion period, the children were reminded to look at the question and see whether they were still talking about that question. No difference in reading ability was discernible in the seriousness of discussion in the groups. After approximately seven or eight minutes of discussion the groups were alerted to prepare to report. The results astonished the teacher. The strongest differences of opinion were expressed by the two groups comprising those whom the teacher regarded as the least able students. Their reporters gave cogent statements, spirited and to the point. In contrast, the three groups considered the "good, second-reader" groups seemed less stimulated by their discussion and had no difference of opinion within the group.

An experiment in discussion as simple as this revealed a readiness on the part of young readers scarcely past the beginning stage to weigh, consider, argue, and recall accurately for reporting. It also demonstrated convictions on the part of some. It raised some questions about too-bland or too-ready acceptance by some readers, and the teacher planned to examine the reasons for these attitudes.

Some comments revealed surprising facets of children's thinking. One of the reporters for a first-reader group said, "None of the stories are like us because they are about five-year-old kids." When asked how it was possible to recognize the children in the stories as five-year-olds, he said, "You can tell by the pictures." Another reporter said, "We can't tell if the kids are like us because we can't see where they live." Ideas such as these indicate the kind of thinking children are ready to use in examining some simple accounts in beginning readers.

Furthermore, the teacher was frank to admit her surprise at the language ability the so-called slow readers displayed. Jeanette, one of the able readers, a fragile-looking girl with a troubled expression, said to the teacher: "Those first-reader reports were as good as ours." Another important observation was made by the teacher: The entire procedure took approximately twenty-five minutes, and during that time *all* were actively participating. In evaluating her observations, the teacher raised the question: "Is it possible that common teaching procedures in primary reading obscure the true picture of a child's ability and also deny him a chance to think?"

Techniques of Involvement More experiments are needed to help teachers overcome the handicaps created by class size. Techniques that involve youngsters so that they feel themselves a part of the work are essential. Sharing in planning work is now a widely used technique and helps to achieve involvement. Breaking a class quickly into groups of three or four for a short discussion of one point or a key question also has promising value.

Eager teachers in a school where improving reading comprehension was a year-after-year concern used small-group discussion frequently as the need arose to achieve more participation and more pupil reactions to key matters. An outstanding contribution to this school's growth, according to the teachers' observations, was the decrease in flabby attention and a marked increase in learning by all youngsters. Techniques of involvement comprise another area where more research would bring valuable assistance to today's teachers and their pupils.

GUIDELINES FOR DISCUSSING HOT ISSUES

The previous descriptions of children's learning to use discussion show how discussion stimulates children to greater intellectual activity in their reading. They notice more, react more personally, grow in ability to express their ideas, and learn to listen to ideas of others. Earlier in this chapter the reactions of intermediate-grade youngsters to an adult demonstration of inadequate discussion techniques were cited. Few of today's adults received specific help in learning these techniques. Perhaps all too few children today do. When matters we deem important are in controversy, we may find difficulty in reading about them in order to clarify our thinking and may find ourselves awkward in discussing them. At the very time when comprehension should come to our aid, we may be compelled to admit that it will not function, that emotions and unreasonable behavior take command of our decisions.

Beginning in the intermediate grades and even before, many school, community, and national affairs attract youngsters' attention: the new school ruling about riding bicycles to school published in the local daily; the report of a local citizens' committee opposing collection of money for UNICEF by children on Halloween; the school newspaper report of a controversy over all-school assemblies; the story in a school magazine about cheating in sports; and so on. When interests are stimulated in events of this kind and children reveal strong feelings, unanimous or mixed, a wise teacher utilizes the occasion as an opportunity to teach ways of discussing a subject even when feelings are extremely strong.

Just as in sports, where strong partisan feelings are often stirred, rules for the "game" must be made beforehand, and an umpire or discussion leader must be selected. With newcomers to the experience of discussion, the teacher, of necessity, must be the leader. As children grow in competence, however, the class may select youngsters as discussion leaders and evaluate their effectiveness.

With a teacher's help, a group may make original guidelines to test out, then revise them if or when the need is demonstrated. Among commonly accepted regulations are these:

1. *All must be prepared to discuss the point.*

Some questions or topics demand a background of information. Perhaps the group has been reading and investing real study in the topic, perhaps not. If not, discussion should be deferred until there has been time for participants to become informed. Such emphasis on gathering needed information is essential to good discussion. It will counter in today's children the contagion of opinionation we find in adults. At times, trips may be necessary for gathering information; this was the case in a Kansas school when controversy arose over the safety of a new highway circle. Some sixth-graders had not seen it and, without going to see the site, could not understand what the local controversy was about.

At other times, when there are two or more distinct sides in an affair close to children's interests, leaders of the differing positions may be asked to appear before the class and to give their views and reasons for them. "Get the facts first" is an essential policy for children to learn to respect from experience. All methods required for gathering information are followed in today's good schools. The topic or issue under consideration will determine the variety of resources the students must examine in order to ready themselves for later consideration.

2. *A clear statement of the topic of discussion should be written on the blackboard or chart.*

This action has a twofold purpose. First, it helps clarify exactly what the group is discussing; second, having the topic always in view serves as an aid to individuals within the group who wander from the topic and inject irrelevant ideas. Such errors are common also to readers doing reference reading or those who are reading to answer a given question. There is excellent discipline in keeping to the point both in discussion and in reading.

3. *Before talking, each individual must wait to be recognized by the chairman.*

A fair chairman tries to recognize youngsters in turn. Adults, including teachers, violate this point in guiding discussion; at times they tend to show preference for individuals as persons or for others because they hold certain points of view. Such displays of preference are obviously poor leadership techniques.

4. *While one member of the group is talking, the rest must keep hands down and listen.*

This is a point desperately in need of attention in all classroom communication. When one youngster is talking, others who wish to talk often engage in a frenzied hand-waving, meanwhile paying no attention to the child who is speaking. Attention to what is being said is encouraged by the teacher who calls on others to react to the speaker's comments. This practice manages to get the lines of conversation from a pupil to other pupils, not always from one pupil to the teacher.

5. *Each participant has a right to his own personal view, granted his information is correct.*

Children need to be taught a respect for viewpoints that differ from theirs. A teacher, whose conduct exerts great influence on a group, must also demonstrate this quality. On many points of difference, neither side may be wrong or right; the question may be merely one of preference.

6. *Courtesy is a "must."*

Rude interruptions, outbursts of objection or approval, personal criticisms, or any derogatory remarks are taboo. We all experience strong feelings at times. An educated person strives to control his conduct.

7. *If data are used, sources should be quoted, or the speaker should be ready to cite them if questioned.*

8. *After the discussion, or at a reasonable time, the group must decide:*

   (a) Do we know enough to decide upon the answer to our question or feel adequately informed on the topic?

   (b) Are we ready to make a decision or do we need more information and time to discuss?

   (c) In what way was our discussion good? Not good? Is there a need to change or extend rules?

(d) Has the discussion experience produced any helpful suggestions for future study?

Making Discoveries Through Discussion Guidelines for beginners in second or third grade must be simpler, but it is amazing to follow a plan similar to the one proposed here for an intermediate grade and note the ability of younger children in managing the discussion. A procedure similar to that just described was observed in a fourth grade where the reasonableness of arithmetic examples was under discussion. The topic was phrased, "Some of us think our arithmetic examples don't make sense." Those who agreed with this idea cited specific examples from the textbook to prove their point, then elaborated on why they believed the examples to be unreasonable. Others gave examples which to them seemed reasonable; among such examples were some that had previously been cited by other pupils as senseless.

After a fifteen-minute period, the teacher asked, "Has this discussion so far given anyone a helpful answer?" A wide-eyed boy answered, "Yes, it shows that an example may seem reasonable to some kids and foolish or unreasonable to others." Another boy observed, "You can't say *all* examples are senseless. Some are, some are not." Imagine the quality of thinking that can develop in youngsters nurtured for a year in this type of discussion atmosphere.

A tendency toward tolerance will rub off on all. Many will grow to recognize specific elements of straight thinking, such as being cautious about making sweeping generalizations. Once aware of points in good thinking in discussion, youngsters are readier to be alert to those in the press, texts, reference books, bulletins, and magazines. The halo that they may have placed over anything in print is being transferred to their own thinking heads.

Practice in Probing Critically Boys and girls in all grades need frequent experiences in which they take time to examine a story or article carefully. During such times, the teacher leads the way with good questioning and encourages ample expenditure of time for children to *think* about their answers.

For example, a sixth-grade committee was compiling a list of books to suggest to the library for purchase. They gathered book reviews that were read to the class; the entire group then shared in deciding which books to place on the recommended list.

A sentence in a review about a biography of General Lee stated: "The genuine admiration for Lee expressed may come as a surprise to readers who know the author to be a descendant of an active abolitionist." The teacher suggested that the class take time out to examine this sentence. Some surprising comments were offered, such as, "It's so long since the Civil War, everybody now is neutral," a statement challenged by several members of the group. "An author must always be neutral when he writes" also brought forth challenges. Great discussion followed the comment that "Abolitionists were like Communists today."

The teacher of this group was not only a skilled discussion leader but was also gifted in discovering short excerpts that would stimulate good discussion and rich learning. Her concern was that much material read, accepted, and given back on tests was as little understood as the sentence from the book review cited. It was, therefore, her policy to encourage wide reading but from time to time to ask pupils to slow down and take time to do some extremely careful analyzing. "You can see these boys and girls grow sharper before your very eyes," she observed.

AID TO TEACHERS A NECESSITY

Help to teachers who desire to grow as discussion leaders must be specific. From experience, the author has found that to encourage the teachers to use discussion, but not to open up, elaborate, and even demonstrate some of the many ways of conducting discussion leaves these teachers with the desire but not with the "know-how."

The medical profession has pointed the way to educators. Physicians conduct clinics in which the "how-to-do" is carefully demonstrated. True, we in education have become cautious because we have seen the destructive effects in teacher education when teachers became imitative, rather than creative.

It is sound teacher education to prepare teachers to meet the countless unpredictable situations in classrooms and to think out the best ways of handling them. However, in our fear that demonstrating would stimulate imitation, we may have relied too exclusively on verbal suggestions and exhortation. More direct help is obviously needed in an area as important as that of developing thinking discussants who will then become more powerful readers. As a starting point, teachers might be helped by observing an experienced discussion leader guiding in discussion an age group at the same grade level as the one they themselves teach.

Textbooks and study guides contain suggestions for additional experiences that stimulate discussion. Planning projects in science and social studies stimulates much need to talk things over. Many other excellent opportunities occur in following up interests in current affairs. Children also bring to school items from home reading, movies, television programs, and civic programs that spark good discussion. There has been a marked increase in opportunities to discuss children's experiences in recent years.

Reducing Compulsion in the Classroom To encourage and increase children's powers of critical thinking and careful reading, two assets are imperative: a thinking teacher and time. Current in-service and pre-service education practices are focusing attention directly on the first factor, the teacher. The time factor is one commonly recognized, but the changes necessary to take the compulsion out of classrooms seem slow in coming. A hurried atmosphere puts a premium upon short either-or answers, snap judgments, opinionation, and many of the other errors described in Chapter 10.

Some schools are studying and experimenting with a longer school day, but more time is in itself not the answer. Children and teachers may spend more hours in the same hectic fashion in which they now spend a shorter day. Instead, a studied approach to key teaching situations to see how to inject time for youngsters to pause, think out answers, suspend judgment—and to listen—may go directly to the heart of the need. Within family life a similar attempt at living so as to encourage time to think is due. A child who enjoys a slower-paced life at home and also experiences it in the classroom is given a genuine opportunity to become a sound, straight thinker and an able critical reader. Add to this the privilege of exposure to intelligent teaching efforts, and the results should be noticeable in a child's entire education.

The development in our time of readers who can demonstrate

independent powers as critical selectors of material and who can be trusted to read widely on their own is both a slow and a difficult process. The entire personality of the child is involved. He needs to grow into wanting to be informed, wanting to think through ideas before accepting them, and wanting to understand the reactions of others. No short exercises, machines, or quick methods will accomplish this ambitious task. Only the careful, day-after-day, often laborious efforts of teachers and other adults, as described and implied in this chapter, will even approach this goal.

SUGGESTED READINGS ON GROUP DISCUSSION

CHASE, STUART. *Guides to Straight Thinking.* New York: Harper & Brothers, 1956. Chapters 4, 5, and 7.
Three key points involved in discussion are interestingly described: finding the fact; overgeneralizing; and getting personal. Examples are from adult experiences, but descriptions will help teacher and parent in guiding discussion of intermediate-grade children.

MIEL, ALICE, and BROGAN, PEGGY. *More Than Social Studies.* Englewood Cliffs, N. J.: Prentice-Hall, Inc., 1957. Chapters 1, 2, 3.
Gives conditions that enhance discussion and some helpful tips for teachers. Entire book includes descriptions of incidents and examples of help to teachers interested in deepening children's comprehension through stimulating the intellectual climate of the classroom.

ROTHSTEIN, EDWARD. "The Techniques of Teaching Controversial Issues." *Social Education,* February 13, 1949. P. 82.
One of the few writings of help to teachers on guiding pupils' thinking in areas of disagreement. Suggestions are of value for teachers of all age groups and for those who lead adult discussions.

RUCKER, W. RAY. *Curriculum Development in the Elementary School.* New York: Harper & Brothers, 1960. Chapters 2 and 3.
A classroom climate conducive to discussion and one in which children are challenged to think is described in Chapter 2. Guidelines for organized work with suggestions for reading and reporting are included in Chapter 3.

STRICKLAND, RUTH G. *The Language Arts.* Rev. ed. Boston: D. C. Heath and Company, 1957. Pp. 177-192.
Short description of the function of discussion in social studies and science, how to guide it, and its bearing on clear thinking and critical reading. Written in clear text style.

CHAPTER 12

Motivation in Reading—and Conflicting Pressures

Today's growing reader is confronted with problems vastly different from those faced by the young learner of former years, when there were no school buses, school libraries, inexpensive books, and chore-saving devices. Today's youngster grows up with fewer miles to walk, many more books, magazines, and pamphlets accessible, and, quite commonly, "nothing to do" at home. To a casual observer, it would appear that these conditions should promote more time for voluntary reading, plus a greater desire to read. Such may be the case for some, but for the majority, the contrary may be true.

NEGATIVE VALUES IN SOCIETY THAT AFFECT READING MOTIVATION

Many influences, some direct, others subtle and less direct, exert pressure on children. Concern is frequently expressed over the crowded, scheduled lives of youngsters, usually as they reach the age of nine. Time to sit and read seems to diminish in present life.

One of the current influences on children is the emphasis placed on education as a means of developing one's self, not as a knowledgeable, competent person, but rather as a person adorned with diplomas and degrees for "personal advancement." "Read so that you can get into the next grade," "Read so you'll get into high school," "Read so you can get into the right college," are exhortations heard by today's children and youth. Reading as a pursuit of personal pleasure and worth is bypassed, as is all education. In former times, the personal motivation for reading had more intrinsic value than does today's pressure to read for a vaguely felt extrinsic value.

But wherever youngsters are building the habit of reading into their living for its value to them as persons, then home and school, probably working together, have used good judgment and proper techniques for countering negative influences and utilizing a genuine respect for education as motivation. A child wanting to learn to read is like an automobile with its engine running; a child who is not eager resembles the car with a dead motor—it must be pulled, pushed, or dragged.

THREE BASES FOR A SOUND READING PROGRAM

A sound reading program draws upon three sources: first, the nature of those for whom it is planned, with variations for the youngest, the intermediate age, youth, and adults; second, the kind of world that is influencing children's and adults' interests and efforts; and, third, the aspirations for children and the world future toward which we are reaching. This, on the face of it, is a big order, yet forthright workers in the entire field of education accept this responsibility, from teachers to school superintendents, research workers, various educational specialists, writers, editors, and many parents. To the degree to which motivation of children's reading draws intelligently upon this triple base, to that same degree does a child's reading approach the highest hopes we entertain for it.

The nature of the aspirations in teaching reading need to be kept uppermost in all teachers' minds lest the end be children who read solely for school purposes and only when required to do so. A teacher with high aspirations aims to develop readers who enjoy and will continue to enjoy reading as a personal satisfaction, who will want to be informed persons, and who will use reading, in addition to other media, as a means of keeping up to date, and as a means of growing in their own proficiency, be it expressed in industry, home-making, religion, the arts, or professional work.

A school reading program should develop the basic skills, shape comprehension abilities, and encourage the self-propelling and continuing personal use of reading. Implicit in every part of these three phases of reading work with children are the books and other materials to which they are exposed. A genuine understanding of children requires that materials appropriate for them be selected and made available, with ample time for their use. A concern for societal influences on children requires us to reckon with the reading influences upon them, from the least desirable to the finest, and to guide children to select the preferable.

KEEPING YOUNG LEARNERS EAGER

For the youngest learners coming from what we commonly regard as a "good home," very little motivation to read is needed. In fact, with them our responsibility may be just the opposite. Once a young preschooler has sampled the pleasure of sitting close to an adult who reads to him, he wants more of this satisfaction. His pleasure may come from a mixture of enjoying the closeness to an adult whom he likes, the individual attention he is receiving, the soothing effect of hearing the adult's voice, and the pleasure in the book itself.

If he has been receiving books as gifts, his pride in the ownership of them is obvious. At the early age of two or three he has already become a book browser, one who can enjoy being alone and looking at a book. For those less experienced in such early contacts with books at home, the kindergarten does the job. Thus, either through home or school, or both, a child upon entrance to first grade is eager to proceed in becoming a reader, many even before this age. Those few who have had too much pressure at home or who are too timid will, with careful guidance in school, doubtless capture the spirit.

At this age the child's world is bounded by home, the closest neighborhood, and school. Within this realm a majority have contacts with books of many kinds, as well as signs and symbols. They also catch the urge to read from older brothers and sisters who are the symbol of "bigness" toward which they are stretching.

The association of "bigness" with reading is a powerful aid to children's efforts in overcoming the difficulties in learning to read. Many young five- and six-year-olds have been heard to say, "I want to go to school and I want to learn to read." So strong is the desire that some first graders are keenly disappointed if after two or three days in first grade they have "no reading yet." An excellent first-grade teacher, who referred to herself as an old-timer, said she always had a *reading lesson* on the first day of school. She sent each youngster home with a booklet, made of a folded sheet of construction paper on which she had printed with a hand press *I go to school* or *I am big*. She and her new pupils would "read" this together, chant it perhaps, and the youngsters would go home thrilled—they had begun to read.

Cultural Origin of the Desire to Read The child's desire to read is not a natural condition that occurs at the approximate age of six. It is the subtle, and often not so subtle, cultural expectation of our country. A child born into a New Guinea tribe has no such yearning. A child born in a European country where youngsters start school when they are seven may not express a desire to read as early as do the young children in the United States. One of the problems we Americans must face is that for many the customary expectancy is too difficult at six. For such children, it would be better if our mores were different, if, perhaps, we placed more emphasis on the continued reading in adult life rather than the early beginnings among children.

Even with the eagerness to read almost ready-made, a good first-grade teacher does much planning to keep this spirit alive for the eager, stimulate it for some, and rekindle it for others. The process of learning to read is a difficult undertaking even for the quick learners. Unfortunately, an attitude that first-grade learning is light work too often prevails. It is unfortunate that more people who have this attitude cannot have the experience of a father who visited the first grade in which his daughter was a pupil. The school had been labeled by local critics as a "progressive" school. This parent said he thought of himself as an opponent of progressive education, but he was amazed at the industry of the children in his daughter's classroom. He was surprised to see the spirit of work and the varied quality of work six-year-olds accomplished in one day. He was astounded by the amount of learning achieved in reading, writing, science, numbers, art, cooking, and music. Later, he described his visit with considerable excitement. "What surprised me most," he said, "was not only that they worked like beavers, but also that they knew what they were doing and got a kick out of being able to do it."

The teacher commented: "Well, this is my brand of progressive education. The children talk over and plan the day's work with me at the beginning. Later, they help decide if they've done a good job. So, of course, they are prepared to go about their work in a businesslike way."

A child included in planning his work can catch the spirit of work and thus add to his own sense of importance. A child not so included but rather told what to do is denied such an appeal to learning and to his importance. Teachers give much thought and study to keeping the spirit of industriousness high. They recognize that even eager learners in the first grade need continued motivation.

ENTER COMPETITION WITH READING INTERESTS

When the young reader reaches seven, eight, and nine, the world has expanded for him. He has grown socially so that he is mindful of what other youngsters say and do. He is growing increasingly aware of how they regard him, whether or not they like and admire him. He needs to feel *right* with his group. This need often serves to motivate him to put forth more effort at school. He also has grown in self-management and can range away from home and know many people, adults and youngsters, whom his parents or guardians do not know. He is aware of a wider number of skills to master, not only in school but out of it. He has sampled comic books and a variety of TV programs, and is discovering popular brands of food, clothing, cars, and transistor radios. The world seems to be opening up to him and revealing many fascinating new things to know about.

By now, for a few, even after only a short time in the second grade, school, books, and assembly programs are "old stuff." The word "teacher" has lost some of its glamor. The child is becoming more aware of and affected by the attitudes of adults and youth toward reading and school in general.

It is only natural that a child realign his interests as this bigger world opens up to him. The excitement of learning to read, the fun of being able to write the whole alphabet, and the fascination with numbers must give way in part to meeting two new boys who have moved in next door, or riding a two-wheeler, or saving coupons from some packaged food for a set of miniature cars. Teachers and parents are aware of this change; they expect it.

If those responsible for guiding the child are alert and aim high, they study methods of keeping each child's work in school challenging and rewarding. His other interests are recognized as essential to his growth, and, if wisely guided, they contribute to his learning. This sensible viewpoint was expressed by a breezy teacher advising a student teacher working with her in a rural area in Vermont: "You might as well face it; once they lose their belief in Santa Claus, they are no longer the eager beavers who came to first grade. From there on, it's up to us to show them how important school is, and not merely by telling them."

Unwise Attempts to Motivate Many of us can recall when some of our teachers considered that they were warming up cooling ardor about school by telling us how important school was. Others may have prescribed more homework to be sure that learning efforts came in for their proportionate share of time. Still others, and unfortunately this is still all too prevalent, applied fear as the technique of recharging lagging learners.

Low grades, threat of failure, notes to parents, as well as public scolding and ridicule, were (and still are) the processes whereby the inferior teachers attempted to stimulate increased eagerness to learn. Levels of motivation and their use have been studied by Ray Simpson,[1] who defines the highest level as *the ability to define goals clearly and work for them wisely with a minimum of help from others.* This was true of the first grade visited by the father. The lowest level identified by Simpson is *working because of fear.*

Motivation Is Everybody's Business Deeper insights in how to motivate constructive behavior—which includes learning to be a better reader—have now come to the attention of teachers, no matter what their vintage. With this new knowledge, there has been

[1] Ray H. Simpson, *Improving Teaching-Learning Processes.* New York: Longmans, Green and Co., 1953, ch. 6.

a corresponding decline in the use of fear as a force and an increasing disfavor toward its use. Instead of threatening a plodder or a "reader-on-vacation," teachers give encouraging help, introduce new materials, and offer youngsters new and challenging work. Sometimes all that is needed is a bit of individual attention from a pleasant teacher. Thus, with the best methods within their knowledge, teachers in the primary grades aim to start youngsters off toward the successful life to be found in the personal enjoyment of reading. They employ such practices as helping youngsters establish regular use of library books, encouraging ease in talking about their reading with others, and providing books to take home to enjoy with the family.

Reading at home is now properly considered essential in a child's reading life. Efforts are made to link home and school reading into a single pattern. To accomplish this goal, books read at home are shared in the classroom. Reactions by the family to the child's reading become a part of classroom discussion. So interwoven was the reading program with family living in one Western school that a third-grader who was a newcomer to the school said, "Everybody all over reads here, even at home."

A program in which so much enthusiasm about reading is obvious makes reading such respectable business that some of the conflicting pressures upon the child are reduced. Moreover, his world takes on more unity; everyone is involved in his school business. If a child senses that his reading is "little business" and of little account with adults, he may take on a similar attitude. A wise parent reported at a parent-teacher gathering, "Going to school is the kids' business and just as important as my business. So, at the dinner table in the evening I tell them some things about my business, and I want them to tell me some things about theirs. They feel just as important about their work as I do about mine."

AS HARRIED LIFE BEGINS AND READING EXITS

By the time the child enters the fourth grade, his life has lost some of the simple streamlining of home-school boundaries. At this stage a child is approaching the psychological need to demonstrate his independence from home, especially from mother. In upper economic groups it is common for boys and girls of nine and ten and older to have a full schedule for after-school hours and Saturdays, with recreation clubs, dancing, and music and riding lessons. These youngsters are often so highly scheduled that they may not even find adequate time in which to do homework or watch a favorite television show.

A tense, bright boy in a large Eastern city reported at school that he had two hours per week to do as he chose—on Sunday afternoons. The teacher inquired into the situation and found his report to be true. In such a crowded life the possibility of finding time to enjoy a story or even to page through a magazine is unlikely. Children in lower economic brackets may not belong to as many clubs or take as many lessons, but many of them, too, complain of too little time to follow pursuits of their selection.

Part of the pressure for time comes from bus travel, which uses up time twice a day for thousands of children. Not infrequently, adults are shocked to find that young children leave home to catch a school bus shortly after seven o'clock in the morning and return toward five o'clock in the afternoon. Add to this long day a few hours of homework, which unfortunately some schools require, and the question naturally comes to mind: How do children manage to accomplish so much?

When they do find free time at their disposal, children, reacting as we do to the fast tempo of contemporary life, may be too weary to read even an appealing short story; reading may require too much effort. The television program, radio, or record player may make less demand on their depleted energy.

The surprising fact is that wide and wholesome use of reading goes on despite such harried lives. This is gratifying proof that, given even marginal opportunity, children will read. Their persistence in reading also reflects favorably on the strength of the schools' reading programs and the appeal of today's reading materials.

SENSIBLE PLANNING FOR SUSTAINED MOTIVATION

Countless ways are used to motivate a strong desire to read on the part of this age group. Some that are helpful include:

1. *Planning the day to be sure to include ideas from the children:*

A child is thus helped to feel that he is identified with the school's work and important to it. School work is not "something the teacher wants me to do" but becomes "something I've set myself to do." A teacher adds suggestions and helps youngsters plan wisely but is careful to encourage the child to share in making decisions.

By sharing in the planning of self-improvement tasks, children can help to select the types of drills they need to work on or the rereading they will do. They can also set for themselves the responsibility of doing further reading on certain topics and reporting on given pages, articles, or chapters in a book. Part of the teacher's responsibility is to see that some do not plan too enthusiastically, but rather that they set reasonable goals for themselves. For the less interested, help is given to find work they can do that involves them more closely in the learning process.

Sharing in planning raises the level of work morale in children as it does the morale of adults in industry. Teachers have observed that teaching methods that involve children in planning the class program stimulate and encourage a freer use of energy and an increase in learning.

2. *Helping the child understand what he is doing and ascertaining that he sees the value in it:*

The value in reading to our life is evident all about us. If its importance is attached only to its use in school, then the child who loses his fondness for school may dump out his fondness for reading too. The old chant on the last day of school—"No more lessons, no more books, no more teacher's homely looks"—has much to ponder in it.

Of course a *good* school aims never to be rejected by any one of the children attending it. But reading if honestly taught should not draw its value from school use only; instilling such an attitude is erroneous teaching because it ignores what reading does for a child's respect for himself and for the world in which he functions as a reader.

The teacher in the following example was considered an excellent reading teacher–the description reveals why. Her children, second-graders, early one fall were preparing for a birthday party. They decided to make a trip to a self-service local grocery store to see how much reading they could do in order to purchase a list of items needed for a lunch. They asked the manager, "Do you help people read the prices and find the things they are looking for?" The manager answered in the right key. He said that at times he did help someone who could not read well or who had come from another country and was not yet at home in English, but "Sometimes when I'm busy, they just have to wait a while."

Later, when his answer was discussed at school, these seven-year-olds saw the value of being able, through their own reading, to help themselves as shoppers. In experience after experience of a similar nature, this teacher built up youngsters' awareness of reading as a powerful tool for promoting their independence in carrying out important daily tasks.

A fifth grade at this same school visited a New York City television studio to watch a program. They interviewed the announcer and asked him, "What special talents did you need to get this job?" He said, "Well, you noticed that I had to read a lot, including two commercials, so the first talent needed, I'd say, is to be able to read well, orally as well as silently."

To these fifth-graders, the fact that the ability to read well orally was demanded in work as modern as that of a television announcer came as a surprise. Some youngsters had come to regard oral reading as the "small-kid-stuff" that they left behind in first and second grade.

Science and social studies, if properly taught, stimulate the type of inquiry that frequently seeks outside sources of information. A sixth grade on a trip to a large radio factory for such information observed at noontime that the men received a news bulletin as they passed through the entrance to the lunchroom. Their guide told them this was a daily news sheet distributed to them through their union leaders, who expected each member to keep up to date on current affairs by reading it.

Any class that, with helpful leadership, makes a study of the uses of reading outside of school will be impressed by the necessity for using reading in daily life. A study of this kind can have a twofold effect upon the young observers: It will raise their respect for the importance of reading in out-of-school life, and it will incite in them a wider use of reading in some similar ways. For boys especially it will discourage the sad attitude they meet that "reading is sissy business." All children's education is quickened and becomes more practical as well as visionary if the community is drawn upon properly. An eye-opening curriculum quickly erases the old idea that education is stuffy, even for teachers, and has a mind-closing effect.

In general, as highlighted by the incidents described above, pupils learn better, faster, and more adequately if they sense the reason for what they are doing. To see the skills they are acquiring in reading regarded as essential tools in the adult business and professional world exerts a very good influence upon them. The time and effort expended by teachers in arranging for contacts with the adult community pays high dividends. Teachers themselves find that such experiences are of real value to them, too.

3. *Developing methods of checking, testing, and self-testing to reveal progress:*

A child who can feel progress in his work is stimulated by such success and inspired to put forth more energy. "Nothing succeeds like success" is sound psychology. Because reading is a large, rather vague area of learning with many facets to it, a child may not feel he is gaining ground in it. He needs to be spurred on by the assurance gained from specific evidence that he is improving. Therefore, the teacher who gives periodic, simple tests or checks on progress or who helps children check themselves is motivating more effort.

Before much was known about the skills involved in reading, it was common to refer to a child's reading as "good," "not so good," or "poor." What made it good or poor? How would a child know what to do to make it better? How could he tell that he was making progress in the right direction? Undoubtedly, many normal boys and girls put forth real effort but sensed no progress and finally grew discouraged and gave up. Today an effort is made to understand each child's reading progress so that if he meets a specific hurdle he can be given appropriate help to get over it. Remedial programs have given teachers and youngsters much help at this point.

To beginners, the specific words they know, the letter sounds they have learned, and the pages they can read independently are milestones that indicate to them real progress. To a third-grade child who had been a careless reader, the ability to read a story in his reader and to answer correctly all ten test questions about specific items in the story was proof to him of improvement. To a child who previously had looked at books, read here and there, and had become intrigued enough by reading to cope with a whole book, finally to read all of E. B. White's *Charlotte's Web* was a big step forward. A general statement such as "You are getting better" may occasionally be gratifying to a youngster, but it is the specific evidence that whets a struggling reader's eagerness to work at reading with determination.

The need to recognize milestones in each child's growth demands that teachers organize their work so that they can follow individual reading efforts closely enough to give help and commendation at strategic times. A beginner or one who has had difficulty needs a cheery word more frequently than do those who are sufficiently advanced to feel and see themselves progress. For them, their own awareness of their many satisfactions in reading is all the boosting they need.

4. *Stimulating and supporting interests that thrive on reading:*

The curriculum in good schools of today is filled with studies that catch pupils' interests and add to the number of topics or fields they can list among their interests. A visit to a nearby school during Education Week stimulated a free-lance writer on education to such a degree that in mentioning the visit at a social gathering, he pulled a paper from his pocket and read a bit of the "different things these kids were studying in the rooms I visited." His list included: dinosaurs—second grade; preserving foods, before and now—third grade; machines we use in daily living—fourth grade; existing colonies in today's world—fifth grade; Antarctica, what we can find out about it—sixth grade.

Other learnings were going on too, but this visitor was impressed with the range of the topics about which the youngsters had the opportunity to learn. He added that he was in complete agreement with one of the teachers, who commented, "It ought to be so interesting that I, too, keep interested and keep learning."

When children study topics of vital interest to them, they become challenged to look for relevant material and read to the degree their ability permits. Many teachers and parents have been surprised to find a child "digging" out meaning from reading that they had considered too difficult for him. They may comment, "He is so interested and eager he can get the meaning." A real measure of reading power is the quality of reading a child can do under such highly favorable conditions. We adults have experienced this. What means much to us excites our keenest alertness, our wholehearted attention, and our best reading powers. At times we say, "we accomplished the impossible."

So too with children, even the youngest. We have seen a toddler who wished to get something that had been intentionally placed on a table out of his reach push a chair to the table, climb on it, and then pull himself within reach of his objective. He could do this without yet having acquired the language with which to tell what he aimed to do. The desire to do something releases "full steam ahead."

5. *Inviting reading through the appealing quality of books and other reading materials:*

Visual appeal has long been recognized as one of the most natural ways of stirring a desire in children to read. Many of us have seen examples of this motivation. In doctors' and dentists' offices, for example, where good magazines and books for all ages are handy, children read eagerly to cover as much as possible before being called to take their turn with the doctor. Children in libraries are almost reverent as they handle the new books, and many teachers and parents have seen youngsters at annual new book exhibits almost breathless with the excitement created by seeing so many attractive books.

A third-grade teacher in a New York City public school who took some of her least interested readers to a book fair later reported the effect this trip had upon their interest in reading. Her observation, expressed to a class of experienced teachers studying for an advanced degree, is worth remembering: "Most children if given a chance to look at our new, beautiful, and interesting books and if given enough time to look at them without interruption will want to read."

CREATIVE TEACHERS AT WORK

Teachers have demonstrated unique abilities in creating interest in lackadaisical or half-hearted learners. In a large first grade in New York State's suburban Westchester County, where grades were divided homogeneously, a teacher who taught "the plodders" year after year improvised much material calculated to have special appeal to her six-year-old pupils.

She successfully motivated the reading of these slow starters by writing a simple story about each one. The story might be "My name is Ellen. I have two dogs. I have red hair," or "My name is Bruce. I lost my front tooth." Each story contained the child's name and one fact the teacher had gathered that was unique to this child. Each story was bound with a folded paper cover on which was written plainly (in manuscript writing) the child's first name and below it: *A Story About Me.* Children prized these "books," exchanged them, and in many cases learned to recognize and spell their names and to read their own story and those of others. They were eager to take their books home to display their budding reading powers. Of course some books "got lost," but the teacher cheerfully made new ones.

The personal element in this experience was the factor that caught the interest of the youngsters. Although interest in ourselves may be lessened as we grow older, some keen observers deny it. They say we remain deeply interested in ourselves but grow sophisticated and conceal this interest. It should not surprise us, then, to find children motivated by materials written for them and about them. Such materials must be homemade; therefore, they demand an imaginative and dedicated teacher. Fortunately, many youngsters are taught by such teachers.

Sampling Real Scholarship In a school where children are encouraged to select topics for study or pursue appealing inquiries, the more independent readers have a chance to experience the excitement of gathering a rich fund of information on one topic or related to one idea. Young Christie in a busy third grade in a Virginia school became interested in the Civil War. He began to collect pictures, news items, stories, books, and all types of replicas, including caps and guns. When his collection grew, he found it necessary to organize and bind his pictures and clippings in a scrapbook. He pursued his study until the end of the fourth grade, when he reported that he had read every article and book dealing with the Civil War he could locate. His friends, their parents, his grandparents, classmates, and teachers aided his search for materials.

The curriculum that emphasizes continuing studies of important topics serves as a great influence in starting reading pursuits like Christie's. Once a child has sampled learning-a-lot-about-one-topic, he has experienced that good feeling which approaches real scholarship. Something important has been added to his self-respect and to his standard of education for himself. He has learned the difference between "knowing a little about one thing" and "knowing a lot about one thing." Many educated and fairly mature adults have not acquired the basis for making this judgment.

VALUES GAINED BY MOTIVATED READERS

Returning to the previous point made of the narrow margin of time in the life of today's child, one can see that if practices of motivation such as those described here are followed, a youngster's desire to read helps him to overcome some of the time limitations and to sandwich reading into his busy life. Filling a youngster with such persisting desire is important not only for the value of the specific reading but also for the help he acquires in regarding himself as an informed person.

Experiences through which youngsters acquire a respect for thorough study, prolonged inquiry, and continuing interests will help establish in them some fundamental attitudes. They will acquire a respect for *knowing facts about* or *having an opinion about* a subject. Tasting the satisfaction of gathering information and feeling adequately informed on a subject will remain important to them. They are on the way to becoming readers who continue to read newspapers and magazines to be informed and who read in fields related to their work so they may increase their personal competence.

Increased Morale—Increased Learning Studies of how to arouse more zest for one's work have frequently been made in industry and in the military services. A motivated worker is a greater asset than one not "in it." A motivated person in military service has been found to be more inventive, more resourceful, more creative, possessed of more endurance, and more capable of looking out for his own safety. Educators have shown good judgment in applying data gathered from industry, military service, and other areas to educational efforts with children.

Teachers have discovered that properly motivated youngsters have high morale and that they express it through eagerness and effectiveness in learning. These qualities seem to influence the quality of their behavior in school. It is noticeable in the effort they put forth. They "try harder," to use the child's way of putting it. They come up with ideas of their own. Imagination becomes stimulated and brought into the process. As one excited girl answered when asked how it occurred to her to ask an adult acquaintance for books about whaling and old maps of Connecticut: "I just got so interested in finding more good books on whaling and more old maps that I asked myself, 'Who has lived here a long time who might have things like this?' And I came up with the idea—Miss L———." One boy said he "laid awake nights" thinking of where else good materials on the topic of his interest might be found.

Hard Work Can Be Fun Such responses result when a group is truly interested in a study and feels so much a part of it that class members think of the study in and out of school. An observer may be surprised to note how seldom they refer to such studies as "hard work." The satisfactions are so great that the effort involved is diminished in proportion.

Many of us have experienced, as have children, the effort that we must put into work that does not appeal to us—the chore such work becomes, in the negative sense of that word. John Dewey developed this point clearly in a brief book written years ago called *Interest and Effort.*[2] The idea is commonplace, yet what a powerful generation we would now be sprouting if all children were given the continuing impetus of positive motivation. Creative thinking and full release of effort are generated by genuine interest and can truly be described as "Operation Hard Work."

Deriving deep pleasure from work influences future efforts. There is an old saw that "The right expenditure of energy begets more energy." A ten-year-old child who had been rewarded by his thorough enjoyment of a study of butterflies while at a summer camp said to his teacher that September, "I'd like to find something else to study that will be as much fun as my study of butterflies." He then added, "Something on which I can find several books." Reading had already made itself known to him as the tool for continuing education. Moreover, he had sampled more inclusive learning than thousands who may graduate from schools via the short-assignment route and who may join the ranks of those uninformed people who read a sketchy article on a topic in a popular magazine and thereafter speak with authority on the subject.

In schools that stress day-to-day lessons in which the child has little or no hand in planning and little or no opportunity to develop persisting interests, a youngster is denied such stimulation. Formerly this was the common school curriculum pattern, but today it is giving place to the other patterns described in Chapter 6. However, children under all types of curriculum emphases may become the continuing, selective, and critical readers we envision. They catch the spark in good homes, from friends, from some chance contact or from some satisfying experience, as did other boys and girls in former days in a dreary school program. Good schools do not leave such growth to the element of chance, however. The examples we have given were taken from schools that guarantee the development of good readers by making it possible for children to read with real satisfaction in their present life.

Credit should be given to those good teachers and wise parents who, in years past, employed many practices that served to motivate offspring. They persuaded children "to want to do their

[2] John Dewey, *Interest and Effort.* Cambridge: The Riverside Press, 1913.

work." Today's informed educators bring to the understanding of the process of motivation more knowledge and a larger collection of skills. Some of the resulting work may be misunderstood. Periodically, newspapers or magazines publish a complaint that "School is not hard enough because the youngsters enjoy their work." Such criticism reveals a hangover from the day when it was considered that whatever was good for one, like medicine, had to taste bad.

An astute observation was made by a mother whose four children had recently transferred from a school where the homework was growing to be "too much for the parents" to a school where each child was looking up articles in the encyclopedia, dusting off the family reference books, and becoming excited about his part of a study. This mother, with surprise registered in her voice, told the principal at the new school, "Why, they go at their reading like grownups."

Guiding children to work under favorable stimulation helps them to develop a type of maturity that used to be rare in children. If such work becomes common to most schools, the estimation of children's potential reading power must be revised upward. Continued efforts to motivate each child to work toward his best will pay dividends in literacy.

SUGGESTED READINGS ON MOTIVATION

MOORE, LILLIAN. "Reader in the Making," in *The Children's Bookshelf.* New York: Bantam Books, 1962. Pp. 25-33.
Sprightly description of how to induct young child into a yearning to read and how reading begets more reading. Parents and teachers can be influenced by this brief account.

RYAN, DAVID G. "Motivation in Learning," in *Psychology of Learning*: Forty-first Yearbook of The National Society for the Study of Education. Chicago: University of Chicago Press, 1942. Part II, Chapter 8.
Excellent technical description of motivation and evidence from researches of the effect on learning of motivation.

SIMPSON, RAY H. *Improving Teaching-Learning Processes.* New York: Longmans Green and Co., 1953.
An invaluable book for teachers. Abundant analysis of classroom procedures,

with concrete suggestions for increasing learning through use of proper techniques of motivation.

WILES, KIMBALL. *Teaching for Better Schools.* 2nd ed. Englewood Cliffs, N. J.: Prentice-Hall, Inc., 1959. Chapters 10 and 11.
Suggestions included for establishing intellectual climate and encouraging youngsters to set goals that stretch their learning. Nontechnical language.

CHAPTER 13

Satisfying Whetted Reading Appetites

There is an extremely close link between the nature of the young readers we are developing year after year in today's schools and the nature of the reading materials selected for their learning. Over the past two or three decades vast changes have been made in the amount and variety of these materials, as well as in the ways in which they are selected.

Let us look first at the growth in demand for materials often described as library reading. This begins with the yearning for another book so frequently heard by those who look after very young book-owners at home. To a preschooler, each book is a novel experience, something good to explore. If it is truly satisfying to the child, he will look at it repeatedly and will ask to have it read to him again and again. Then it may take its place in the lengthening shelf of books that receive a periodic review. Even with the addition of more companions with whom he can play and many exciting trips and other adventures, books continue to hold the interest of the well-cared-for preschool child.

Youngsters who come from homes where a mother works by day and crowds household duties into early and late evening hours come into their own with books during regular periods in nursery schools and children's centers. This is the age when a taste for books gets started. The library table in these child-oriented centers is a popular spot, and books are pored over as if they were being read. Often, two youngsters talk about a book, pointing out items in pictures and laughing over some. Lois Lenski's *The Little*

Fire Engine was so frequently fought over in a certain nursery school that the teacher bought another copy.

In the kindergarten-primary grades, where books and time for reading them are available, the interest previously developed continues. The desire to own books also continues if the home assists in nurturing it. At this period, some parents may feel their support in supplying books is no longer needed; the school will take over the role the parent formerly had. It is true that schools with adequate budgets do furnish a wide array of books used individually by children. Many a child, with no other source of books, has most of his reading needs fulfilled at school.

BOOKS ON THE BUDGET

Understandably, when a child's personal wants make increasing demands upon a family budget, a choice must be made: books or puzzles, books or a new part to a train, books or ice-skates, and so on. Only a more than adequate budget can finance all. Yet to stop adding to the young child's growing library is to cut off a desirable trend that is limitless in its rewards.

In the third and fourth grades, children may become book collectors, purchasing all books on a particular topic, such as dogs, dinosaurs, airplanes, or all the books by certain authors, or a series, such as the *You Were There* series. Wholesome interest in books often crowds out the undesirable pastimes that may be seized upon as something to do by a child who has not put roots down in other worthy pursuits.

The expanding interests of children between eight and twelve, the intermediate-grade years, create a demand that good school libraries and public libraries help to fill. Even in an economically privileged home, if a child is an avid reader, he will need books over and beyond his own library. Not only that, but many books that he will enjoy reading will not fall into the category of those he wishes to own. Children may have periods in which books with humor appeal; at other times they may be intrigued only by straight, honestly written information; and at still other times only by fiction. Only well-stocked school and public libraries can serve the changing reading appetite and the volume of consumption of real readers of this age.

Sales personnel in bookstores often comment on the care with which children buy books. One salesman described them as so "cautious" that they frequently hold a spot at a book counter while they read long parts of the book before deciding to invest their money in it. Many are learning the essential lesson of spending carefully the money they earn and save for books. This is good consumer education.

As an aid to young book buyers and also to their parents and teachers who are eager that a child read what is desirable, book clubs for the various age groups have become popular. The books for most of the clubs are carefully selected and serve a highly important function for some of today's eager book owners. Fine inexpensive paperback books are also increasing in number. Good magazines, too, have appeared for the various ages, so that youngsters can now enjoy the pleasure of receiving a magazine regularly in the mail. The fact that these ventures planned to furnish children with good reading succeed financially offers excellent evidence that we are building avid, functional readers.

PROBLEMS IN GUIDING TASTE

Once children themselves become book selectors, parents and teachers face another kind of problem—namely, the quality of the books selected by children. The teacher has an easier row to hoe with this problem than does the parent. The books supplied for school library and classroom use are carefully selected on merit. The child in going to the school bookshelf has a selected list from which to choose. Not so in all bookstores. On shelves he may find books that critics consider inferior—or books for which he is not yet ready.

The Freedom to Choose Guiding a child's choice is not easy, at best. With some youngsters it is extremely difficult. They may feel tightly yoked to adults in too much of their lives, with not enough opportunity to develop their own powers in making decisions, so that choosing a book becomes an exercise in defiance. Some of us can vividly recall the effect on us of taboos. When we were told, "That book is too old for you," the desire for the book was multiplied immeasurably in our estimation. All the furor in the past over comics, only some of the concern valid, excited children's appetites. Comics were "bootlegged" into schools, traded in locker rooms, sold for exorbitant prices in back lots, and collected by the hundreds by many youngsters who seldom read them but needed to be part of the pro-and-con crusade.

Although it is not always true that wholesome school and home environments safeguard a child's taste for his growing years, they do protect the majority of youngsters from using their choices of reading material to degrade themselves. An occasional journey into the *verboten* seems to leave unaffected the many children carefully reared and educated. A wise teacher who taught in a school embattled over comics observed, "I've found that if we carry on our regular work with proper attention to the big ideas, and if I don't keep beating my drum against these awful comics, they settle down to their work and their library books as usual with only an occasional nod at trash." Her observation was borne out by the research on children's comic reading done by Josette Frank,[1] who found that children who read comics read other things widely and maintained the "reading-as-usual" life of wholesome children.

Countering Undesirable Materials Several wise policies that have been found helpful by parents and teachers in countering the selection of trashy and undesirable materials should be stated here:

1. Create no stir over the first discovery of poor material selected by the child.
2. If a child resorts to "sneaking" in undesirable reading matter, suggest that no material needs to be smuggled in. If the child thinks it is worth reading, let the teacher or parent also read it and talk about it.
3. If the material is trashy but not sordid, ignore it, or at most make some bland comment, such as, "A book like this may not be one of the best you'll read."
4. If the material is objectionable, ask a child how he rates it and what its appeal is. He may like it for points that are not objectionable. He may say, "All the guys read this stuff" or "I just wanted to see why the kids say it's so bad." The adult needs to take a cue from the child's answers and what other facts are known about him. The child may

[1] Josette Frank, *Your Child's Reading Today*. Doubleday, 1960, pp. 185-196.

need to prove to his pals that he is not a sissy. He may have a deep curiosity created by too many restrictions in his life. He may be testing himself out, not knowing why. Parent or teacher may terminate the episode by saying, "You have good judgment and know why books like this are not wanted in homes or schools."

5. If such an incident is not an isolated one but a persisting trend with one child or a fad within a group, follow-up measures may be necessary. The situation should be studied to see if enough good, exciting books and magazines are available, if a new source for undesirable material has entered the child's neighborhood, and if certain children are becoming the stimulators and purveyors. Steps taken in light of any such findings need to be carefully planned and must be acted on without fanfare. Contagion runs high in matters of this kind.

Both homes and schools should share in plans to redirect children's interests, except in situations in which relations between adult and child are tense. Parents and teachers who are inclined to become wrought up over behavior involving taboos should defer to others who can remain calm, matter-of-fact, but firm in talking with children. If a child's departure into the realm of undesirable reading is met with unharried good judgment, it usually lasts but a short time. In many homes and schools with honest child-adult relationships, in which children select for themselves from an adequate supply of good reading, the problem never arises.

Children at times startle us with the common sense implied in the questions they ask. In a community where a three-meal-a-day discussion of the evils of comics was going on, a fourth-grade girl asked her teacher during a discussion of the anticomics crusade in the town, "What if a girl like me has nothing at all to read, not even a comic book, then does anybody care?" How often is this question raised? Do those who go to battle against undesirable trash in books and pamphlets also carry the banner for more money for school-library books and a more adequate budget for the public library?

MAKING SURE THAT CHILDREN MEET BOOKS

Citizens concerned with children's reading can play an important role in supporting wholesome choices of materials by examining the amount of money made available in the community for children's voluntary or free reading. In some communities this already has been done. Leaders of elementary-school programs often deplore the small amount allocated in the budget for library books. In some schools the textbook budget, which is listed separately, also is pinched. Yet studies of children's reading for personal satisfaction indicate that today's children, given time and books, become wide readers and select good literature.

The Important Function of the Public Library Another evidence of children's expanding reading is to be found in the increased space in public libraries that is now devoted to children's reading rooms and children's books. Teachers now commonly introduce their groups to the public library and help each child to become a card-carrying book borrower. Even if a school has excellent library facilities, it is good education to establish the habit of public-library use during elementary-school age, preferably as soon as a youngster can travel to the library in his community without parental assistance.

A public library operates on a twelve-month plan. Unfortunately, far too many school libraries still operate on a school-year schedule, remaining closed not only on Saturdays throughout the school year but all through summer months. A growing number of schools, however, are reversing this policy. With the help of parents and juvenile volunteers, school libraries are open for a scheduled number of hours on Saturdays and at stated intervals during all vacation periods. To facilitate year-round library services, some elementary schools now build the library on the ground floor with an outdoor exit, so that it can be used while the remainder of the building is closed. It is encouraging to notice that buildings are being planned to accommodate the pressing reading demands of our young readers.

Motivation Through Attractive Books In the previous chapter on motivation, the relation between desire and effort was described. Here we are describing the relation between desire and the availability of appealing materials to read. To urge a child to read but to withhold the very materials that would quicken his desires is certainly a frustrating procedure. Common sense should tell responsible adults that, once whetted, the child's appetite needs an ever-expanding array of the finest books, magazines, pamphlets, newspapers, and other materials. He will not only gain deep personal satisfactions in reading but will also sharpen his skills through the best kind of practice. The shelf with a meager handful of dingy books is disappearing. There is still room, however, for more shelves with more books for eager readers to reach for and relish.

Many teachers have described what happened when lukewarm readers were exposed to an array of new, appealing books on a variety of topics with no further instruction than to look at them. The results were more gratifying than these teachers' expectations. Writers, artists, and publishers have produced children's material of such fine quality that even to some dubious or already jaded readers the appeals are irresistible.

A teacher, listening to a complaint of a fellow teacher from another school system that "today's fifth-graders don't care to read," asked incredulously, "Even if they are surrounded with the wonderful books written for them?" There may be some who even in a paradise of books will resist being tempted, but before they are diagnosed as nonreaders, we should be sure they have received the proper overtures and invitations to read. It is a tragic fact that in our country, in which desirable materials for children are the envy of all other lands, we have children who have had not one chance in their entire school career to browse through a new, beautiful book. A corollary to this fact is that in thousands of communities there is not one store that sells good books. A narrowly educated public makes a poor consumer market.

SUCCESS WITH SKILLS INCREASES READING APPETITES

Not only have library or trade books for children become extremely appealing in recent years, but the materials designed primarily as teaching materials also have increased their appeal. To a child eager to be a good reader, materials that give him a chance to improve himself are valuable. Even before they have started the serious job of learning to read in school, youngsters need to demonstrate their power from time to time. A mother described the way her four-year-old hunted through a box of plastic letters until he found *D*, carried it to the dining-room table and placed it on his place mat, which had a *D*, the family initial, on it. He looked at his mother and sister and fairly crowed with success. This, to him, was as thrilling an accomplishment as the driving of a golf ball three hundred yards straight down a fairway in front of a fringe of spectators would be to an adult. There are many moments in learning to read when a child needs to see for himself that he is "coming along fine," and needs a chance to prove it to someone.

Getting Specific Proof of Improvement Skill-building materials that incorporate methods of proving to a worker his degree of success are essential, especially for beginners and slow movers. Some exercises include score cards or pages on which the child can keep his own record of achievement. The idea that a child be responsible for keeping track of his own progress is sound education. This technique shifts the relationship from a teacher-tells-how-I'm-doing to a self-motivated one: I-can-see-how-I'm-doing. Children frequently set specific work for themselves to see how well they do. Beginners may set a goal to see how far they can read in a personally selected book before finding it necessary to ask help in identifying a word. This is the sort of tangible evidence children need as proof of accomplishment.

Some speedy learners may not need as frequent assurances of progress as do beginners and slow learners. They too, however, as they acquire new skills and more advanced techniques, periodically need to feel a boost to the ego through the assurance that they do well on tests and checks of these newer learnings. The teacher's comment, "You are doing all right," or "You are above grade," may be too vague to be helpful, even for them.

Continued skill development in the intermediate grades in recent decades has given pre-teen-agers not only more mature power but also added incentives for more extensive reading. Through skill-building exercises included in texts, fourth-, fifth-, and sixth-graders have developed greater competence in the use of the library and in the use of dictionaries, encyclopedias, atlases, globes, maps, charts, and other reference material. As a result, these readers handle newspapers, magazines, books, and a variety of information materials with an ease formerly considered adult.

Extending Reading Interests Beyond Firsthand Experiences
Slides, film strips, moving pictures, and television have enriched learning for all ages. Intermediate-grade youngsters, in particular, can become acquainted with many topics on their interest level but perhaps difficult to read about. Stimulating new and wider interests at the age that precedes the difficult adolescent years is highly desirable in order to establish long-range reading habits.

Students of intermediate years are also acquiring the ability to handle the new audiovisual machines in connection with their work. Sixth-graders in New Rochelle, New York, extended their learning through wise use of a tape recorder. Five committees recorded on tape the historical background of our national holidays. The entire class offered suggestions for revision after auditioning each report, and the final reports were utilized as part of an all-school assembly. The management of the tape recorder for each step was in the hands of the boys and girls.

Moving pictures viewed by an entire class can be an excellent basis for discussion and can lead into follow-up reading. Film strips with challenging points can also be used for class reading and discussion. Children's interests can be stirred and widened through proper use of audiovisual equipment.

GROWTH IN REFERENCE READING

The success of extended research projects invariably depends upon the availability of enough good reference materials and the guidance of boys and girls in their proper use. Schools with narrow programs consider only textbooks as essential. A school with a high standard of education equates reference material with texts in importance. In some fields of study, both are essential.

Suggested references for further reading are now common in textbooks, and they provide great help to teachers and librarians in stocking book supplies. Standard reference works, such as the encyclopedia, the atlas, and the dictionary, are, and will continue to be, of utmost importance to genuine education of today's young.

School librarians not only teach the use of reference materials but also take on new work, as the following example shows:

A group in Connecticut had been studying weather. The study had its origin in the science textbook, but as the students' interest grew they soon exhausted the information in the text and its suggested additional readings. They proceeded to gather books, maps, pamphlets, models of weather vanes, charts with tables of weather data, and a generous supply of magazine and newspaper clippings. At the completion of their study, the question arose: What shall we do with these materials? The librarian took all the books, pamphlets, and models. A new display case was ordered for the models that had permanent value for the school. The clippings were carefully organized by class members with the help of the librarian and were placed in a "Curriculum Materials" file also housed in the library.

Not all studies lend themselves to fruitful gathering of relevant materials. When they do, the process can become a rich part of what the youngsters learn under wise teacher guidance. Some elementary-school children of today are more aware of appropriate sources for information than are their elders, and they seem to have a nose for materials that are free. The bargain-hunting of children should delight us.

In schools with a curriculum emphasis bounded more completely by textbooks, obviously the techniques of hunting down sources and checking their relevance remain undeveloped. An emphasis on textbooks to the exclusion of reference reading, it is argued, increases learning. Such reasoning is almost like arguing that a person who reads one book carefully gathers more knowledge than if he read several books carefully. Youngsters who become adept in reference reading are acquiring, in addition to much valuable information, study techniques that add a new dimension to their growing competence. The proof of their growth in reading power can be observed in schools with well-planned curriculum programs. Children who are denied such experiences in schools because their materials are handed to them may fail to learn to be selective.

CHILDREN AS CRITICS AND SELECTORS

In school systems where the curriculum is continually being brought up to date and where the most promising ideas currently known are tried out in the classroom, real strides have been made in teaching pupils to select many types of material. Administrators, teachers, and school-board members need to be encouraged to explore these ventures and to make note of the effect upon youngsters. The examples that follow reveal the inherent educational value to children of selecting books.

Choosing Their Own Books In a school on Long Island, New York, each grade, under the teacher's guidance, made a list of the new books the members wished included in their biannual order. To further the work of book selection the school subscribed to the *Horn Book*, the book-review sections of the New York *Times* and the *Herald Tribune*, and the *Wilson Bulletin*. Other reviews brought in by teachers and children were added to the list. With the younger children, the teacher read reviews and mentioned the cost of the book. Children grew in their ability to react to the content of the review and also became aware of book costs. The older children read the reviews themselves and grew rapidly in knowledge of such facts as backgrounds of authors, costs of books, and names of publishers. They also grew to appreciate lacks in their library resources and the cost problem of keeping library resources ample and up to date.

At a given date all lists were sent to a book-supply house for "immediate" delivery. From that day until the books arrived, the children expressed much anticipation. Young children found the waiting time long. Once the books arrived, seventh- and eighth-grade youngsters sorted them according to class orders. No pressure was put on the committees to hurry with the work because the principal, a booklover and an inspiring reader, appreciated the rich experience it was for these youngsters on the committees to handle so many fascinating books.

In the sorting committees were several boys, recent transfers to the school, who had not seemed interested in books. They followed the method used by other workers, looking through each book as it was taken from the carton before placing it with the right collection. Squeals of delight came from the basement supply room as these sorters did their work. One boy announced loudly, "Young kids today get the breaks."

The books were placed on display in the classrooms for their selectors, older brothers and sisters, and friends to see. Older children were asked to react to the selection of the primary grades. They also could borrow books that looked extremely appealing in order to "catch up with what you missed because you are now out of the primary grades." The principal told youngsters he prevented himself from becoming envious of young children by reading some of their books when he could get at them. His comment provides a clue for motivating and aiding slower, less eager readers.

Discussion among the children in this school about books, authors, illustrators, and book prices resembled that carried on by literate adults. The teachers and principal attributed the high interest in reading and the ultimate effect—"not one truly poor reader in the school"—to the experience each child in the school had with buying books for the school library.

Making Comparisons A fourth-grade class in a Wisconsin parochial school had a different sort of experience in selecting books. They made a study of three arithmetic books that were under consideration for purchase by a committee of teachers. The teachers asked the children who had been studying and discussing the books to report on any "good" or "not good" features they had found. The youngsters surprised the committee of teachers by indicating a preference for the clarity with which one of the books provided instructions to the reader. They cited examples and compared them with the books in the other two series. One fourth-grade teacher reported that those who had shared in this study had greater interest in all other texts. "The books came to life" for them, she said.

Choosing Other Materials Another experience in selecting material was carried out by a fifth grade in a rural area of upper New York State. The teacher and her students were taking turns in reading orally Anne Morrow Lindbergh's *North to the Orient*, which appealed to the entire group. The route of the flight intrigued them. They talked about the maps of the Lindbergh flight drawn by Charles Lindbergh. Then one of the children asked, "Do we have a big map in school that shows the world round, not stretched out at the poles?"

This question triggered a study of the maps and globes available to the approximately four hundred children in this school. The fifth-graders made some interesting discoveries. A map of the United States in one grade showed "The Indian Territory." China appeared on one map in an upper-grade room of the school, but the map, because of its age, had to be handled carefully. Only maps of Mercator's projection were available.

The fifth-graders made a report of this investigation at an assembly meeting, after which the principal made available to all classes, from fourth through eighth grade, catalogues describing new and available maps and globes. The students, with teachers' aid, made recommendations for purchasing. The school board approved the recommendations. The entire study, with a display of maps and globes, provided the basis for an interesting, informative, and well-attended evening P.T.A. meeting. Anyone attending the adult meeting who did not know these children would naturally have asked, "Are these particularly astute children?" Actually they were demonstrating astuteness that they had acquired through a highly stimulating, worthwhile venture in their reading program.

Many teachers in schools where work of a similar kind is encouraged could add accounts of intellectually provocative work that excited youngsters to go even beyond the teachers' highest expectations. As sharing in planning has been found to stir greater interest and success in learning, so will sharing in the selection of materials.

The child who remains spoon-fed probably refrains from turning on his full learning potential. He may even grow to prefer spoon-feeding to being self-reliant. He will not have a chance to develop a respect for good books, good magazines, and good newspapers and, therefore, may fall into that group of readers who are patrons of the trashy and tawdry—which, in a free-reading society, are available. Involving more children in certain parts of book and supply selection is of such promise to their reading maturity and safety that the obstacles (and there are many) must be faced.

SCHOOL PRACTICES IN BOOK BUYING

Until the present time, the practice of supplying each classroom with all the books, supplies, and equipment needed has been thought of as an administrative responsibility. The tools for learning were made available to teachers and their pupils; the teachers were to supervise their use and care. As schools became larger and school systems and districts became more complex, the buying and distributing of all necessary materials became increasingly institutionalized.

It is important to recall that most of today's purchasing policies were established when the school curriculum was relatively static and practically delineated by what was in the textbooks provided. Textbooks were adopted by the state, county, or locality for periods of approximately five years. This practice is waning; teachers in many schools at the present time are asked in the spring to send to the principal's office their suggestions and requests for the coming year. Some schools have a printed or mimeographed form for this request.

With many budgets textbooks are not included in the classroom teacher's list; they may be recommended by a teacher committee and/or school administrators and are listed separately. Requests from the classroom are, therefore, often considered in addition to basic texts. It is not uncommon for the school budget for the ensuing year to be made and approved before the spring requests by teachers are submitted. In some localities teachers are given the approximate amount that will be available for their needs; in others, not.

Except in rare cases, such as these described, children do not directly assist in selecting texts, library books, or other working materials, although their preferences may influence a teacher in his recommendations for purchase. Learning how to choose books, maps, and all other materials wisely as early as children seem ready to do so should, however, be considered an integral part of educating today's youngsters as functional readers. To teach children by merely handing them the materials as though these fall like manna from heaven may encourage them as adults to join those who, out of ignorance, would limit budgets and hamper education.

Changing Buying Policies As previously indicated, school leaders in some localities are taking steps to change outmoded policies of material selection, particularly those features of the process that are closest to children's potential learning. The ideal toward which one would wish them to move is for children from early years to share in the purchasing of materials and for this role to expand as their maturity increases. If this were common practice, by the time such well-educated elementary groups reached high school they would have arrived at some mature standards of judging books and other materials. They would also have acquired a close identity with and some knowledge of the large and difficult process of maintaining and financing their schools.

Today's inexperienced youngsters cannot be blamed for assuming that books are a matter for remote educational "higher-ups." As a result of this assumption, however, they often abuse materials, thereby reflecting their detachment from one aspect of the cost of education. Looking back to goals in education, we properly ask: What kind of citizens are they becoming?

Changes in the complicated established method of buying books and other supplies must be based upon an adequate understanding of all that is involved. For example, a P.T.A. in an alert community made fifty dollars per classroom available for teachers and children to spend on books that they were to select together and with care. An excellent bookstore was within easy travel distance. The majority of groups made trip after trip to the shop, buying books to add to their favorite reading list as well as some to further certain studies. They spent cautiously lest crucial book needs might appear later in the year. Not so with two teachers, however. They hurried into the shop one day after school and, without any discussion with their pupils, spent the entire amount. These two thus deprived their pupils of an extremely valuable educational experience.

Teachers' Buying Responsibilities Careful administrative planning with teachers must be a prelude to their guidance of children's participation in the selection of any kind of important material. What standards will they as individuals hold in mind? How will they help children make careful, wise selections? How broad is their own knowledge, for example, of books available? What plans can be made to make information about new publications and productions available to them? How should meetings be planned, keeping in mind the importance of conserving teachers' time and energy, to give them aid in this responsible phase of teaching reading?

Teachers in an up-to-date curriculum program already take a greater share of responsibility in the selection of materials than was formerly common because many needs cannot be anticipated in advance. Month-by-month buying demands not only changes in requisition procedures but also the availability of money for cash purchases. Recommending such purchasing as policy will stir the question, already frequently raised, of who bears the responsibility for money allocated to teachers to spend. Of course, teachers for years have been accountable for money collected from children for daily milk, lunch money, and various community drives. Nevertheless, delegating to them responsibility for purchases traditionally thought of as administrative and/or board duty is a major step away from tradition and controlled practice.

Obviously no one method will fit all purchasing needs. Some standard reference materials, such as atlases, encyclopedias, maps, and globes, will serve the needs of groups year after year. Books on periods of history and on lives of great individuals also retain a rather permanent value. Many groups of students can have experience in purchasing them and take adequate time for the work. Other materials that are contemporary, especially on topics high in current importance, must be purchased as needed. Current-events magazines, special bulletins, and books on such topics of present-day interest as nuclear development and exploration of space are of this nature. Schools with no cash funds or without a quick-purchase policy cannot make certain informational content available; they thus limit children's learning. Students and teachers often finance such needs in ways of their own devising, but this procedure seems questionable in publicly financed education.

INCREASED BOOK BUDGETS FOR INCREASED LEARNING

The total amount of money allocated to books must come under careful scrutiny. Not only must there be a process whereby materials can be rented, and at times purchased, but the financial resources for all the materials must be adequate. Changes in this direction have already occurred in locality after locality.

Sometimes the need requires dramatization of the sort utilized by one teacher. She made a study of the budget allocation for textbooks and all learning materials per pupil, applied this to her class of twenty-eight fourth-graders, and arrived at the shocking conclusion that it cost the community five cents per day per child for his reading materials. It is a tragic but true fact that this meager amount is above that allocated per pupil in thousands of other communities, including one of our largest metropolitan cities. In another school system, where the amount in the budget for books and supplies was eight dollars per pupil, which was considered "generous," the teachers in that system met with the school board to report, "We are unable to teach adequately because we are too short of material." The board increased the book budget promptly.

Inherent in the problem of supplying enough materials is the dilemma of meeting the reading ability of those who are plodders as well as of those who are lopers. "Grade level" is a term that, to an alert teacher, has little value. When the concept is strictly applied for purchasing books per class, it is not uncommon to find ten to forty per cent of a class unable to read any of the books with any workable degree of success. Aside from the waste of such purchasing, think of the frustration caused by the utter futility a child meets day after day in trying to glean something from books beyond his reading ability. Think, too, of the boredom of the bright reader who meets no challenge.

In an up-to-date school system we are developing more active readers, we are encouraging book buyers, we are guiding more selective readers. Our next major steps are (1) to stop spoon-feeding them as rapidly as they grow in independence and can share in selecting; (2) to enlarge school and library budgets to be sure that we have sufficient food for growing reading appetites; and (3) to make the changes in school finance policy required to hasten such added opportunities in every child's reading program.

If our purposes in education are consistent with the needs of this rising generation, and if we see increased incentive in children's reading after including them more fully in judging and selecting their own reading, then whatever the effort, we shall feel rewarded. When children participate more actively in choosing books and other materials and in understanding costs, they are likely to become the kind of citizens who will favor adequate school budgets and proper financing of both school and public libraries.

SUGGESTED READINGS ON BOOK SELECTION AND INDIVIDUAL READING

BURROWS, ALVIRA T. *Teaching Children in the Middle Grades.* Boston: D. C. Heath and Company, 1952. Chapter 10.
Description of individual approaches to children through their interests, preferences, and reading abilities. An invaluable aid to a teacher eager to keep up with demands created by a roomful of eager readers.

FRANK, JOSETTE. *Your Child's Reading Today.* Garden City, New York: Doubleday & Co., Inc., 1960.
The author's genuine understanding of children and her rich knowledge of books are combined in well-organized, readable style. An excellent reference for parents and teachers eager to stimulate and broaden children's reading in this age of mass media.

LARRICK, NANCY. *A Parent's Guide to Children's Reading.* Garden City, New York: Doubleday & Co., Inc., 1958.
Guidelines for stimulating youngsters to read, to understand, and to develop good taste. Excellent list of books and periodicals.

LAZAR, M., DRAPER, M., and SCHWIETERT, L. *A Practical Guide to Individualized Reading.* New York: Bureau of Educational Research, Board of Education, 1960.
Planned to be of help to teachers even in large classes. Suggestions for independent reading in relation to curriculum studies.

WOLLNER, MARY HAYDEN BOWEN. *Children's Voluntary Reading as an Expression of Individuality.* New York: Bureau of Publications, Teachers College, Columbia University, 1949.

The "voluntary" reading of 11- to 13-year-olds was studied and revealed some strong personal qualities in their reading habits that prevent parents and teachers from making generalizations about their reading without an adequate personal profile of each. Technical.

CHAPTER 14

Parent Responsibility and the Child's Reading

Opinion about the role of the parent in helping his child become a reader varies from those who caution, "Don't try to teach your child to read; teaching him to read is a technical matter that only teachers are prepared to handle," to those who assert, "Today's parents are able to read, so they can teach their children to read without the help of a teacher." Each contender can prove his opinion by a child who is a good reader, and each has strong convictions that only his position is sound.

As a matter of fact, thousands of children have become successful readers despite their parents' indifference to their reading or their parents' happy abdication from any responsibility in favor of trusting this matter entirely to the teachers. Other thousands have become successful readers with the help of parents' teaching, at either the child's persistence or the parents' suggestion or both. There are also some who, even with the aid of helpful parents and earnest teachers, barely inch along and fail ever to become interested readers.

Too often adults, including specialists, who become imbued with a sure-fire theory are upset when confronted by the surprising power in some children to resist their theories by not learning to read, while others may be taught with methods that violate all the canons of good teaching, yet step off blithely into a fine reading career. Youngsters have tremendous adaptability. This is fortunate for them because they need to adjust to the firm ideas well-intentioned adults have toward them and about teaching them.

HOME INFLUENCES ON READING

Family life exerts an influence on children that they carry along into all future phases of learning. The very nature of the child's outlook on his world starts under the home's guidance, as was discussed in Chapter 2. His early interests in reading, his acquisition of a growing vocabulary, his wide-awake eagerness to understand the world about him, his respect for a wide use of reading, and his many contacts with books and magazines—these are among the contributions of a good home to a child's success as a reader.

All too often eager parents overlook the contagious learning in family life. In a home where life is punctuated with enthusiasm for new experiences, happy ventures in looking up information, animated discussions of reading, and respect for each individual's reading moments, a child naturally catches the spirit. One cannot imagine a child from such family living exclaiming with disgust, as did one eight-year-old to his teacher, "Why should I get so hot about my reading? My Mother and Dad never read." In today's family, which operates under the many pressures of contemporary life, time can still be found to protect an intelligent way of living that keeps reading established as everybody's business.

Much assistance and advice on general child rearing have been offered by pediatricians, the Children's Bureau of the U. S. Government, the Child Study Association, some family magazines, the official bulletin of the National Congress for Parents and Teachers, and religious and social agencies. Many schools issue bulletins on how to help a child with his reading that offer to parents both advice and assurance on specific points, and parent-teacher meetings and child-study clubs discuss troublesome problems.

As a result, we doubtless have the largest number of best-informed parents supervising today's children ever to live in any land. They are an invaluable resource for the child's wholesome growth as a reader.

OFFERING HELP AT HOME

A number of facts need to be taken into consideration when examining the parents' role with a young and budding reader in his home. Despite emphasis in recent years on common-sense responses to children's questions about reading, a strange fear still persists on the part of many otherwise sensible parents. It is not uncommon for parents to relate how, in their quandary when a child asks a specific question such as, "Spell this for me" or "Where does it say *bunny*"? they dodge the request or feel uneasy about answering it. One cannot help wondering what passes through a four-year-old's mind when he asks his mother, "What does it say?" as she reads the directions on a can of soup, and his mother responds, "I mustn't tell you. Wait until you get to school. Then you'll find out." This same child may ask, "Whose car is that?" or "Where did George go?" and receive a sensible answer. To receive such a peculiar response to a question as simple as the others must be puzzling to him, to say the least.

Help—But Don't Push Beginnings in reading are so closely interwoven in child-parent relationships and sibling relationships that common sense should tell us to answer a child's question about reading or spelling as promptly and as simply as possible. As long as an adult takes the cue from the child, the path will be a reasonable one. If a parent is tense and unduly eager to get a child to demonstrate precocious tendencies by pushing him in reading—or in any other endeavor—the damage that ensues is more serious than impairing the child's attitude toward reading. It may certainly do that, but it may also rob the child of his own self-assurance and perhaps create tense and even resentful feelings toward the high-pressure parent.

Instances of children who were made tense and fearful through unwise pressure at home were called to the attention of school officials in some cities. These educators then proceeded to establish policies equally unwise, urging all parents to "Keep Hands Off Your Child's Reading." The hangover from such unwise admonitions still persists in some localities. However, thanks to the good judgment prevalent in many of today's homes, we have a rising generation of children between the ages of two and five who gather many helpful specifics about reading simply by asking questions and receiving direct, matter-of-fact answers.

The excitement of a child in learning to read is a privilege to see. Nothing else in life at that period seems important. He literally lives it. He may no sooner be home from school than he sits down, preferably near an adult, and starts to read, usually exploding words with vigorous breathiness. It is fortunate for a child to find a parent or other sympathetic, listening adult at home upon such occasions. This ultra-excited period may persist for four to six weeks. While it lasts the child derives great satisfaction from finding patient adult listeners available.

Meeting a Child's Specific Requests If the child asks for some specific help during these reading moments, his request should be answered. "What's this word?" is one of the most common requests. If the parent is near enough to look at the indicated word, he should pronounce the word clearly. If the child asks again, the pronunciation of the word should be given again. It may not be advisable to ask a beginner to spell the word, because he may not yet be able to identify all the letters.

Some youngsters want an adult to read a passage for them slowly while they follow. Then they like to try reading the passage themselves. Some educators have qualms about such a procedure, fearing that it will encourage a child to memorize the passage and hinder him from becoming adept at recognizing words. This may happen occasionally but need not cause alarm if one thinks of all the other words and sentences a child will meet through which he can be taught how to recognize words. Memorizing takes place with a majority of children who read a story again and again and conclude by "knowing this whole story by heart." In fact, it is impossible to prevent some children from quickly memorizing what appeals to them. They learn to read by first memorizing appealing parts of a book, then connecting the word they say with its correct identity in the book. This is a common process through which bright youngsters learn to read. If a child continues to memorize but makes no headway in recognizing words by himself, his teacher should be told so that she may give sensible help.

Sharing the First School Book A recent widespread practice is the school's refusal to permit a first-grade child to take home his beginning reading book. Parents have found this policy difficult to understand. Schools following this rule evidently wish to keep the beginning reading experiences with basal readers exclusively within the teacher's supervision. Perhaps they fear that parents may coach a child, help him to memorize the beginning stories, or confuse him. Parents may profit from some suggestions at this time. A page-length letter from the school on "How to enjoy your child's first reading," with some "do's" and "don'ts" would help parents at this important time in a beginner's life. However, denying a child who is filled with enthusiasm the right to take his book home and demonstrate his important new power is a policy based on ignorance of children or a failure to consider them with due respect.

How does this policy affect the beginner? He may not yet have the verbal ability to answer an inquiring parent's question, "What did you do in reading today?" One child, when asked each day by a nervous parent, "Did you read today?" answered, "No." This perhaps was the simplest way out for him. The mother wisely had a conference with the teacher, who assured the parent, "We are getting along nicely in our first preprimer."

Many a child loses some of the excitement of beginning reading that he can catch from displaying his budding new skill to anyone at home who will listen to him. To deny him these opportunities seems similar to asking a new golf player to park his clubs in a locker and not display his new skill or handle the new clubs while he is with those who are most interested in his progress. Some better way to solve the problem can surely be found. The fact that many schools do not follow this practice is assuring and also indicates that no problem necessarily exists around the use of beginning reading books at home.

Establishing Take-Home Policies One element in the problem may be budgetary. Six-year-olds lose books on the way to and from school and misplace them at home. Responsible parents help children by reminding them to take books back to school and also by establishing a proper place for books so that they do not become misplaced. A school with many pupils reared in neglectful homes needs a policy of allowing more money for book losses than do other schools. Teachers, mindful of the plight of children who come from such homes, suggest to the youngsters helpful ways of taking good care of books while using them at home and also provide some cues for remembering to bring them back. Nagging and threatening these children adds to their already heavy burdens in life and may make them withdraw interest from books.

Fortunately many schools operate in a way that is psychologically sounder. Children are encouraged to decide which books they wish to take home to share with the family. Close ties between home and school on all matters relating to a child's reading are fostered. In such schools basal systems, if used, are not used in a rigid lesson-by-lesson manner, nor are they read by all children. They are fitted to the needs of individual children. Close adherence to a reading system as the *authoritative* approach to beginning reading is doubtlessly responsible for the rise of the inhibiting practice of not allowing children to take home their beginning reading books.

Lastly, a proper respect for preschool experiences should help determine policy. Many a child before entering school has had close associations with his parents in using books. The home plate still remains for him the first place to bring all matters that are important to him. Therefore, his first *real* reading book should be shared with parents and other family members. Intelligent school practices thus reflect good understanding of a child's early learning needs and also a respect for the child's family.

Today's Child—A Book Connoisseur Experienced kindergarten teachers notice a difference in the book knowledge of today's children as contrasted with that of children beginning before World War II. The rapid increase in production of attractive books for preschool age has added new stimuli to young-child life. Many children now entering kindergarten reflect these publishing trends.

Good schools, mindful of this new richness in child life, continue to alter their programs to fit the youngsters who enroll in kindergartens and first grades already sparked as experienced book-lovers. For some of the alert youngsters, this means earlier attention to words, letters, and printed materials about the kindergarten room. It also means a larger and more varied supply of good books for children to look at and browse through. Story hours, too, have become enriched with comments made by children drawn from the stories and information they have received at home.

PLANNING FOR HOME-SCHOOL CONTACTS

If home and school become a relaxed working team with the child, his world is more streamlined and therefore less confusing. He can use his energy to forge ahead, instead of hesitating and feeling his way, unsure of what is expected of him in either place. Many ways are used to build a team approach. Parent-teacher conferences in which there is mutual respect of parents for teachers and teachers for parents foster good team work. Parents learn much by visiting schools for part of a day when the regular daily program is in operation. Of great importance is the chance for a parent with a question to have some legitimate time in which to ask it. One extremely assuring teacher sent a mimeographed note home with all first-grade children in the first week of school: "Your child may not yet be able to tell what goes on in school. Should you have a question, call on me at my home, Franklin 6-8166, on Tuesday afternoons between 4:30 and 5:30."

Parents appreciate a prearranged way of having a brief talk with a teacher over questions, even simple ones, that arise. Teachers, too, feel more ready to answer questions if such contacts can be regularized. Even when there are no questions, it is good for parents and teacher to report personally, "All is going well." Some schools have after-school "telephone hours" at which teachers are available. The practice of group conferences offers several advantages. Parents can exchange questions and share suggestions. The hesitant parent finds the group conference a help in overcoming school-shyness. Schools with a high percentage of working mothers find early-evening conferences for small groups an aid to both parents and teachers. One rigidly set time or one type of social setting for all parent contacts is wisely being replaced by a variety of relaxed and convenient meetings. Some regulations, however, are essential, not only for parents, but for teachers as well.

PARENT AND CHILD LEARNING TOGETHER

Once the beginning reading period has passed, the family can enter into a child's reading life in other constructive ways. A simple way is to read the books the child brings home for his personal reading. Talking over common reading in a relaxed, informal way can develop excellent bonds of understanding between parents and child. The child who shares his reading with his parents starting at the age of six or seven, when conversations are still psychologically easy, will be more inclined to continue to keep this channel of communication open during the later, more difficult years of adolescence.

Today's good books for children also make good reading for adults. A young father at a book fair stated publicly, "Now that I have two children going to school and bringing home their books I have made Marjorie Flack, Jean de Brunhoff, and Virginia Lee Burton my favorite authors." A mother announced that for the first time in her life, science was coming alive. She had always "detested" it, but after reading Branley's *Rockets and Satellites* and several other science books brought home by her seven-year-old son, she was learning science with him.

It can be expected that children's interests in topics will capture parents' interests and that together they may enjoy functioning as a research team. New findings in archaeology, the islands of the South Pacific, new experiments in agriculture, water fluoridation, history programs on television, were among studies which parents at a Colorado evening party cited as examples of "getting educated with our children." Many adults can tell interesting stories about becoming re-educated through contacts with their children's learning.

A grandmother, who previously had led a sheltered life, was praised at a summer church fair supper table for her contemporary outlook on life. She was interested in the coming World Series, Geiger counters, good radio and television programs, and the United Nations. She was asked how she managed to keep up to date. She replied, "I look after three grandchildren when they come home from school, before their parents come home from work."

One can summarize this role of the adult simply by stating that parents and others who supervise children at home can encourage children's worthy interests and broaden their own by keeping informed about children's studies and the books they read and by joining them in some of their intellectual pursuits.

PARENTS AND HOMEWORK

Homework is frequently a matter of concern from the point of view of the child, parent, and teacher. The tasks set for the child to do after school hours should be appropriate to his years and should seem reasonable and worthwhile to him. Some schools have no assigned homework; the children decide what books they will take home and what work they will do. In such schools, motivated children are consciously being developed. The finest home study emerges from self-assigned work, and able teachers and observing parents are aware of this.

Unfortunately, some teachers and school leaders may still assume that the more homework can be made to resemble punishment, the better for a child's learning. That there are educators who display such retardation in understanding children—and all human beings for that matter—is difficult to accept in a learned profession, but such there are. They may be supported by parents who pursue a similar course in guiding their children. As a result, children so burdened may work longer hours than do their parents or teachers. It is only natural that children facing such treatment learn to dislike school.

Protecting the Value of Homework One of the main reasons often offered for homework is that it gives a child a chance to work independently, away from his chums and in a home setting not as ready-made for study as is the schoolroom. If this purpose is to be realized, three factors must be present:

1. *The child must bring some eagerness or at least willingness to the work.* Sensitive teachers put forth effort in challenging and stimulating youngsters to work at home with good attitudes. Parents, too, can kindle interest. Homework done under duress may have only negative effects.

If a child seldom reacts favorably, the homework program may need to be reconsidered. First consideration should be given the total quality of the child's day. How sedentary is his school life? What opportunities does he have for informal play, investigating personal interests, and dawdling? What lessons, such as music and dancing, does he take? What home chores must he meet? Such inquiry has led some responsible education leaders to minimize or omit homework.

2. *The home must be conducive to study.* A quiet, comfortable spot, proper lighting, books and tools for work, and freedom from interruption are necessary. In families with several children, regular quiet times can be established to facilitate the work of young students.

Controlling such matters as the use of television and noisy socializing is only fair to a child who may find it difficult to get into a proper frame of mind for work. A good atmosphere for work is created by many families even in crowded homes chiefly because parents respect the value of this period for the child and also understand what is needed for a good study atmosphere. Under proper conditions a child can get the satisfaction of getting work done.

3. *Parents should perceive when it is wise to give encouragement and assistance.* With an eager worker, this is a simple matter. With a child who is easily discouraged, the parents' role requires more sensitivity.

A dependent reader, for example, needs to be urged to "try it for yourself first and see how well you do." If the task is utterly beyond his ability, it is sensible to face that fact and help the child also to accept it. To do all the work for him may increase his dependence. If he shows resentment toward the teacher for expecting too much of him, the parent can ease his feelings by helping him to realize that a teacher with dozens of pupils cannot always cut the cloth to fit each child. If he is frequently in deep water, a conference with the teacher is advisable, and the question of continuing homework should be raised.

Gauging the Amount of Help Needed The desire of parents to help each child become a competent, independent worker serves as a guide in sensing when and when not to enter into the child's homework and also helps to regulate the degree and nature of help. Parents with this motive will not impair their youngster morally by doing all the work and permitting the child to claim it as his own. The destructive effect of this conduct on a child is too serious to overlook.

In a good home climate it is possible for a child to ask questions and seek help in understanding matters about which he finds insufficient opportunity to gain information in a busy classroom. When youngsters between the ages of eight and twelve do this, they indicate, by so doing, that they have confidence in their elders at home. This, for them, is an ideal home-study situation. Parents often feel more at ease in answering questions with children in this age group than they do with the beginners. For one reason, among others, older children tend to express their problems with a clarity of which younger sprouts may still be incapable, and they are often quite specific as to what type of help they want.

Older children may present another dilemma for parents, however: namely, that they are learning some things their parents do not know. A fifth-grader in looking up the meaning of *halyard*, a word noted in a story he was reading, found the abbreviation *Naut.* in the definition. He immediately turned to the introductory pages of the dictionary to find out the complete word for *Naut.* His mother commented, "In all my college days, I never once used a dictionary with the skill my child has." Adults who are secure and who do not feel threatened when a child's ability and information go beyond theirs can derive satisfaction from such incidents.

Facing Pressures for Increasing Homework Questions between home and school do arise over homework. In one community, parents sought more extensive home assignments, protesting that the absence of such assignments was resulting in a too-soft brand of education for their children. Teachers and the guidance director considered the children's lives already too crowded. After a careful study of children's use of after-school hours, a new homework plan was proposed. This plan included definite time limits for work, with the understanding that children were not to be encouraged to work beyond such limits. It was also suggested that informal socializing be encouraged to offset children's scheduled days.

Some parents seek longer home assignments as an aid in keeping their youngsters off the streets, thereby easing supervision responsibilities. One can understand this desire from their viewpoint, but a child's day needs the proper balance between various activities. Some children, perhaps too many, lead a sedentary life, are overburdened with prescribed work that puts excessive demands upon them, and become weary, disheartened, and uninterested in learning. A strict schedule of after-school assignments can deny a child his chance to learn to explore, to plan his time, and to evaluate his own work. Where the necessity for time for such personal growth is respected, homework problems are not present.

PARENTS' DOUBTS, QUESTIONS, AND CONCERNS

Because confident relations between home and school affect a child's success in learning, some observations related to the need for such a relationship belong here. It is desirable to keep misunderstandings from arising between the two agencies, the home and the school, both so vitally interested in the progress of a child's education. Many of these misunderstandings can occur during the beginning school years, particularly in the first grade, and may concern methods of teaching reading. "How can Ellen learn to read when she doesn't know the letters?" "If my boy can't sound out a word, how can he read it?" "How am I supposed to know how well Jack is doing if he doesn't bring his reader home?" "Why don't they teach writing any more? It's print now." Questions such as these are legitimate and deserve a careful answer.

Caution: Protect the Child's Confidence in the School Parents who ask questions of this sort are expressing a rightful concern. But how they reveal their concerns about the teacher's efforts may have a serious effect upon a child. It is essential for a youngster to feel not only that he is "all right" and is a going concern but that his teacher, too, is competent. To rob him of this confidence is to do a great disservice to his free release of effort in learning. A child who is led to doubt the competence of his teacher and to lose respect for his school can scarcely be expected to invest a wholesome effort in his work.

In light of this last point, parents need to discipline themselves to withhold doubt or disapproval of school methods and school affairs from their children for the good of the children. Their questions should be resolved through contact with the teacher or other staff member with whom they may be asked to meet. If a genuine difference of opinion persists, it is hoped adults can accept that fact. It is not uncommon for a teacher to meet several parents who have widely divergent views. What then? In order to teach, a teacher must be free to operate in a way he believes best suited to the group. But no matter what the ultimate decision, a child's confidence in his teacher and his school must remain secure.

There are difficult situations that may arise when, according to a parent's view, a child's belief in himself is being threatened by a teacher. For example, a first-grade child came home greatly upset. "My teacher says I'll never be a good reader because I point." The devastating effect of this comment upon her young six-year-old daughter was evident to the mother. She tried to ease the child's distress by saying, "Your teacher means that if you stop pointing you'll be a better reader." The child would not let herself be soothed.

A visit by the mother to the teacher revealed that the teacher did believe that those who relied upon pointing in the second semester of the first grade "never got to be good readers." Nothing the mother said altered her firm opinion. The mother, a more mature and informed person than the teacher, assuringly told her daughter, "Your teacher does think as you say, but I don't think so. I think you will become a good reader. I'll help you. Your teacher will help you too."

It is good policy to follow up a child's report, as did this mother, when the child seems disturbed. Often children misunderstand a teacher, as they frequently do parents. At times the shoe is on the other foot; the child relays to the teacher comments from home that he has confused. A teacher uses good judgment in either disregarding them or, at times, making a contact with the home. Misunderstandings can eat deeply into a child's ability to pay attention to his work and can have a negative effect on his progress. Keeping home-school ties on a good, friendly basis is, therefore, worth the time and effort spent by both parents and teachers.

Children Who Abdicate Finally, a problem causing deep concern arises when youngsters who, for a number of reasons that may be understood or for some unknown reasons, lose interest in school work. They may spend time being orderly but idling, or they may be disruptive in school, home, and neighborhood. Such defection from normal behavior may be sudden, and the cause a mystery to parents and teachers. It may stop as suddenly as it begins. Brief "off" periods are normal in the life of many children. The youngsters themselves may not know why, but they seem to take a breathing spell by indulging in behavior unlike that which is normal for them.

When indifference to school responsibility persists, home and school together should probe honestly to see if there is a cause. The cause may reveal itself as too much tension or excitement at home or a new friend who has upsetting tendencies. It is helpful if home and school can plan cooperatively to help the child return to his normal behavior, the nature of the plan depending upon the tentative hunches about the causes of the change in attitude.

It often helps if the child sits in with adults for a part of the conference. The spirit of such meetings needs to be warm and friendly. The purpose of the meeting may be introduced by a comment such as, "We've come together to talk over with you how to help you back to business." A child may be asked in what way the teachers and parents might be helpful. Even seven-year-olds may startle us with their good suggestions. Some ideas, like Ruth's, may be hard to follow: "Keep Jimmie from being sick and crying all the time." Jimmie was a young brother who had been "colicky." Other youngsters may be extremely reluctant to participate and will make no helpful proposals. They may not feel at ease with the parent, or the teacher, or with both.

A Scoutmaster whose son while in the fifth grade suddenly stopped working found him unresponsive in the interview held at school with his teacher. A plan was worked out without the boy's help. It was decided that he should spend two thirty-minute periods a day on homework, the time to be set regularly for each day but selected by the boy. If his schedule worked out satisfactorily, at the end of one week his case was to be reviewed to see if less time were needed or if a more favorable schedule could be made. The plan worked successfully.

Setting Consistent Controls Parents need to establish some controls, such as limiting telephone calls and television viewing time, but they should respect some prized social contacts and favorite television programs. A complete denial may only add to a child's rejection of his work. If the upsetting factor comes from a neighborhood influence, parents teaming together can create a supportive climate for their youngsters. A problem frequently arises from widely divergent parental control commonly expressed by different hours for bedtime. A private-school P.T.A. in New York City solved this problem by establishing uniform retirement hours by grade levels for the entire elementary school. This single decision eliminated a difficult problem in individual homes and also erased the problem of contagion caused by one nine-year-old who relayed to his assembled chums each day the information that he had again retired at midnight.

Some of the foregoing points may seem completely irrelevant to parents' responsibility in relation to a child's success in reading. To those who understand what makes children tick successfully, however, these points will be accepted as appropriate.

THE CONTAGION OF PARENTS' READING

The impact of present-day hurried, almost breathless, living has left a marked effect on reading in the family. Surveys of adults and children often reveal a narrow margin of time devoted to home reading. Newspapers, if available, may be hastily read, and little or no time may be spent in talking over items of interest to the family. Sharing the reading of a book with appeal to the entire family is a delight that tragically few children experience. Many children never see either parent or other adult family member sit quietly enjoying a book. No wonder that to some children reading has become "kid stuff" that they too can skip once they reach adulthood.

The fact that many families have two breadwinners who are often not on the same work schedule has added to an interrupted quality in the home that is not conducive to relaxed reading and discussion. Unwise use of television has further vitiated the calmer side of family life.

Yet, with the existence of all these factors, parents who cherish reading see that it remains a rewarding part of the family schedule. At a school P.T.A. meeting scheduled to discuss children's reading, parents shared their ways of maintaining reading as a part of the crowded daily life. It was generally accepted that if parents protected time for their own reading, children also tended to do so. Reading was discussed as a privilege rather than an assigned chore. The use of the public and school libraries by parents and children on a year-round basis was heartily endorsed. The majority of parents at the meeting felt that no matter how hectic life about them became, they could encourage and safeguard their own and their children's personal reading.

The more clearly a child's growth in reading is recognized as an integral part of his family life, his general school life, and his own deep inner concerns, the more understanding and helpful our relations to him can be. With the out-of-school world becoming increasingly appealing to the child and demanding of his interest, home influence on a child's reading will take on more importance. Direct attention to the increase of the family's effectiveness is of such importance that it should be on every home-school program for consideration. Instead of sealing parents off from working with children on reading, adding to their willingness and drawing upon their effectiveness is in order.

SUGGESTED READINGS ON PARENT ROLES IN READING

ALMY, MILLIE. *Children's Experiences Prior to First Grade and Success in Beginning Reading.* New York: Bureau of Publications, Teachers College, Columbia University, 1949.

The results of this study show the positive relationship between pre-first-grade contacts with reading in the home and later success in reading in the first grade. Those studying the role of parents in kindergarten and primary grades will profit from this study.

ARBUTHNOT, MAY HILL. *Children and Books.* New York: Whitman, 1957.

A college text, clearly written. An invaluable source for teachers and parents who are interested in a child's in- and out-of-school reading.

GANS, ROMA. *Reading Is Fun.* New York: Bureau of Publications, Teachers College, Columbia University, 1949.

A pamphlet written for parents and teachers with suggestions for stimulating and maintaining children's eagerness to read from preschool years to adolescence. Easy reading.

MILNER, ESTHER. "A Study of the Relationships Between Reading Readiness in Grade One School Children and Patterns of Parent-Child Interaction." *Child Development,* 22, No. 2, June 1951.

Children who lived in a verbal home climate, had books to look at, and were read to scored higher on tests in first grade than did children less privileged. A technical study which underscores the importance of parental relationships to a young child's success in reading.

NATIONAL CONGRESS OF PARENTS AND TEACHERS AND AMERICAN LIBRARY ASSOCIATION (Special Service Division). *Let's Read Together.* Chicago, 1960.
An annotated list of 500 carefully selected books from which parents and children can select those that a family can enjoy together. A good list for teachers as well as parents to use as a guide.

RASEY, MARIE I., and MENGE, J. W. *What We Learn From Children.* New York: Harper & Brothers, 1956.
Authors examine their own assumptions about children's learning and report how, upon closer contacts with children, they found the assumptions to be wrong. Parents and teachers will be heartened by this book.

TOOZE, RUTH. *Your Children Want to Read.* Englewood Cliffs, N. J.: Prentice-Hall, Inc., 1957.
Excellent understanding of children and books which appeal to them. Genuine respect shown for parents' help to children in reading. Fine book lists.

CHAPTER 15

Some Spots for Reasonable Concern

There is room for reasonable concern, intelligent inquiry, and solid research in assessing the entire field of reading, ranging from the manner in which a child grows into a literate reader to the use of reading in all the myriad ways current in a society as educated as we in the United States have become.

To a parent with a child who is not becoming a successful reader, the number-one concern, quite naturally, is how to help the child to do better. Interest in children's reading progress is also a rightful concern of good citizens. The functioning of our democracy at home and abroad demands the quality of enlightenment that reading helps build and keep alive. Therefore, the knowledge that one child is not succeeding in learning to read frequently evokes the attention of many beyond his family. Educators and those particularly interested in the teaching and functioning of reading express concern over a number of additional aspects.

INSURING SUCCESS THROUGH REMEDIAL HELP

Widespread interest and active support have been given schools testing out new ventures in teaching reading and in helping children who have reading difficulties. The rapid growth of remedial programs and the increased number of reading specialists added to school staffs reflect the public respect for educating not only the facile learners but all today's children. The former policy of failing the straggler and absolving the school of further responsibility would find few supporters today. Genuine progress in teaching reading can be attributed, in part, to the wholesome regard parents and the general public have given educators studying new approaches to the complicated field of reading.

A parent whose child seems unable to get a good start or who seems to be lagging behind in reading now commonly asks to talk the matter over with the child's teacher. The majority of individual cases are of a minor or temporary nature. A conference initiated either by parent or teacher, with good two-way suggestions made between them, often results in putting the young reader on a regular road to progress. Many simple problems, if ignored, would grow into more serious, even retarding, influences.

Some children, even with early recognition of and proper attention to their reading problem, continue to have trouble. For these, reading specialists and special help programs called "remedial" are becoming available in an ever-increasing number of schools. A special reading teacher works with the child or assists the regular teacher in working with him. The nature of the child's difficulty is examined, and measures planned to correct his problem are then followed, either in the classroom or in a special reading room.

Under good leadership such specific help is not only accepted but often sought by children themselves and by their teachers. The negative title "remedial" does not repel if those closely related to the work establish good relationships with children. A favorable attitude toward the work is essential if the child is to profit from it. Educators, like pediatricians and pediatric dentists, recognize the importance of an inviting approach to the child.

Although *individual* help in reading, which is a more appropriate title than *remedial* work, is relatively new, many experiments and careful studies have already been made, with the focus on providing the best aid with the least delay to all youngsters who can profit from it.

RESEARCH HELP WANTED

Some problems in the field of reading are of another order, although not unrelated. They include some difficult questions for which research or experimental programs or both are needed.

What About the Controlled Vocabulary? A problem frequently cited concerns the vocabulary controls in beginning reading materials discussed in Chapter 7. Preprimers, primers, and primary books are printed utilizing a limited number of words found to be common to children's language and other books. These words are introduced and repeated according to a formula. Often the result is uninteresting content for today's live wires whose vocabulary may show a strong influence from television programs, many rich experiences, early contacts with books, and peer-group interests.

The concept that high frequency of words is associated with ease in learning seems to have gained wide acceptance, although research workers who helped establish controlled vocabularies have not made this association. Such a concept is a good example of crooked thinking. Intelligent teachers of beginning reading have for many years challenged the idea. They frequently noticed that a child might recognize *Halloween* and *Fudgesicle* more quickly than *one* and *see*. The all-phonics and controlled-vocabulary specialists notwithstanding, the child comes alive at words which convey ideas charged with interest for him. As a result, he turns on full powers of alertness, and these words become firmly fixed—he then knows them. More studies including children of varied backgrounds and verbal aptitude are urgently needed in the area of understanding vocabulary selection for beginners.

Should First Books Be Teaching-How-to-Read Books? Such probing raises the question of whether worthwhile content and word-teaching materials are mutually exclusive. At this vital period in a young child's life his reading interests can be divided roughly between learning-how-to-read and enjoying reading. Pre-primers, primers, and first readers, using a restricted vocabulary and attempting to use a content of universal appeal, have grown increasingly vapid and repetitive. Just as the medical profession was stalled for decades on a plateau, attempting to cure tuberculosis through rest, fresh air, and essential foods until the event of wonder drugs, so too, with a controlled, repeated vocabulary, are the educators stalled in their quest for simplified beginning reading materials until the birth of a new "wonder" idea comes to the fore.

Should the Entire Beginning Reading Process be Re-examined? A third question that arises is whether the beginning-reading period should come in the first-grade year, or at approximately age six. Although some schools no longer operate on that assumption but, rather, teach the child when he shows sufficient interest and verbal power to begin, the beginning period seems largely fixed in the minds of educators, parents, and children as occurring with entrance to first grade. In recent years pressures to include more formal reading work in kindergarten have gained ascendancy.

For the majority of six-year-olds, beginning to read may be a simple matter that they meet with success. For others, it may be the beginning of a series of difficulties that follow them throughout the years of their education. At best, those who experience difficulty may be faced with a period of "adjustment" for several years, which, for a young child coping with stress, is a long period. Some preliminary research in a limited situation has shown that youngsters whose beginning reading was delayed two years leaped ahead when they did start and at the end of the third grade had matched or passed beyond those taught the conventional first-, second-, and third-grade reading programs.

More humane promotion policies have eased the problem faced by slower beginners. Children who, despite lack of success in reading, seem able to mix with other six-year-olds are sent on to second grade. Teachers in second grades and beyond are given both aid and appropriate materials with which to meet the needs of the later beginners. Merely liberalizing promotion policies without changing succeeding grade programs can only add to the dilemma the child faces. Where such forthright measures are not established, many a child may labor unsuccessfully through year after year of schooling, growing increasingly unfitted for work expected of him and developing negative attitudes toward school, family, and even his entire community. Research to examine the established attitude of beginning reading for all at their sixth year or in the first grade is long overdue.

Relation of Teaching Methods to Reading Independence Other traditional practices need re-examination. Opportunities to grow in the ability to select materials should become a part of every child's education in reading. The process whereby the teacher prescribes the book, the pages to be read, and even the purposes for reading has a legitimate place at times in some parts of school work. Such an assignment as "Read the account of *Farming in the*

New England States on pages 66-68 and be ready to talk about your own observations of farming here in Maine and the description on these pages in your geography" may at times be desirable. An entire group can focus on the assignment, discuss the question, and also reveal to the teacher their degree of ability to respond to this type of critical reading.

There are other facets to the child's growth as a mature reader, however, that cannot be developed in a program that relies too exclusively on such methods. Extensive use of assigned reading tasks can become spoon-feeding. To expect a child so taught to be a selective, intelligent reader once freed of assignments is wishful. Cutting the apron string in family-child relationships has long been recognized as an essential step for the child in the process of growing toward adulthood. In education, too, there are some apron strings that need cutting. The cooperation of youngsters in planning their reading, sharing in recommending books for purchase, and using their growing skills in a library should be expected activities in every child's reading program. Today it is a part of the education of only a small percentage.

There is a mistaken idea that elementary-age children are not yet mature enough to assume responsibility in choosing what they read. Children of nursery-school age select books for adults to read to them and reveal beginnings of individual preference. Occasionally we may hear about a first- or second-grade youngster who bursts in upon the family and excitedly says, "Look, this is the book I picked to read next." The more active a child can be in choosing books for his personal use and for information related to curriculum projects, the more eager to read will he become and the more competence will he acquire in managing himself in communities rich in reading materials. Growth in selecting reference readings pertinent to their studies in content areas should be a result of the regular method of school work for all children.

CENSORSHIP OR SELECTION?

One interesting reflection on this matter of school-controlled reading is its contradiction of the deep grass-roots attitude toward censorship in the United States. Periodically, an incident occurs in which a book is questioned and its free distribution is challenged. Protective procedures for proper use of censorship are quite well established in such incidents; their main purposes are to protect the right of an author to distribute his ideas, the right to publish what some consider undesirable. We are not and, God willing, we will never be a society in which censorship can be ruthlessly applied. Yet from kindergarten through high school our programs all too often resemble those through which young people are being taught to function as if they were going to continue to be nonselecting readers, turning the pages of only that which the censors permit or authorities prescribe.

Common sense should tell us that in our free land the education of children and youth for twelve and more of their most impressionable years should not be dominated by prescribed reading programs that disregard the need to become competent, continuing readers of good materials. In that classic book *The Freedom to Read*, the authors challenge the educators in the statement:

> Sensitivity and response to the better is an effective protection against the more superficial attractions and grosser influences of the worse. A positive program of education for the appreciation of moral and aesthetic values would go far toward making prohibitions unnecessary; without such a program, moreover, prohibitions are of doubtful efficacy.[1]

Controversy and Discussion The problem of censorship is closely related to children's studies. In good schools, current affairs and problems related to major issues form an important part of the elementary school's program. In the process of keeping informed on a question, ideas from the press, pamphlets, radio, and television may be evaluated. A teacher must be ready to help boys and girls deal with conflicting points of view. Some information and points of view may support values we hold dear; others may oppose them. It is not uncommon for children to recommend that materials contrary to their views be ruled out of classroom use. At this point, children are ready to learn about censorship—when and when not

[1] Richard McKeon, Robert K. Merton, and Walter Gellhorn, *The Freedom to Read*. Bowker, 1957, pp. xiii and xiv.

to rule out. Their decisions upon such matters as adult citizens will reflect the help received for such responsibilities throughout education started in the elementary-school years.

As a rule, the time used for this part of the curriculum is expanded from grade to grade as boys and girls develop greater interest in important happenings and increased ability in understanding them. Proper study of most matters of this sort includes reading and discussion. At times, a study may be placed on a to-be-continued list, pending receipt of additional information or further developments; at other times, tentative conclusions can be made; and, at still other times, youngsters may be helped to realize that the problem is beyond their ability. Students who are so taught are receiving throughout their active school years the type of help in facing crucial issues that will affect the way they approach serious problems in later years.

Reading and Informed Citizenship There are students who do become educated in this important phase of reading as it functions in decision-making. However, they are in the favored schools of our nation, and they probably represent a small percentage of our total student population rather than a majority. The expansion of the schools' reading programs to meet this individual citizenship need in our country must be given far more specific consideration. Once the child has grown to adulthood, he should not only be free to select materials to suit his choice, but he should have values that lead him to make good choices. Demands for good reading material will decrease demand for the less desirable. The child should also be so educated that he can bring an enlightened point of view to questions about censorship.

It is a valid assumption that adequate help in reading to acquire adequate understanding of one topic should produce more readiness to study other topics. Too often we hear at election time, "I didn't vote. I was not sure enough." Many such inactive residents are able to read well, but the process of arriving at a decision strikes them as too difficult. Rather than discipline themselves to acquire this power, they recede from responsibility. Some would like to be told what to believe. Doubtless, many who do cast ballots have been told what position to take. Perhaps this is to be expected in light of past emphasis in schools of carrying out assigned tasks to the neglect of stimulating interests and learning how to think independently about them. Stuart Chase in summing up American opinion according to opinion polls makes the shocking statement:

> Among the subjects where interest has not been aroused, and where this study shows excessive ignorance and confusion, are these: Unawareness of the imperatives of a nuclear age; Unawareness of the massive effects of technology on our lives and our future . . . Unawareness of the true goals of education . . . Ignorance of the Bill of Rights . . . Gross inability to define "Communism" and so intelligently assess its threat.[2]

No one would argue against the essential need in our country to educate all youngsters for high-level performance as citizens. Neither would one deny the contribution of wise reading to the effectiveness of good citizens. It is, therefore, logical to urge that those responsible for teaching reading include classroom experiences that develop awareness of important issues, interest in them, and critical reading on them. Those problems and issues in controversy, including politics, should be made an essential part of intermediate grade work.

PLANNING FUTURE PROGRAMS

Much progress will continue to be made on the first concern cited at the beginning of this chapter—the aid to individual children whose progress in acquiring reading skill falls below what seems proper for them. The other questions and problems listed here require something more than mere "normal progress." School budgets should grow to include adequate financing of research. Teachers and administrators in general do a fine and conscientious job of checking on the progress of youngsters in reading growth, in assessing the school curriculum to see where there are weak spots that need revision, and in trying out promising new procedures. To go beyond what is done today, as some studies will require, will demand a budget adequate to include research workers and to free competent teachers and staff members to carry out research projects.

[2] Stuart Chase, *American Credos*. Harper, 1962, p. 202.

Some projects, it has been found, can effectively be carried out on a state level rather than by a local unit. More state-supported research is greatly needed. An examination of carefully planned programs in which there are bold new approaches to beginning reading might be a project for state-planned research. A broadly based reading program centered around science and social-science studies and followed for several years would also be a promising large-scale venture. This latter study would meet the recommendation of the authors of *The Freedom to Read,* who propose a study of:

the ways in which interests and tastes are formed, for it is these which, through self-selection, go far toward determining whether books are read at all, what kind of books are read, and what is derived from the books which are read. This inquiry would have major significance in providing a sound basis for identifying the sources and consequences of various patterns of reading and of related patterns of exposure to the other mass media.[3]

Teachers' Growth and Research Direct assistance to classroom teachers in changing from some established practices to others more promising is a widespread need. The point is crucial. Anyone who visits schools across the country can notice that where teachers have assistance in translating helpful ideas into classroom procedures, good teaching is prevalent. In schools with twelve to twenty teachers, professional principals aid teachers through good planning and classroom visits, with excellent results. Principals who offer such helpful services have an educational background for their work. All too often, however, in large schools principals are understaffed and have insufficient time to spend in classrooms. A more adequate concept of staffing schools is long overdue. Continued growth on the part of a school staff and school-planned research cannot be expected when all hands available are essential merely to keep the school holding its own.

In former years, the supervisory help given teachers prescribed methods in teaching reading and demanded careful attention to specific requirements. Teachers did not share in planning, discussing, and making changes about their work but were handed instructions as to revisions in methods. In some systems they were

[3] McKeon, Merton, and Gellhorn, *op. cit.,* p. 76.

checked to be sure they were obediently following instructions. Such procedures put a premium on being dutiful but not open-minded, alert, and creative.

The proposed inquiries into reading programs suggested in this chapter will be achieved to the degree that teachers grow in their own insights into straight thinking and extensive critical reading. The closer they come to appraising programs and planning suggestions for revisions and sharing in essential research, the more will their professional thinking be stimulated. Teachers eager to explore ways to teach youngsters to become active critical readers need to be encouraged and helped by staff members. Work that helps us grow in understanding children and in seeing the crucial reading needs of our society offers excellent starting points.

SUGGESTED READINGS ON RESEARCH PROBLEMS

BOND, GUY, and TINKER, MILES A. *Reading Difficulties, Their Diagnosis and Correction.* New York: Appleton-Century-Crofts, Inc., 1957. Chapter 17.
A general but helpful treatment of how to stimulate greater interest in reading and improving taste.

CHASE, STUART. *American Credos.* New York: Harper & Brothers, 1962. Chapters 8 and 12.
For an evaluation of the type of adult readers home and schools are educating, these two chapters offer evidence that indicates key shortages. Entire book challenging reading for professionals and other adults interested in education.

MCKEON, RICHARD, MERTON, ROBERT K., and GELLHORN, WALTER. *The Freedom to Read.* New York: R. R. Bowker Company (published for the National Book Committee), 1957.
The authors present the difficulties inherent in censorship and the error in assuming that censorship can be substituted for educating readers to be selective. Essential reading for those setting goals for reading programs.

ROBINSON, HELEN M. *Corrective Reading in Classroom and Clinic,* Supplementary Educational Monographs, No. 29. Chicago: University of Chicago Press, 1953.
The nature of reading difficulties and the function of classroom teachers and various specialists in their correction. An essential pamphlet for reading teachers and those responsible for planning remedial programs in schools.

STRICKLAND, RUTH. *The Language Arts.* 2nd ed. Boston: D. C. Heath and Company, 1957. Pp. 248-252.
Brief but excellent comments on appropriateness of vocabulary of beginning reading books in relation to intellectual and language growth of children.

VERNON, M. D. *Backwardness in Reading—A Study of Its Nature and Origin.* Cambridge: Harvard University Press, 1957.
Research and analysis related to children's difficulty in reading, applicable to children of all ages. A valuable book for interested teachers and reading specialists.

INDEX